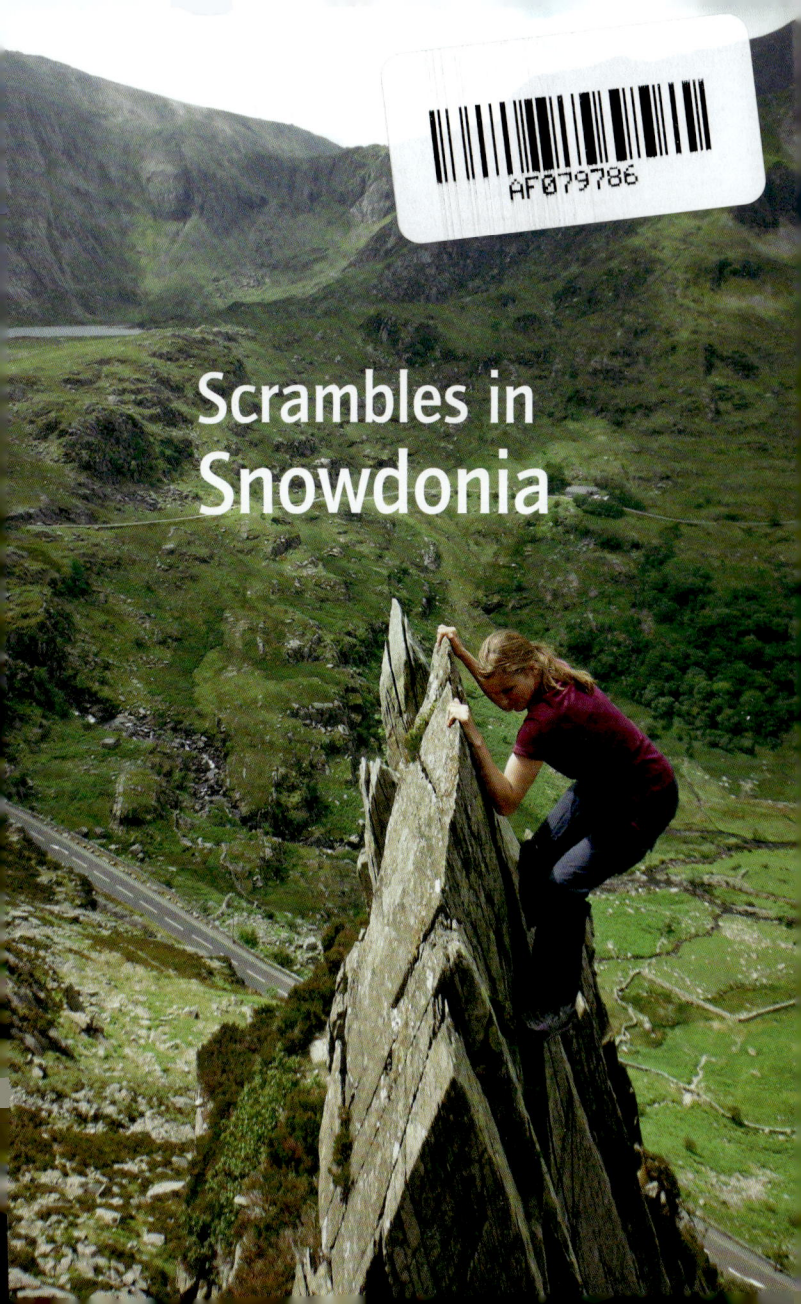

Scrambles in Snowdonia

Warning! Scrambling can be dangerous
Scrambling can be a dangerous activity carrying a risk of personal injury or death. It should be undertaken only by those with a full understanding of the risks involved and with the training and experience to evaluate them. Scramblers should be appropriately equipped for the routes undertaken. Whilst every care and effort has been taken in the preparation of this book, the user should be aware that conditions are highly variable and can change quickly. Holds may become loose or fall off, rockfall can affect the character of a route, and in winter, snow and avalanche conditions must be carefully considered. These can materially affect the seriousness of a scramble, tour or expedition.

Therefore, except for any liability which cannot be excluded by law, neither Cicerone nor the author and updaters accept liability for damage of any nature including damage to property, personal injury or death arising directly or indirectly from the information in this book.

Acknowledgements
The updaters would like to thank the inspirational group of people who accompanied us on scrambles, let us photograph them or helped out in other ways. Special thanks go to Stephanie Crolla, who supported us on numerous trips to Wales with the children and without whom this update would have been considerably more difficult. Also thanks to: Casey McKeating and James Wilby; Mark Barrett, Sam and Luke; Katie Cole; Charlotte Wilson and Ali Fontbin; Sarah, Mike, Becca and Amy Watton; Neil Butterton; Spencer Cullis and Chris Corcoran; Ali Lee; Dan 'rabbit' Williams and Darren Beever; Marc Yeoman; Jo Rochester and Sophie Nunn; Ben Wood, Lee Wales and Rachel Varney from RAF Valley Mountain Rescue; Luke Jackson, Dave Noble, Ged Heaton and Dominic McKenzie; Monika Kucerova and the late Keith Archman; Robert Bromley (as Adam) and Laura Long (as Eve); Helena and Christian Bird; Huw Gilbert; Ed Sutton and Theia the dog; Chris Aynsworth and Tim Harrop; the Dinsell family; Ella Williams; Steve Smith and Phil Timms; Heather and Rosa Crolla. Finally, a massive thank you to Anna Fleming for literally being a lifesaver with her Heimlich manoeuvre on Glyder Fach!

Eryri/Yr Wyddfa
Since this book was published in 2022, the Snowdonia National Park has officially reverted back to its Welsh name and is now known as Eryri, while Snowdon is now Yr Wyddfa. This will be amended in the next edition.

Scrambles in Snowdonia

by Steve Ashton
updated by Carl McKeating and Rachel Crolla

Juniper House, Murley Moss,
Oxenholme Road, Kendal, Cumbria LA9 7RL

www.cicerone.co.uk

© Steve Ashton, Carl McKeating
and Rachel Crolla 2022

Fourth edition 2022
ISBN: 978 1 78631 136 8
Reprinted 2024 (with updates)
Third edition 2017
Second edition 1992
First edition 1980

MIX
Paper | Supporting
responsible forestry
FSC® C014138

Printed in Czechia on responsibly sourced paper on behalf of Latitude Press Ltd.

A catalogue record for this book is available from the British Library.

© Crown copyright and database rights 2022 OS AC0000810376

All photographs are by the updaters unless otherwise stated.

Front cover: Superb positions on Glyder Fach's East Gully Ridge with Tryfan beyond (Route 34)

Half title page: Traversing the second pinnacle of Braich Ty Du Face (Route 2)

Updates to this guide

While every effort is made by our authors to ensure the accuracy of guidebooks as they go to print, changes can occur during the lifetime of an edition. Any updates that we know of for this guide will be on the Cicerone website (www.cicerone.co.uk/1136/updates), so please check before planning your trip. We also advise that you check information about such things as transport, accommodation and shops locally. Even rights of way can be altered over time. We are always grateful for information about any discrepancies between a guidebook and the facts on the ground, sent by email to updates@cicerone.co.uk.

Register your book: To sign up to receive free updates, special offers and GPX files where available, create a Cicerone account and register your purchase via the 'My Account' tab at www.cicerone.co.uk.

Contents

Map key	8
Preface to the second edition	11
Updaters' note	13

INTRODUCTION 15
Area covered by the guide 15
Selection of routes 15
Using this guide (including explanation of grades) 15
Equipment 19
Basic rope technique 22
Maps 22
Access 22
Bases 22
Public transport 23
Accidents and emergencies 23
A final cautionary note 26

THE CARNEDDAU 27
Route 1   Southern Ridge Circuit .... 1- ✪✪✪ ... 31

Pen yr Ole Wen 33
Route 2   Braich Ty Du Face
           (including Pinnacle Ridge and Porcupine Ridge) .... 2+ ✪✪ ... 33
Route 3   Broad Gully Ridge .... 2+ ✪✪ ... 37
Route 4   Craig Lloer Spur .... 3- ✪✪ ... 41

Carnedd Dafydd 43
Route 5   Crib Lem (Llech Ddu Spur) .... 1 ✪✪✪ ... 43
Route 6   Eastern Ridge of Black Ladders .... 2 ✪ ... 47

Carnedd Llewelyn 49
Route 7   Craig yr Ysfa Amphitheatre .... 2+ ✪ ... 50

THE GLYDERAU 53
Route 8   Cwm Bochlwyd Horseshoe .... 1 ✪✪✪ CB 🔵 ... 56

Tryfan 59
Tryfan East Face 61
Route 9   Tryfan Bach Approach .... 3 ✪✪✪ ... 61
Approach and orientation for the Heather Terrace, East face of Tryfan 64

Route 10	Bastow Buttress Variant	2+ ✪✪✪ ... 68
Route 11	Nor' Nor' Buttress Variant	3 ✪✪ or 3S ✪✪ ... 70
Route 12	Nor' Nor' Gully	2+ ✪ ... 73
Route 13	Nor' Nor' Groove	1+ ✪ ... 75
Route 14	North Buttress Variant	2 ✪✪ ... 77
Route 15	Little and North Gullies	1 ✪✪ ... 79
Route 16	Pinnacle Rib Variant	3 ✪✪ ... 81
Route 17	South Gully	3- ✪ ... 83
Route 18	South Buttress	3 ✪✪ ... 85

Tryfan West Face 87

Route 19	North Ridge	1 ✪✪✪ CB 🆄 ... 87
Route 20	Milestone Buttress Approach	3 ✪✪ ... 93
Route 21	Milestone Gully Approach	2- ✪✪ ... 95
Route 22	Milestone Continuation	3 ✪✪ ... 97
Route 23	Wrinkled Tower (aka Wrinkled Slabs and Castle Chimney)	3S ✪✪✪ ... 99
Route 24	West Face Route	3 ✪ ... 101
Route 25	V Buttress	3 ✪✪✪ ... 105
Route 26	V Arête	3 ✪ ... 106
Route 27	Notch Arête	2 ✪✪✪ ... 108
Route 28	Y Gully	2 ✪ ... 111
Route 29	South Ridge Direct	1 ✪ CB 🆄 ... 112

Glyder Fach 114

Route 30	Bristly Ridge	1 ✪✪✪ CB 🆄 ... 115
Route 31	The Chasm Face	3 ✪✪✪ ... 118
Route 32	Main Gully	2 ✪✪ ... 122
Route 33	Main Gully Ridge	3 ✪✪✪ or 2 ✪✪✪ ... 124
Route 34	East Gully Ridge	3 ✪✪✪ ... 125
Route 35	East Gully	1+ ✪ ... 127
Route 36	Shark Buttress	3S ✪✪✪ ... 129
Route 37	Dolmen Ridge	3 ✪✪✪ ... 132

Glyder Fawr 134

Route 38	Gribin Ridge	1 ✪ CB 🆄 ... 135
Route 39	False Gribin	1 ✪ ... 138
Route 40	Cneifion Arête	3 ✪✪✪ ... 142
Route 41	Maybe Tower Rib	3 ✪ ... 144
Route 42	Seniors' Ridge	1 ✪ ... 146
Route 43	Seniors' Gully	1- ✪ ... 148
Route 44	Direct Approach to Seniors' Ridge	2 ✪ ... 149
Route 45	Idwal Staircase and Continuation	2+ ✪✪✪ ... 152
Route 46	North West Face Route (aka Idwal Buttress)	2 ✪✪ ... 154

Route 47	Bryant's Gully	2+ ✪✪✪ ♠	157
Route 48	Esgair Felen Direct	2+ ✪ ♠	161

Y Garn ... 164
Route 49	Devil's Kitchen and the Sheep Walk	3S ✪✪✪ or 1- ✪	165
Route 50	East Ridge	2 ✪✪	168

Foel Goch ... 170
Route 51	South Arête	1+ ✪	170
Route 52	Needle's Eye Arête	3 ✪	173
Route 53	Yr Esgair	3S ✪	175

Carnedd y Filiast ... 177
Route 54	The Ridge (aka Atlantic Ridge)	2+ ✪✪	177

SNOWDON GROUP ... 181
Route 55	The Snowdon Horseshoe	1 ✪✪✪ S 🅄	185

Crib Goch ... 188
Route 56	East Ridge	1 ✪ S 🅄	189
Route 57	North Ridge	1 ✪	191
Route 58	Jammed Boulder Gully	3S ✪✪	193
Route 59	Traverse of Crib Goch	1 ✪✪✪ S 🅄	196

Crib y Ddysgl (Garnedd Ugain) ... 198
Route 60	Crib y Ddysgl	1 ✪✪ S 🅄	198
Route 61	Cwm Glas Mawr Approach	1+ ✪ or 3S ✪	200
Route 62	Clogwyn y Person Arête (including Parson's Nose options)	3 ✪✪✪ or 3S ✪✪✪	203
Route 63	Cwm Glas Ridge	1- ✪	206
Route 64	Llechog Buttress	2 ✪✪	208
Route 65	Llechog Ridge	2- ✪	211
Route 66	Eastern Terrace of Clogwyn Du'r Arddu	1+ ✪✪	213
Route 67	Western Terrace of Clogwyn Du'r Arddu	3 ✪	217

Snowdon ... 219
Route 68	Tregalan Couloir	2 ✪	219
Route 69	Y Gribin and the East Ridge	1 ✪✪	222

Lliwedd ... 225
Route 70	Traverse of Lliwedd	1 ✪✪ S 🅄	225
Route 71	West Peak via Bilberry Terrace	3S ✪✪✪	227

EIFIONYDD ... 231
Route 72	Nantlle Ridge	1- ✪✪✪	234

Craig Cwm Silyn ... 236
Route 73	Craig Fawr Rib (aka LMH)	3 ✪	236

Mynydd Mawr 240
Route 74   Sentries' Ridge and Continuation .... 3- ✪✪✪ .. 240
Route 75   Bear Buttress .... 3S ✪ .. 245

OUTLYING AREAS 247

The Moelwyns 248
Route 76   Moel Siabod Ridge Circuit (including Daear Ddu Ridge) . 1- ✪✪✪ .. 248

The Rhinogs 251
Route 77   South Face of Rhinog Fawr .... 2- ✪ .. 251
Route 78   South Ridge Variant, Rhinog Fach (aka Hywel Ridge) ...... 3- ✪✪ .. 258

Cadair Idris 262
Route 79   Cyfrwy Arête (including Table Direct option) 3 ✪✪✪ or 3S ✪✪✪ .. 262

Conwy 267
Route 80   Penmaenbach Arête .... 1+ ✪✪ .. 267

Appendix A   Summary of routes in grade order 271
Appendix B   Longer combination ideas 274
Appendix C   Useful contacts 274

Routes marked **CB** 🔽 and **S** 🔽 form part of the Cwm Bochlwyd and Snowdon Horseshoes. ♠ Route is accessed from the Pass of Llanberis, not from the Ogwen Valley.

Route symbols
(for OS legend see printed OS maps)

- 〰️ route
- 〰️ alternative route
- 🔴80 scrambles on longer routes
- 🚶 start/finish point
- 🚶 start point
- 🚶 finish point
- ▶ route direction

Route symbols on photo topos

- 〰️ the route of the scramble
- ⋯ line of the scramble where it is not visible (through routes etc)
- ⋯ approaches and descents (walking)
- ⋯ scrambling approaches and descents that are not part of the route
- 〰️ alternative routes
- ㉒ route numbers
- ⇨ notable features

Looking out to sea from the Llech Ddu Spur (Route 5)

About the Author

Steve Ashton began climbing in 1969 in the Lancashire quarries, wearing hiking boots and 'protected' by a tow rope retrieved from a council tip. Within two years, he was grappling with grade VI routes in the Dolomites and narrowly surviving storm-bound bivouacs.

While living in Snowdonia, he wrote regularly for the outdoor press and later produced numerous guidebooks and instructional manuals on climbing and hill walking. The first of these – *Scrambles in Snowdonia* – helped revive this neglected facet of mountaineering and introduced the now ubiquitous grading system.

After retiring from mountain writing, he spent several years as an actor and playwright before turning to fiction.

Other Cicerone guides by Steve
Ridges of Snowdonia

A summer's evening on Tryfan's South Ridge (Route 29)

Preface

What criteria should be used to define a scramble? General agreement could be reached on the lower limit – that we must also expect to use our hands on the rock – but fixing the upper limit is always going to be controversial. My own interpretation, reflected in the cut-off point for this guide, is that the technical interest of the climbing (which in any case ought not to exceed Moderate or short passages of Difficult standard in the rock climbing classification) must be superseded by the wider interests of scenery, position and atmosphere. In other words, seeking out difficulty for its own sake, without regard to line or position on the mountain, is not scrambling but rock climbing.

Since its first publication in 1980, *Scrambles in Snowdonia* has served thousands of existing scrambling enthusiasts, and no doubt helped to convert many more from the ranks of hill walkers and rock climbers. This is not an entirely comforting thought. Unroped scrambling, however exhilarating it may be, is potentially the most dangerous form of mountaineering. There have been times when – alone, unroped and in trouble halfway up some remote and uncharted face – I have vowed never to go into the mountains again. I break the vow regularly, but grow ever more cautious. There is no way of entirely eliminating the risk, only of reducing it. No mountain is worth a life, yet without mountains perhaps no worthwhile life remains to be lived.

Steve Ashton, 1992

About the Updaters

Carl McKeating and Rachel Crolla live at the edge of the Yorkshire Dales. Having grown up scrambling on local gritstone they first ventured to the Welsh mountains as teenagers, where they sampled the delights of Tryfan and the Glyderau, along with witnessing a dramatic helicopter rescue from Crib Goch. They have since hiked, scrambled and climbed all over Europe, exploring the major mountain ranges. In 2007, Rachel became the first woman to climb to the highest point of every country in Europe. The couple's resulting guidebook, *Europe's High Points*, was published by Cicerone in 2009. In 2010, Carl and Rachel completed a long-standing ambition to climb all the routes in Ken Wilson's *Classic Rock*. This was followed by a three-month climbing tour of America and Carl has since worked on a Yorkshire gritstone guide. In 2013, *Walking in the Auvergne* – the couple's guide to the hills of the Massif Central in France – was published by Cicerone. In among roaming the steeper parts of Snowdonia, Carl completed a doctorate about Mont Blanc and the couple are both teachers.

Other Cicerone guides by Carl and Rachel
Cycling the Reivers Route
Europe's High Points
Hadrian's Cycleway
Outdoor Adventures with Children – Lake District
Walking in the Auvergne

Updaters' note

It has been a privilege to work on this inspirational book, and one that we have not taken lightly. In preparation for this extensively updated third edition, we have climbed and checked all the original routes, some of them many times. Grades have been reappraised and descriptions revised as necessary. After much thought, five of the routes from the previous edition have been relocated to the book's supporting webpage on the Cicerone website, www.cicerone.co.uk/1136/updates. In contrast, 16 additional routes have been included in the book. All are in keeping with the original premise of the book and allow scramblers to venture onto the best lines in a wider area of the national park, as well as to explore a greater number of excellent lines on the northern mountains.

We share Steve's sobering sentiment regarding the use of this guide. Although grade 3 scrambles are now more commonly climbed with a rope, we have tried to clarify where there is a higher element of risk by introducing the 3S grade – the 'S' being severe, serious or, when tackling their hardest parts, an expletive of your choice! Taking into account scramblers' feedback about the last edition, we have tried to provide extra information about finding and following the routes that are less frequented. Ultimately though, the difference between a superb mountain day and an unmitigated disaster is the experience and common sense of the party. The freedom of scrambling is life-affirming, yet it must be taken seriously.

Carl McKeating and Rachel Crolla

A fine crest on the Cyfrwy Arête with Llyn y Gadair beyond (Route 79)

Introduction

Area covered by the guide

Nearly all the described routes lie within the northern half of the Snowdonia National Park, where the most rugged mountains are found. Good scrambling in the southern half is scarce, the rock here being typically loose or vegetated, but a handful of good routes have been included.

Northern Snowdonia naturally divides into four regions. From north to south these are: the Carneddau, the Glyderau, the Snowdon group and Eifionydd. The best scrambles will be found in the Glyderau, with the large majority concentrated on Tryfan, Glyder Fach and Glyder Fawr. The Snowdon group also boasts many excellent routes, whereas the Carneddau and the Eifionydd regions provide only a handful. In this book, each region is introduced by a general description of the terrain and an indication of the scrambling potential. The best routes in the outlying areas of the Rhinogs, Moelwyns and Cadair Idris have been added to the updated edition of this guide to give wider coverage of the Snowdonia National Park.

Selection of routes

The choice of routes is, by necessity and design, a selective one. All the best scrambles, along with the most worthwhile routes in the outlying areas, have been included. The range of difficulty extends from scrambly walks to short sections of proper rock climbing. Average fitness and a head for heights will suffice at one end of the scale, whereas nothing short of mountaineer's skill and daring will do at the other. Some routes fit neither category: scrambling over loose rock and up dripping, vegetated gullies seems to require a special cunning, for which neither hill walking nor rock climbing provides adequate preparation. The proficient all-round scrambler is a unique beast with some cautionary tales to tell.

Using this guide (including explanation of grades)

Route information boxes

Basic information has been included in a box at the start of each route in order to help readers decide whether the scramble is suitable for them. The headings are fairly self-explanatory: 'Location' refers to the mountain or mountain group where the scramble can be found and the grid references given here refer to the location of the actual scramble. (Parking details and corresponding grid references can be found in the longer 'Approach' section at the start of the main route description.) 'Approach time' is provided from the point at which most people would begin walking, up until the start of the scrambling. 'Altitude' is the height at which the scrambling, rather than the approach, begins. 'Aspect' simply refers to the approximate direction the route faces. The 'Route length' information is a rather subjective estimate of how much scrambling you can expect to find and whether the route is a long or short outing. This should be treated with caution because people move at vastly different speeds on steep ground, especially if ropework is sometimes involved. Approximate scrambling vertical height gains are often included, but again it is worth bearing in mind that scrambles are rarely vertical. The 'Conditions' heading is essential reading; it takes account of aspects such as rock quality and weather.

For the longer ridge circuits that include more than one scramble, such as the Snowdon Horseshoe, a rough circuit time based on an average unroped party has also been included.

Route descriptions

After an introduction and approach description, the routes are described generally or in detail according to the intricacy of the terrain. **Remember that the described line is often only one of several ways of ascending the face.** Use it as a guide, but be prepared to find easier or harder variations as the situation demands. A 'Descent by this route' section gives advice on using the route as a descent; if this section is not present, a descent is impractical or unduly difficult.

Descents and combinations have been given for all the routes to suggest interesting combinations for those seeking a longer mountaineering day. (See also Appendix B.)

Within route descriptions, alternative options are given as bullet points.

Route classification

The routes have been classified 1, 2, 3 or 3S, according to difficulty and level of risk. The progression from the very easiest grade 1 routes, such as the Southern Ridge Circuit or Seniors' Gully, through to the hardest grade 2 routes, such as Bastow Buttress or Bryant's Gully, is considerable; this increase in standard should not be underestimated. To give as much detail as possible we have sub-divided the grades for this edition. Borderline cases formally indicated by a grade of 1/2 or 2/3 are now indicated by the use of + or - symbols. However, it is impossible to apply any grading system

Early on the Cwm Glas Ridge with Esgair Felen behind (Route 63)

Above the Great Pinnacle Gap on Bristly Ridge (Routes 8 and 30)

The initial slabs on Direct Approach to Seniors' Ridge (Route 44)

rigorously, and at best it can serve only as a rough guide.

Grade 1: This grade denotes routes that require no special mountaineering skills (eg Snowdon Horseshoe, Tryfan North Ridge, Bristly Ridge), and which should be within the capability of any adventurous and experienced hill walker with a head for heights. These routes are unlikely to require rope protection, and may be considered for descent or during doubtful weather.

Grade 1-: A particularly simple grade 1 route that limits exposure and is ideal as an introduction to scrambling (eg Moel Siabod, Seniors' Gully, Cwm Glas Ridge).

Grade 1+: A grade 1 route likely to have increased steepness, technicality and exposure (eg East Gully, Milestone Gully, Nor' Nor' Groove).

Grade 2: Things are getting much more serious now. These include the difficult gullies and ridges, and the easier face routes (eg Y Gully, Eastern Ridge of Black Ladders, North Buttress Variant). You may have to wait for optimum weather conditions, and even then difficulties that require rope protection may be encountered. Grade 2 routes often involve short passages of Moderate grade rock climbing. A wide experience of scrambling, or a background in mountaineering, is essential. Such routes are rarely suitable for descent. Note also that a grade 2 climbed unroped may be potentially far more dangerous than a grade 3 climbed with rope protection.

Grade 2-: Routes that provide an introduction to the grade (eg Llechog Ridge, South Face of Rhinog Fawr).

Grade 2+: The hardest routes in the grade (eg Bastow Buttress, Bryant's Gully).

Grade 3: These routes have the attributes of grade 2 scrambles but with the additional complication of one or more short 'pitches' of simple rock climbing, often up to Difficult standard, on which rope protection is usual (eg Chasm Face, Dolmen Ridge). Someone whose background is limited to hill walking and scrambling will need to acquire a knowledge of basic rope technique before attempting these routes – in particular an ability to select belay anchors, fix running belays, and, in the event of a forced retreat, to abseil.

Grade 3-: Routes that offer an introduction to the grade (eg Craig Lloer Spur, South Gully, South Ridge Variant Rhinog Fach).

Grade 3S: Particularly challenging grade 3 terrain (eg Yr Esgair, Devil's Kitchen, Jammed Boulder Gully). The scrambles given grade 3S have more sustained or exposed passages of Difficult grade rock climbing or crux sections on wet or suspect rock. They present mountaineering experiences where good judgement and knowledge of rope work are essential. **Experienced climbers who solo grade 3 scrambles should be wary of 3S routes.**

Star ratings

Routes have been allocated a quality rating from zero to three stars. Obviously this is a subjective assessment, although few will argue over the merits or otherwise of routes at either end of the scale:

✪✪✪	acknowledged classics or routes of exceptional quality and interest
✪✪	routes of high quality
✪	routes of merit but which lack continuous interest
no star	routes described for completeness or because they are the best available in that particular region.

Equipment

Small first aid kit: Essential and should include: bandages, plasters, antiseptic cream/wipes, sun cream and surgical swabs. A tiny roll of duct tape can be surprisingly advantageous for holding swabs and plasters in place.

Whistle, compass and **head torch.**

Clothing: Your normal hill-walking clothing will generally be suitable for scrambling, but ensure that it gives adequate free movement for high leg and arm reaches. Mountain weather is changeable; it is wise to always pack a lightweight waterproof. Fingerless gloves or liner gloves that offer sensitivity and grip can be useful for scrambling up cold or wet rock but are no substitute for the sensitivity offered by gloveless hands.

Footwear: Specialist climbing approach shoes designed for scrambling and easy climbs are produced by all the major climbing brands and are recommended for scramblers venturing onto the grade 2 and 3 routes. However, be aware that approach shoes have their downsides: their soft

Practising ropework at the difficult chockstone in Main Gully, Glyder Fach (Route 32)

soles can wear down very quickly; they offer very little ankle support; are no fun during boggy or wet approaches; and are not great on mud, wet grass or angular scree. Lightweight walking boots, particularly those with a firm (not rigid) rather than floppy midsole, are also good for scrambling – especially on easier routes that involve a lot of hiking. Rigid-soled mountaineering boots are unnecessarily clumsy and uncomfortable for scrambling.

Rucksack: Choose a neat daysack, ideally fitted with stabilising waist and chest straps but with as few other fittings as possible. Remember, 'light is right!'

Rope: The typical 50m or 60m single and double ropes used for climbing are unduly heavy and cumbersome for scrambling, where a rope is often needed only for a short section of the overall route. The best compromise might be 30–50m of 9mm diameter half-rope. Half-rope can be used double in ascent and will allow significant abseils. Better, although more expensive, is a specialised superlight 9mm single rope. If using either a half-rope or a narrow diameter single rope, scramblers should be aware of its limitations: it is unlikely to be 'sharp-edge' tested and will wear out faster.

> **Note**
>
> The Devil's Kitchen (Route 49) requires an abseil. Yr Esgair (Route 53) requires exactly 50m of rope to reach a good belay on its hard step.

Equipment

It is essential your rope is a climbing rope with a 'dynamic' quality (in other words it must be capable of stretching to help absorb the energy of a fall), so it is no use buying caving or yachting rope, which has a low-stretch 'static' quality. Note that rope sold off the reel in 8mm diameters or less for making into runners and slings is low-stretch 'static' rope and should not be used as a main rope for scrambling. The rope should carry the UIAA label of approval.

Harness: The days of back breaking by tying a rope around your waist are long gone. Ensure you have a UIAA-rated climbing harness with a belay/abseil loop.

Other protection equipment: On some of the more technical routes, especially grade 3 and 3S routes, it is a good idea to include: three or four Nylon or Dyneema slings of 120cm and 240cm in length with a minimum 22KN rating; three additional screw-gate locking karabiners; two HMS karabiners and two belay devices (although knowing how to use an Italian/Munter hitch belay, a waist belay and a direct belay are essential skills).

The benefits offered by additional gear – such as extra protection and speed in setting up belays – need to be weighed against the hindrance of carrying it. Nonetheless, it is well worth supplementing slings with a very small selection of mixed-sized nuts (for speed of placement include one each of Wild

Strutting up the Catwalk of the Chasm Face (Route 31)

Country or DMM nut sizes 1 to 8 and one larger hex or chock). Include four quickdraws. Cams are not essential, but Wild Country Friend-size cams 1, 2 and 3 can be handy on harder routes. All equipment should conform to the current UIAA and CE standards.

Helmets: The slight irritation experienced when wearing a climbing helmet must be weighed against the partial but valuable protection it offers against falling stones or glancing blows sustained during a fall. Wearing or not wearing a helmet is entirely a matter of personal choice. For routes where friable or 'suspect' rock is noted under 'Conditions', such as Sentries' Ridge or the Western Terrace of Clogwyn Du'r Arddu, a helmet is a good idea even if solo.

Basic rope technique

Instruction in rope technique is beyond the scope of this guide. Rock climbers and mountaineers will be able to adapt their normal belay methods to suit scrambling terrain. Hill walkers will need instruction from experienced companions. Failing that, they may wish to enrol on a course at an outdoor centre (advertised online or in specialist climbing/outdoor magazines). Climbing instruction guidebooks and reputable online videos are invaluable reference points, but are no substitute for face-to-face instruction and practice.

Maps

The vast majority of routes appear on the OS Explorer® OL17 1:25,000 Snowdon – Conwy Valley sheet. The Rhinogs are covered by OL18 and Cadair Idris by OL23. The location of every scramble in this book is shown on OS mapping in the relevant chapters. For longer ridge circuits and lengthy isolated outings, the entire routes are shown on the maps. Do not rely on a smartphone as a substitute for a map.

Access

Approaches have been carefully described to avoid crossing land where access is restricted or in dispute. Improvising unrecognised approaches across lower pastures merely antagonises farmers. Besides, there is plenty of scope for wandering at will on the higher ground.

Bases

For the Carneddau and Glyderau routes, a base in the Ogwen Valley is best. Those with private transport will find anywhere between Capel Curig and Bethesda will do. Both villages provide basic amenities and a range of accommodation can be found throughout the valley, including campsites (those offering facilities are marked on OS maps – enquire locally for other sites); bunkhouses; youth hostels (Idwal and Capel Curig – the latter is now privately run); bed and breakfast; and hotels.

For routes in the Snowdon group, the best bases are the Llanberis Pass and, to a lesser extent, Nant Gwynant. Both have campsites and bunkhouse accommodation (Nant Peris has two campsites and a pub). Bed and breakfast and hotel accommodation, along with amenities, can be found in and

Accidents and emergencies

The remote cliffs of Craig Cwm Du (Route 75)

around Llanberis and Beddgelert and there are youth hostels at Bryn Gwynant, Llanberis, the Snowdon Ranger at Llyn Cwellyn and Pen y Pass.

Most people will visit Eifionydd and the outlying areas from a base in the northern mountains or on separate trips. Dolgellau is a good base for Cadair Idris.

Further information can be found in Appendix C.

Public transport

Regular rail and bus services link Conwy to Bangor and Betws-y-Coed. Bus routes from Caernarfon extend only as far as Nant Peris and Beddgelert. At the time of writing there was no service along the Ogwen Valley road from Bethesda to Capel Curig – a situation likely to change. In summer the Sherpa bus service makes a circuit around the Snowdon group by linking Beddgelert and Nant Peris via Pen y Gwryd. This service is extremely useful, allowing car owners to park and ride up to Pen y Pass and facilitating other unusual combinations of ascent and descent routes (search Sherpa bus timetable for details).

Accidents and emergencies

Always carry a small first aid kit (see 'Equipment') and know how to use

Looking across Nor' Nor' Buttress at a coastguard rescue helicopter, East Face of Tryfan

Accidents and emergencies

it. Consider attending an emergency first aid course including CPR. The National Mountain Centre (www.pyb.co.uk) runs these in Snowdonia and St John Ambulance (www.sja.org.uk) has details of affordable, regular courses across the UK.

With minor injuries, especially during cold or wet weather, it is nearly always best to keep moving – so attempt to descend the mountain by a known route. The danger from hypothermia in mountains is often much greater than the danger from a broken arm or a sprained ankle. Use a whistle to summon help from others on the mountain (sequence of six blasts). Head torch flashes are common on these mountains at night and less likely to raise an alarm (use a sequence of six flashes).

Take responsibility for your own safety. Mountain rescue should only be used as a last resort; teams in Llanberis and Ogwen Valley have seen a massive increase in callouts over the last few years, many of which could easily have been avoided.

To alert mountain rescue

Even in areas with no mobile phone signal, there is a high chance 999 will connect. Dial 999, ask for police/mountain rescue, and try to have the following details ready:

- precise position of the injured person on the crag (eg name of route)
- location of the crag (including grid reference if possible)
- time and nature of accident
- extent of injuries
- indication of prevailing weather at the scene (cloud base, wind strength, visibility, etc).

Keep the phone to hand until met by a member of the emergency services.

Rescue helicopters

- Secure all loose equipment before arrival of helicopter (weight rucksacks and jackets, for example, with stones)
- Identify yourself by raising your arms in a 'V' as helicopter approaches. Do not wave.
- Protect injured person from rotor downdraught (which is intense)
- Allow winchman to land without interfering
- Do not approach helicopter unless directed to do so by one of the crew

Help required
Raise both arms above head to form a 'Y'

Help not required
Raise one arm above head and extend the other downward, to form the diagonal of an 'N'

A final cautionary note

A guidebook of this sort reflects the author's and updaters' reactions and responses to the routes. Not everyone will agree on the exact lines to follow, the levels of difficulty encountered, or the best techniques to apply. The author climbed all the routes personally, specifically with the guide in mind, and at least once in every case without rope protection. All routes have been re-climbed by the updaters for this edition, often several times and in various conditions and ways. Nevertheless, when faced by an unexpected route-finding problem you must be prepared to trust your own mountain sense or judgement.

The same goes for loose rock encountered on the routes. Coping with unstable blocks, shattered rock and treacherous vegetation is all part of the game. Even the easiest scrambles can never be made completely safe, and some are potentially more dangerous than most rock climbs.

All the described scrambles are 'summer' routes. Even the simplest of them would be a totally different proposition in winter conditions, when ice-axe, crampons and winter-climbing skills are required. Remember that even when snow is absent the rocks may be coated in verglas – the thin veneer of ice rendering an ascent extremely difficult and dangerous.

A further consideration: the proliferation of indoor climbing and localised bouldering in the years since the last edition of this guide has led to a generation of technically gifted climbers who have not necessarily served a traditional mountain apprenticeship. Although such gymnastic practice is useful, it does not develop the skills required on an exposed mountainside at 900m in strong winds, a thundershower imminent and nightfall looming. Neither does it teach you to tap holds, to distrust certain blocks, spot the best line and avoid false trails. No grade of scramble should be taken lightly. Experience should be developed gradually: **consider your limitations and the limitations of others in your party before setting out**.

Above all, scrambling demands good judgement of terrain and an ability to assess the potential risk at every stage. These skills are learned gradually, beginning with the grade 1 ridge scrambles. This book can suggest only where the routes go and give advice on how to overcome some of the obstacles you will meet. Knowing when and how to turn back or when to carry on are skills in themselves; no-one can decide for you whether or not it is safe to continue. Ultimately the choices and the adventures are yours.

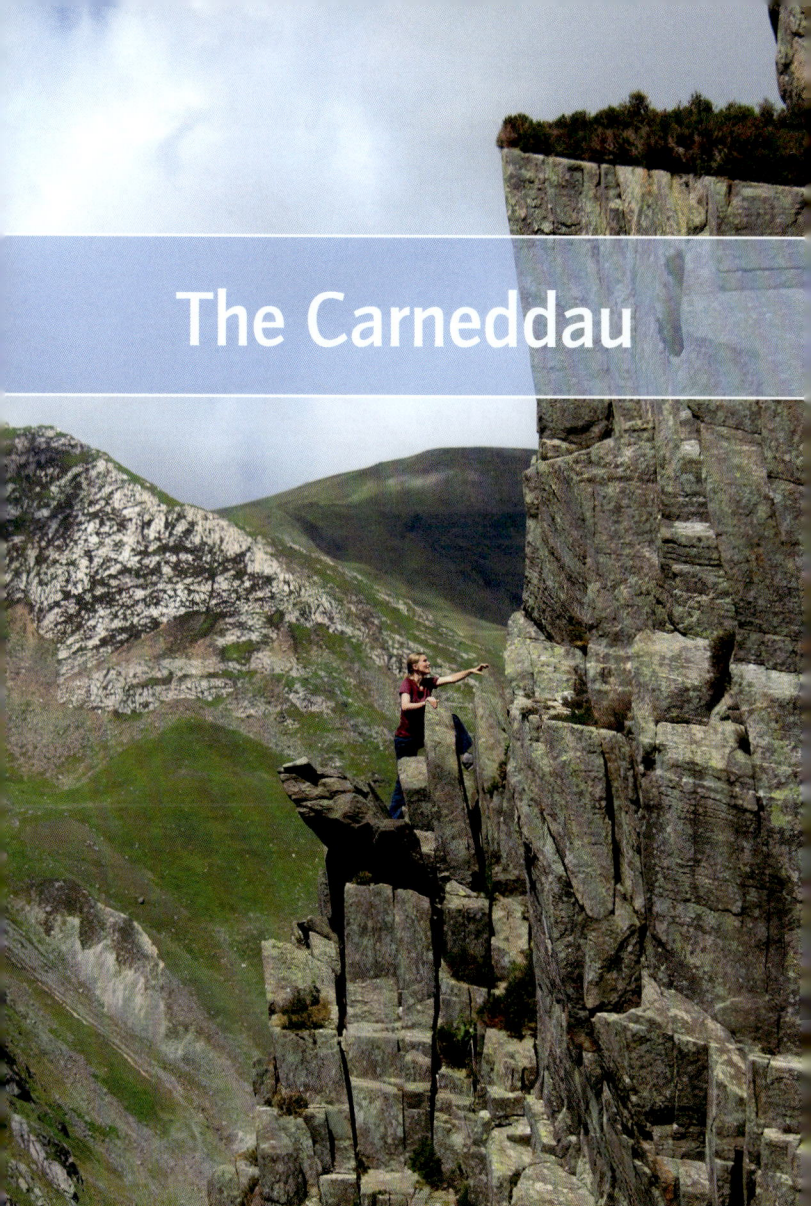

The Carneddau

Not as hard as it looks! On the Pinnacle Ridge of Braich ty du Face (Route 2)

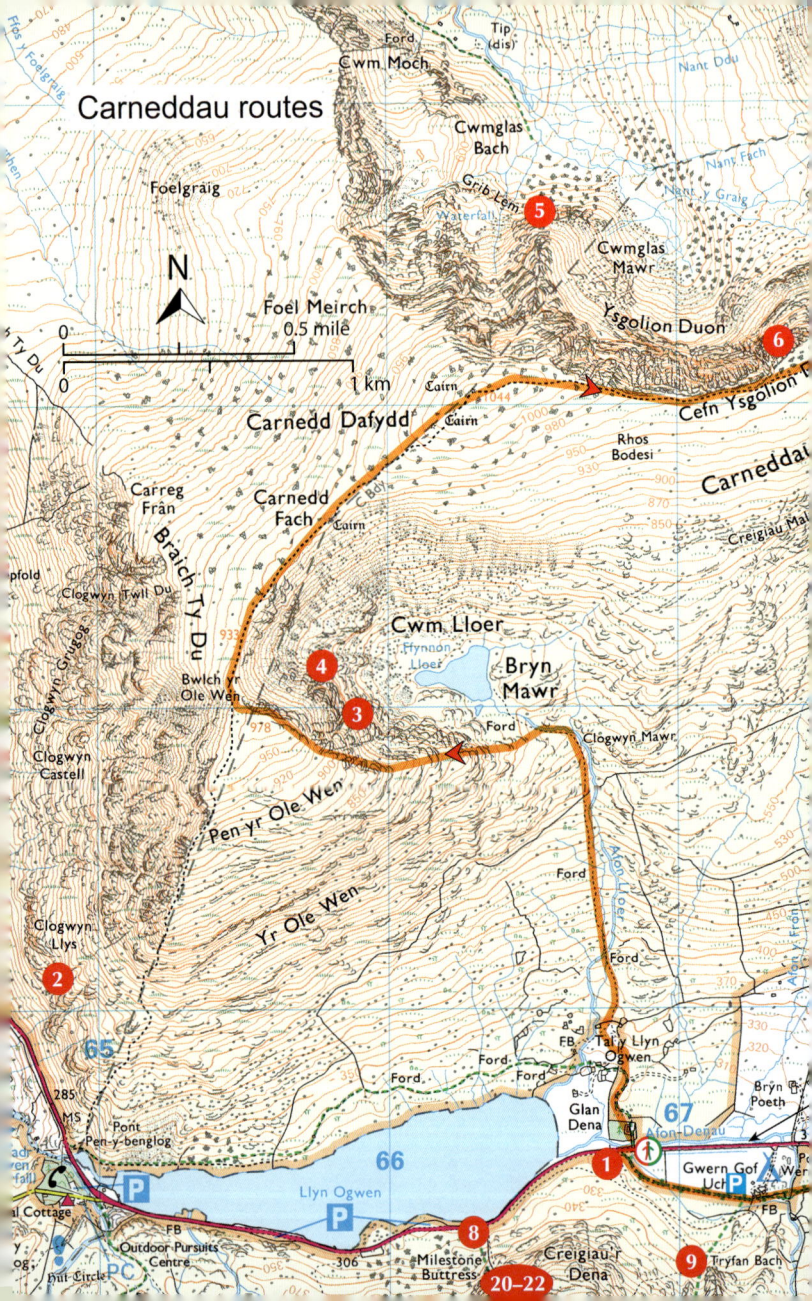

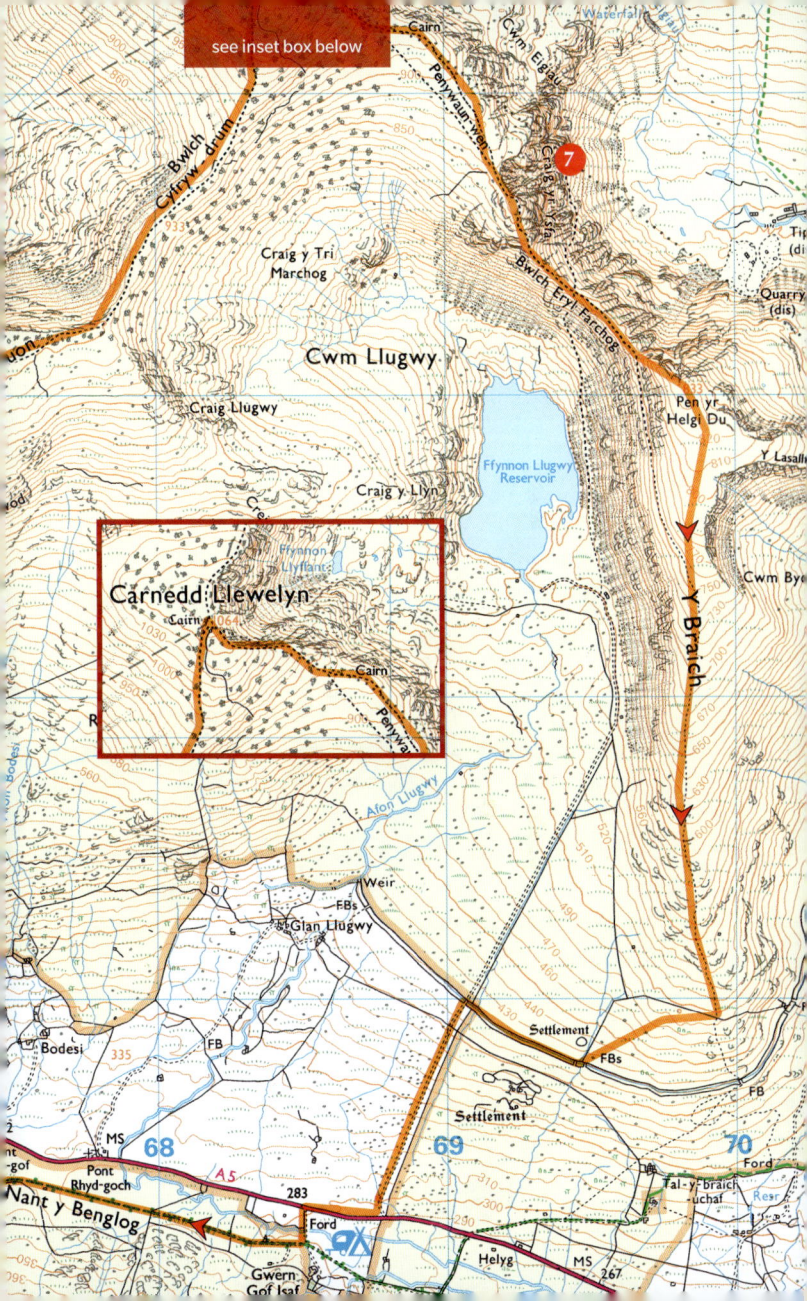

Descending the short step to Bwlch Eyrl Farchog

The Carneddau

The Carneddau form the most northerly hill group in Snowdonia. There are few hints here of the rocky intricacy of the Glyderau, or the rugged splendour of Snowdon; impressions instead are of barren summits and remote valleys.

A fortunate arrangement of ridges means that, having once made the initial height gain, several summits can be strung together in a high-level horseshoe traverse. Unfortunately most of the scrambling potential lies dormant under a blanket of heather, and much of what escapes is either too difficult or too loose. Nevertheless, the few lines worth following are enriched by their remote setting.

In broad terms the group lies within a triangle defined by the coastline between Bangor and Conwy, and the valleys that extend inland from those towns towards Betws-y-Coed. More specifically, the area of particular interest lies to the north of the A5 between Llyn Ogwen and Capel Curig.

The main ridges are aligned roughly in the shape of a T, with Carnedd Llewelyn – the highest peak of the group – appropriately occupying the junction. These ridges and their major intervening cwms – Llugwy, Eigiau and Llafar – provide the usual means of access to the scrambles.

Route 1

Southern Ridge Circuit 1- ✪✪✪

A superb ridge walk over four major Carneddau summits, punctuated by short, easy scrambles.

Location	Carneddau, Ogwen
Grade	1- ✪✪✪
Circuit time	5–6hrs
Route length	16km
Conditions	Much of the route is exposed to strong crosswinds, although nowhere is the ridge particularly narrow or precarious. Take care with route-finding on Carnedd Dafydd and Carnedd Llewelyn in mist. Wet rock does not significantly increase the difficulties.

Scrambles in Snowdonia

This is the classic high-level ridge traverse of the Carneddau, and the best introductory outing in the group. Not only does it ascend four major peaks, but it also previews most of the routes described later in this section. Scrambling interest is spaced, short-lived and of minimal difficulty, although anyone insisting on including something tougher in their mountain day could substitute one of Routes 2 to 4 for their ascent of Pen yr Ole Wen, while Routes 5 to 7 could also be incorporated into the day with a bit of imagination. The route is on mostly good paths across stony ground or grass.

Approach
Via the A5 from Capel Curig or Bethesda. Park on the roadside near the bridge at Glan Dena (SH 668 605).

Ascent/Descent
Follow the track past **Glan Dena** almost to **Tal y Llyn** Farm. Turn right on a path by a stone wall, later crossing the wall by a ladder stile. Several little streams are crossed until the main stream is followed, mostly on its left side (various often-boggy paths), to **Cwm Lloer**. Just as the lake in Cwm Lloer comes into view, take the path left which ascends a broad runnel towards a quartz-veined slab visible above. This gains the left-bounding ridge of the cwm – the East Ridge. The scrambling starts above the quartz and ascends the ridge, in its initial stages via a simple 10m scramble up a rock gully. Follow the ridge to the summit of **Pen yr Ole Wen**, 1hr 15min from the start.

Circle the rim of Cwm Lloer northwards for 700m and ascend a broad ridge for 500m to the summit of **Carnedd Dafydd**. Descend east for 1.5km on a rocky path, then curve north for a further 1km around the rim of Cwm Llafar where a few small steps of scrambling interest can be sought by going over the rocky knobbles on the way to the summit of **Carnedd Llewelyn**. Here there are retrospective views of the Black Ladders and Llech Ddu.

Take the ridge east then south east for 1km, passing around the head of the Craig yr Ysfa Amphitheatre, and descend by a 20m scramble over a gently angled rock nose to **Bwlch Eryl Farchog** (there is a short-cut descent south from here to Ogwen). Walk or scramble very easily up the rocky ridge ahead to the summit of **Pen yr Helgi Du**.

Descend the grass ridge of **Y Braich** southwards for about 2km. On passing through a gap in the transverse stone wall at SH 699 609, contour right on a small path then descend diagonally to cross the leat (manmade watercourse) at a footbridge just left of a stone wall. Turn right and follow the leat to the surfaced Ffynnon Llugwy access road, which leads down to the **A5**. Follow the main road rightwards for 50m or so, but then turn off left up the track towards the Gwern Gof Isaf campsite. After 100m a bridleway on the right is followed to **Gwern Gof Uchaf campsite**, where a choice of two paths leads back to the parking near **Glan Dena**.

Pen yr Ole Wen (978M)

The inelegant bulk of Pen yr Ole Wen protrudes south from the main mass of the Carneddau, introducing a kink into the Ogwen Valley where the outflow from Llyn Ogwen gushes down into the broad U-shaped valley of the Nant Ffrancon. For those based in the Ogwen Valley this is the most accessible of the Carneddau peaks, offering unrivalled views of the northern crags and cwms of the Glyderau.

Unaccountably, the most popular walking route zig-zags up the unpleasant and exhausting south spur from Ogwen Cottage; connoisseurs choose the scenic and comparatively gentle East Ridge. An ascent of Pen yr Ole Wen by either route is generally regarded as a mere preliminary to a traverse of the higher Carneddau peaks.

The featureless south east slope above Llyn Ogwen holds no interest for the scrambler, whereas the pseudo-alpine west (or Braich Ty Du) face, ribbed with ridges and riven with gullies, promises all sorts of adventure. Otherwise the best scrambling will be found at the head of Cwm Lloer, tucked out of sight behind the East Ridge.

Route 2

Braich Ty Du Face
(including Pinnacle Ridge and Porcupine Ridge) 2+ ✪✪

Exposed scrambling on an introductory ridge followed by a big hike to reach the rock arêtes of the upper face that lead, with increasing difficulty and excitement, to the summit slopes.

Location	Pen yr Ole Wen, Ogwen (SH 648 611)
Grade	2+ ✪✪
Approach time	15min
Altitude and aspect	360m, west
Route length	Despite the short approach, a lengthy outing with over 500m of height gain – allow plenty of time. Pinnacle Ridge on its own offers a quick burst of scrambling when time is limited.
Conditions	West-facing and quick-drying, this is a good choice when the north faces are likely to be cold or damp. Nevertheless, it is worth waiting for dry rock, especially for the airy pinnacles. The less-frequented Porcupine Ridge requires an astute judgement of holds, although the rock is generally sound. Good visibility is vital for the approach to Porcupine Ridge.

Route 2 – Braich Ty Du Face

A huge, complex face of ribs and gullies rises above the Nant Ffrancon Pass, appearing to provide endless opportunities for the scrambler. Unfortunately there are two main drawbacks: first, a large part of the lower slope consists of unstable scree which threatens to cascade onto the road at the first ill-judged step and thus limits the access; and second, a wide band of heather at mid-height seriously affects continuity. The selected route does its best to avoid both scree and heather and despite its shortcomings redeems itself with some exciting situations and, on the upper face, a genuine sense of exploration.

Many parties will choose to ascend only the easily accessible and popular Pinnacle Ridge – a good outing when short on time. For those intrepid enough to venture onwards to the Porcupine Ridge, they will find it surpasses the first ridge and is worth every drop of sweat exerted in reaching it. There is, perhaps, no better place to be in the late afternoon sunshine than on the Porcupine Ridge.

Approach

Park at Ogwen Cottage (SH 649 604) – approximately 150m east of YHA Idwal Cottage – or at the overspill parking areas further east. Leave the A5 at the Alfred Embleton stile, on the north side of the road bridge over the stream outlet from Llyn Ogwen, and follow the main Pen yr Ole Wen path for 80m. Turn left on a grassy path near some round stone shelters and follow the well-walked path to the base of the couloir on the right of the distinctive slender twin pinnacles that become identifiable on the approach. Ascend the couloir directly until a low dry stone wall is reached. A clear path accesses a scrappy part of the ridge 10m below the wall, although a pleasant grass gangway 10m above the wall provides the best access to the ridge.

Ascent

Use the gangway to gain the ridge. Follow the crest to a ledge then ascend a 3m step, slightly on the right using large holds, to gain another ledge. An exposed traverse of the pinnacles awaits. They can be taken on their couloir flank leading to a heather shoulder and slender grass col, but few will want to miss the photogenic ascent of the second pinnacle. This can be climbed and traversed on its west side at an exposed and exciting upper-end grade 2. (The first pinnacle is a much trickier undertaking, especially the descent from its top; it receives a V-Diff climbing grade and should only be considered by roped climbing parties.) Pinnacle Ridge ends at the slender grass col, where a path down the couloir leads back to the approach.

For adventurous scramblers the next objective is the cluster of ribs seen on the left side of the upper face – but steel yourself for a big hike. A broad, steep and grassy couloir – often wet and slippery – above and slightly left of Pinnacle Ridge avoids a blocky buttress and emerges onto an open slope of grass and heather. Alternatively, the couloir on the right of the blocky buttress is circuitous but drier and easier

At the first pinnacle of the Braich Ty Du Face, with the profile of Yr Esgair beyond

(its hidden east face offers various lines of roughly Diff standard) – at its top use a sheep path to move back left.

Plod up heather and scree (ignore any well-worn transverse sheep paths) towards a line of low, broken outcrops that are passed on their right. (The first outcrop gives a heathery scramble.) Take a rising leftward line to gain the left skyline ridge with an obvious cracked triangular face near its base set above a collection of spikes which, without stretching our imagination too far, we could call the Porcupine. (There is a second ridge over to the right across a couloir that has an imposing overhanging prow on it.)

Start in the middle of the porcupine spines and head up to reach the cracked triangular face where the rocks coalesce into a continuous ridge. Tackle the triangular face by moving rightwards across it to gain its right edge, which is then followed to its apex. Continue up the crest towards a substantial rise of clean rock, which appears to bar the way. This is craftily surmounted. Bear slightly left to gain height. Then, standing on a block and facing right (east) across the arête just beyond the front of its imposing wall, pull over a rib to land in a groove at the top of which is a well of boulders.

The groove is escaped by means of a shallow rectangular channel leading up to the knife-edged crest of the ridge and an airy position. Continue along the knife-edge and descend to a notch by means of its right side using a prominent shark's tooth-shaped horn. Continue up the crest using an awkward-to-enter sentry box en route to the next impending wall. This is clearly too steep for the scrambler, so head round to its left side and west face where two options present themselves:

- Climb its west face – steep but on excellent holds. Scuttle along the crest and drop down its east side to gain the tilted platform of a large block.
- A wide rectangular ramp leads up to the block. The right side of this is less steep, but more awkward than it looks; its cracks can be disconcertingly greasy. Use the channel formed by its right edge to gain height and at the top of the ramp hand-traverse left on excellent flaky holds beneath the block to gain its top more easily.

The steep, heavily featured wall above the block is – somewhat surprisingly – too difficult. Unfortunately the scrambler must sidle right from the block and gain an awkward heather runnel. Head up this and rejoin the crest.

Eventually the ridge falls back into a knife-edge and finally turns to grass as it abuts the supporting mass of the mountain. The path of the South Spur walking route is close by and soon leads to the summit.

Descents and combinations

The knee-wrecking South Spur provides the quickest and most convenient return to the start. Otherwise, descend by the East Ridge (see Route 1). It is a pity to waste hard-won altitude so this route makes an excellent alternative start to a traverse of the Carneddau ridges (Route 1), although with some imagination and boundless energy the Llech Ddu Spur (Route 5) could be descended and the east ridge of Black Ladders (Route 6) ascended to give a magnificent link-up.

Route 3
Broad Gully Ridge 2+ ✪

An attractive setting with slightly less attractive ridge scrambling.

Location	Cwm Lloer, Pen yr Ole Wen (SH 659 619)
Grade	2+ ✪
Approach time	45min
Altitude and aspect	690m, north
Route length	An undertaking of moderate length. Height gain approximately 210m.
Conditions	This is an unpopular and vegetated north-facing crag and so the rocks, although generally reliable, are occasionally lichenous and greasy. Best after prolonged dry weather.

Scrambles in Snowdonia

> Easy-angled rock on the inner flank of Pen yr Ole Wen is generally too vegetated for much worthwhile scrambling. This route finds the best of the rock, although its main purpose is to prolong time spent within the enchanting hollow of Cwm Lloer. Its merits should be judged accordingly.
>
> Near the left side of the craggy headwall, the prominent couloir of Broad Gully extends from the floor of the cwm to the crest of the East Ridge. The route weaves up the blunt ridge to its left.

Approach

Via the A5 from Capel Curig or Bethesda. Park on the roadside near the bridge at Glan Dena (SH 668 605). Follow the track past Glan Dena almost to Tal y Llyn Farm. Turn right on a path by a stone wall, later crossing the wall by a ladder stile. Follow the stream, generally on its left side to avoid bogs. A faint path branching off from roughly 100m before the steeper rocks of the east face leads to Ffynnon Lloer. Passing the lake on its left side, continue towards the headwall and impressive face of Craig Lloer (Route 4). On nearing Craig Lloer, Broad Gully can be seen properly for the first time hidden on the left. Broad Gully Ridge ascends the blunt arête to the left of Broad Gully.

Ascent

From the lowest point of the left-bounding ridge, move up right 15m to a short compact rib that forms a second toe of the ridge. This is gained from its right side with an awkward step to get off the ground. Above are two longer left-to-right rising ribs with a grassy runnel in the middle. Either ribs or runnel can be climbed, with the upper, longer rib proving the hardest and best route. Continue to a ledge beneath an intimidating blank wall. The wall is too hard. Do not be tempted by the slippery vegetation of the easier-angled terrain on the right. Instead, move left to climb the diagonal left edge of the blank wall (an escape to easy terrain just left is always available). A prominent large pyramid face of compact rock now looms above and bars the way.

Roughly 6m to the left of the pyramid face are two obvious wedged boulders. These are often hazardously greasy and much harder than they look. They can be climbed directly at a tough little grade 3 (a fall from here is unthinkable). Much better is to reach the bottom wedged block, then facing left make a challenging heave to cross over the left-bounding rib. A gentle groove with an untrustworthy spike in it provides recovery. Climb the groove and rib then move right to cross above the line of the wedged boulders and ascend a short crack to gain another rib crest. Above, romp over boulders and heather to a scree shoulder.

Continue towards a short, shallow couloir. It is best to divert right for a final flourish on rock – although the steeper left-hand rock can be climbed or the shallow

Route 3 – Broad Gully Ridge

High above Ffynnon Lloer on Broad Gully Ridge

couloir trudged up – before exiting onto the East Ridge. The upper part of the East Ridge leads to the summit in about 10 minutes.

Descents and combinations

Descend by the East Ridge path. Alternatively, descend steeply angled grass and scree at the head of the cwm, flanking the north side of Craig Lloer (the Craig Lloer Spur (Route 4) can be reached using this alternative descent). See Route 2 for further combinations.

Route 4
Craig Lloer Spur

3- ✪✪

A fine short line of great exposure in a delightfully secluded cwm.

Location	Cwm Lloer, Pen yr Ole Wen (SH 658 621)
Grade	3- ✪✪
Approach time	45min
Altitude and aspect	730m, east
Route length	One of the shorter lines, it goes much more quickly than might be expected from below. Roughly 210m vertical height gain.
Conditions	Craig Lloer catches the morning sun and dries quickly.
Topo	See Route 3

Sustained scrambling begins and ends on the compact buttress of Craig Lloer, a triangular crag truncating the shallow spur that protrudes into the head of the cwm. The airy traverse proves to be the key to an ascent of the buttress. Although of exhilarating exposure, positive holds are always close at hand. An escape is available before the traverse for those unfamiliar with what are essentially rock climbing situations.

Approach

As for Route 3, then head up to gain the left edge of the crag near the entrance to its left-bounding gully (in fact a broad couloir with several branches).

Ascent

Avoid a group of tilted blocks at the foot of the ridge via a 6m slab on the right (the blocks can be avoided more easily on the left, although the slab gives a useful foretaste of the difficulties to come).

Above, ignore easy ground to the left and ascend over small blocks to a larger one split by a 3m crack. A solid hand-jam gets you started and good holds reward a confident step up the crack. There are large belay spikes above if required. Continue easily for 12m or so until stopped by a slabby but hopelessly smooth wall (the last escape into the couloir).

On the exhilaratingly exposed traverse of Craig Lloer Spur

From a belay block, traverse obvious heather ledges rightwards to their end. Continue the traverse via a surprising handrail flake to arrive at a perch on the right edge in a position of breathtaking exposure. Positive holds above offer great reassurance. Pull over the first rise then mantelshelf (or belly flop) onto another flat ledge with a block belay beyond. The major difficulties are now over.

The apex of the buttress is not far above; gain it via heathery scrambling with a few interesting moments on curious, knobbly rock. The tedious scree of the broader upper spur requires a plod to either a simple scrambling exit through the final barrier wall or, better, by tackling the front face of its large left-hand section via a recess and tricky giant flake. Turn right at the top to reach the summit of Pen yr Ole Wen.

Descents and combinations

See Route 3.

Carnedd Dafydd (1044M)

Despite its great bulk, Carnedd Dafydd asserts its character only on the north western approach through Cwm Llafar. Viewed from elsewhere, its summit and flanks blend into the high ground of a ridge system which links the six highest Carneddau peaks. Rarely is it ascended for its own sake.

Scrambling interest is confined to the north face of the mountain – the Cwm Llafar flank. This headwall, evocatively named 'Black Ladders', is one of the most dramatic in Snowdonia. Although a rich source of winter climbs, its dripping tiers of rock do not invite attention in summer. Only on neighbouring Llech Ddu, the truncating cliff of Crib Lem, will you see rock climbers, and then only during the driest weather. With two exceptions the scrambling is disappointing, most of the obvious lines being either too vegetated or too loose for full enjoyment. Remoteness and atmosphere compensate.

Route 5
Crib Lem (Llech Ddu Spur)   1 ✪✪✪

Simple, perfectly situated scrambling on the short and comparatively safe steps of a prominent ridge leading directly to the summit of Carnedd Dafydd.

Location	Llech Ddu, Carnedd Dafydd (SH 665 635)
Grade	1 ✪✪✪
Approach time	1hr
Altitude and aspect	700m, north
Route length	Offers substantial scrambling. Height gain approximately 300m.
Conditions	Despite its north-facing aspect and high altitude, the ridge dries quickly. The rock is reliable, and the route's popularity keeps it clear of moss and lichen.

Scrambles in Snowdonia

An enchanting approach to Carnedd Dafydd through the long, secluded valley of Cwm Llafar abruptly changes to one of menace at the point where Llech Ddu Crag towers above the path. This compact 100m-high cliff guards entry to a long, low-angled ridge of alternating rock and grass arêtes that leads directly to the summit. Flank the cliff and this line – the finest scramble in the Carneddau – is yours.

Approach

Turn uphill off the A5 at the crossroads at the eastern extremity of Bethesda on Braichmelyn Road. Turn right at the crossroads in 1km to Gerlan. There are a few parking spots on the narrow lane, or alternatively park further down the hill. Continue through Gerlan, following the main right-hand fork of the lane and crossing a bridge over the Afon Llafar.

Just before the old waterworks gate follow the footpath sign initially up a private road, and cross a stile on the right. Cross a second stile at the top left corner of the field, and a third shortly after. Follow the track to open ground. Take the path, vague at first, that ascends parallel to the Afon Llafar to enter Cwm Llafar. Continue by a good path to huge boulders below the crag of Llech Ddu (SH 666 637). Ascend to the right of the crag to enter the hollow of Cwmglas Bach.

Carnedd Dafydd
5 Crib Lem or Llech Ddu Spur
6 Eastern Ridge of Black Ladders

Approach from Southern Ridge Circuit
dripping black crag

Route 5 – Crib Lem (Lech Ddu Spur)

Soaring high on the crest of the Llech Ddu Spur

Ascent
Resist gaining the crest of the spur directly and instead ascend into the cwm almost to the level of the deep-cut left-hand gully that splits Craig y Cwmglas Bach, at which point a ramp of grass and stones slanting diagonally left between bands of rock will be revealed. This leads without complication to a shoulder with a large block of quartz on it on the spur above Llech Ddu Crag.

Ascend through seemingly compact rock on the right side of the broad frontage to gain the narrower and less steeply inclined upper crest. Avoiding the many paths, follow the crest and its myriad crampon scars directly over several knife-edges and short steps to the stony summit dome.

Descent by this route
A reasonable proposition once located. When peering down from the convex summit slopes, several similar-looking spurs can be seen protruding into the cwm. Crib Lem protrudes furthest. A band of scree across the broad lower spur signals the approach of Llech Ddu Crag (beware!) and the need to bear left (looking out) to find the grassy ramp at the distinct lump of quartz leading into Cwmglas Bach. Many have chosen a descent to the right (looking out) down soil and scree – ideal if approaching the Eastern Ridge of Black Ladders (Route 6).

Descents and combinations
To return to Bethesda/Gerlan:

Scrambling down the diamond-shaped block on the Llech Ddu Spur

- Best of all, complete the Cwm Llafar horseshoe: follow the ridge east over Black Ladders and round to Carnedd Llewelyn, then head west to Yr Elen. From its summit head north west past the outcrop of Foel Gannol, and at a second outcrop bear west over steady slopes to regain the outward route at the river.
- Descend north west from the summit of Carnedd Dafydd along the delightful Cwm Llafar Ridge over Mynydd Du, joining the approach path at the entrance to the cwm.
- To return to the foot of the cliffs, follow Route 1 east until well beyond the Eastern Ridge of Black Ladders (Route 6) and then descend grass and boulder slopes into the head of Cwm Llafar.

Route 6
Eastern Ridge of Black Ladders 2 ✪

A distinctive outing up shadowy cliffs on the huge headwall of a remote cwm.

Location	Cwm Llafar, Carneddau (SH 673 633)
Grade	2 ✪
Approach time	1hr 15min
Altitude and aspect	800m, north west
Route length	One of the shorter routes, but lengthier than might be expected while approaching it. Height gain approximately 150m.
Conditions	North-facing at high altitude so often wet. The rock is rough and positive, although it is rarely ascended so watch for occasional loose rock. It is worth waiting for dry conditions.
Topo	See Route 5

The upper basin of Cwm Llafar terminates in the crescent walls of the Black Ladders. Upper ridge crests glow attractively in the afternoon sun while shady lower walls ooze ugliness and impregnability. Almost no-one comes here in summer. The solitary scramble on this face takes the right-hand ridge of the left-bounding buttress which, broad and poorly defined, only gathers itself into a recognisable line at two-thirds height. Difficulties need to be sought. Nonetheless, the atmosphere is terrific and the scramble is deceptively interesting.

On Eastern Ridge of Black Ladders with the Menai Strait beyond

Approach

There are two logical approaches:
- As for Route 5 to the huge boulders below Llech Ddu. Continue towards the head of the cwm over man-trapping boulders, then trend left to arrive beneath the easternmost rocks of the face.
- It is also possible to descend from the main Carnedd ridge path, starting around SH 678 634 then trending west north west (if doing so, it is reassuring to drop below the band of black dripping rock to confirm your position on the face).

Ascent

A broad-based buttress tapering to a ridge defines the left side of the Black Ladders. As elsewhere on the cliffs, horizontal bands of dark dripping rock prevent a direct approach to the foot of the buttress proper. These are best flanked on the left, followed by a traverse back right when the terrain eases. This approach gains the buttress at the same level as the start of East Gully, the foot of which is also terminated prematurely by the black-dripping banding.

Although there are many possible lines to take on the buttress, even the easiest of them involves some awkward steps. Stay with the rough steep rock on the crest just to the left of the gully as much as possible. A little higher the gully to your right splits with a rib in its middle: stay left, continuing directly on the narrowing ridge for the best scrambling. A final steepening can be avoided on the left.

The route emerges suddenly onto level ground with the main Carneddau ridge path nearby. The summit of Carnedd Dafydd lies a few minutes away to the west.

Descents and combinations
As for Route 5.

Carnedd Llewelyn (1064M)

Carnedd Llewelyn, the highest peak of the group, occupies a key position at the junction of the two major Carneddau pathways. Its four supporting ridges are aligned approximately south, west, north and east. The southern ridge drops gently to the shallow col of Bwlch Cyfryw-drum (a descent into Cwm Llafar is possible from here) before curving west above the cliffs of Black Ladders and rising to the summit of Carnedd Dafydd. The short west ridge drops only to a high col before rising again to the summit of Yr Elen, a major satellite peak. The north ridge extends in gradual descent towards Foel Grach, Foel Fras and the gentle hills beyond. Finally, the east ridge curves south east, passing above the cliffs of Craig yr Ysfa, and dips to the pronounced col of Bwlch Eryl Farchog before rising again to the summit of Pen yr Helgi Du. All ridges apart from the west ridge carry well-used paths.

The only face of any real interest to the scrambler is that of Craig yr Ysfa, which lies some distance from the summit on the flanks of the east/south east ridge. The cliff is hidden from most viewpoints, and so a special effort is required even to inspect what's on offer. There is even an unlikely story that would have us believe the cliff was discovered by telescope from Scafell.

Although the cliffs are extensive, heather covers much of the easier-angled rock, while loose rock or vegetation fills the most promising gullies. The selected scramble avoids the worst by finding a comparatively uncomplicated exit from the huge central Amphitheatre. The Amphitheatre is in fact a deep, square-cut recess set above a sloping bed of scree. It is bounded on the right by a 90m-high vertical wall of superb rock, Mur y Niwl – host to some of the best Carneddau rock climbs – and on the left by the 300m-long terraced rib of Amphitheatre Buttress – a classic V-Diff rock climb.

Scrambles in Snowdonia

Route 7
Craig yr Ysfa Amphitheatre   2+ ✪

The central ravine of a remote cliff is escaped via slabs, a short gully and a natural staircase of rock steps.

Location	Craig yr Ysfa, Carnedd Llewelyn (SH 694 637)
Grade	2+ ✪
Approach time	1hr 30min from Tal y Bont or 1hr 45min from the Ogwen Valley via Bwlch Eryl Farchog
Altitude and aspect	700m, east
Route length	Surprisingly short considering the crag it breaches. Height gain approximately 150m.
Conditions	One short section of this route has been affected by erosion and requires caution to avoid dislodging hazardous blocks. Otherwise the rock is mainly sound on the difficult bits. The cliff gets the morning sun in summer. Dries relatively quickly.

Hopes for an easy exit from Craig yr Ysfa's Amphitheatre fade when the options are viewed from its confines. None of the lines appear entirely free of complication. The right-hand gully (D Gully) presents the least number of obstacles so received the honour of selection, although some may feel the route lacks stature. The route ought to be valued for its majestic setting more than for the quality of its scrambling, which proves limited.

Approach
- The first option is via Cwm Eigiau. From Tal y Bont on the B5106 between Conwy and Llanrwst, follow a road rising westwards out of the village (not the road to Llanbedr-y-Cennin) for about 5km. Park at the roadhead at the entrance to Cwm Eigiau (SH 732 663), taking care not to obstruct the gate. Walk along a rough track to the Llyn Eigiau dam. Follow the main left branch of the track to cross the outflow. Continue by the lower track and follow it through the cwm to its terminus at ruined quarry buildings. Take a path initially on the left side of the cwm to avoid the worst of the marshy ground. Head up towards the left side of the crag, dodging the bulk of the scree, and join a rising traverse path leading to the Amphitheatre (SH 694 637).

Route 7 – Craig yr Ysfa Amphitheatre

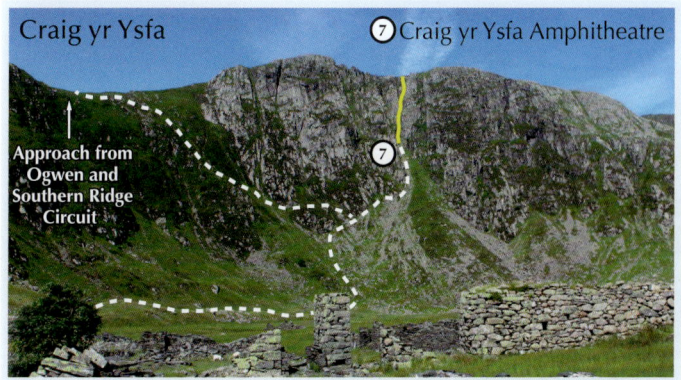

- The second option is from the A5 in the Ogwen Valley. Park in a lay-by at the start of the reservoir access road (SH 688 603) or the car park for the campsite (small fee). Walk up towards Ffynnon Llugwy Reservoir but leave the road where it veers left towards the lake outflow. Continue by the path that rises to the prominent col of Bwlch Eryl Farchog. Descend heather slopes leftwards (looking out) via a path on the far side and follow its arc beneath the main buttress to gain the scree fan below the Amphitheatre.

Ascent

The broad, scree-covered Amphitheatre bed rises steeply to a series of ribs and gullies, at the right-hand side of which will be found a short slimy and mossy gully. It is bounded on its right by an imposing steep crag and has slabs to its left. Use the slabs to gain a small recess above the nasty bottom of the gully. To exit the recess a pile of unstable blocks embedded in eroded soil are hazardous and require caution: ensure seconds are out of the debris line and use the solid rib on the right to progress up to a second recess.

The second recess has two exits:
- For the best and safest line, head up the left gully branch (actually C Gully) for a few metres to a large chockstone. Avoid tackling the chockstone directly; instead use the left wall to gain height before moving back onto it. From here an easy if exposed traverse rightwards leads back to the original gully line.
- A harder exit right via good holds leads up a short, steep wall that is often wet and slippery – at which times it is best avoided. Step left to gain a clean, slanting slab which is climbed with difficulty in a precarious position.

Scrambles in Snowdonia

Foxgloves at the starting slabs of Craig yr Ysfa Ampitheatre

Pick the easiest line leftwards to gain a series of clean rock staircases that zig-zag to the top. A right turn leads up the ridge path up to the summit of Carnedd Llewelyn.

Descent by this route
Not recommended without prior knowledge of the route and a thorough assessment having been made of the hazardous section.

Descents and combinations
From the top of Craig yr Ysfa there are several options:
- After emerging from the Amphitheatre, turn left to follow the ridge path via a simple scramble down a rock nose to Bwlch Eryl Farchog. Refer to the approach notes for continuing the descent into Cwm Eigiau or the Ogwen Valley.
- For a more interesting return to the Ogwen Valley, follow Route 1 in reverse over Carnedd Dafydd and Pen yr Ole Wen or its conclusion over Pen yr Helgi Du.
- Route 6 can be reached using its second approach (from the main Carnedd ridge path).

The Glyderau

Tackling the awkward start of Cneifion Arête (Route 40)

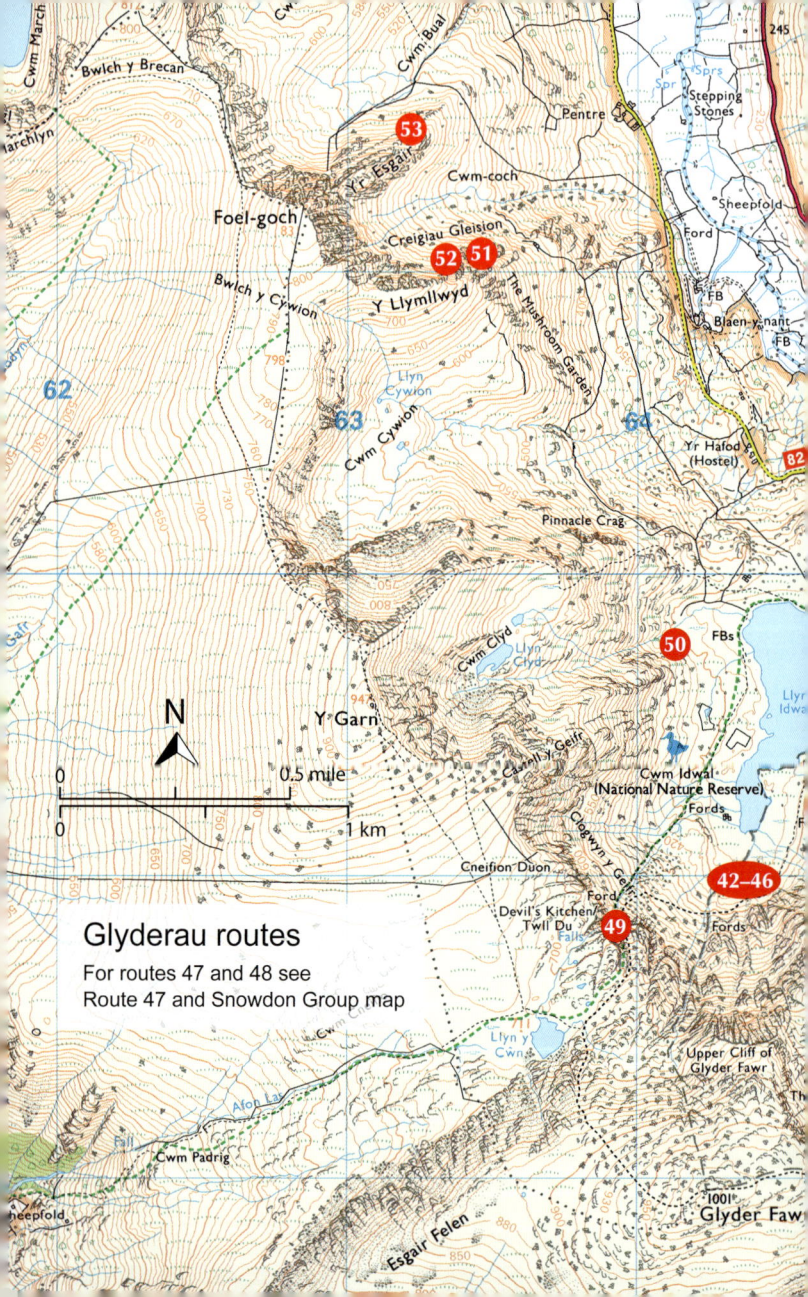

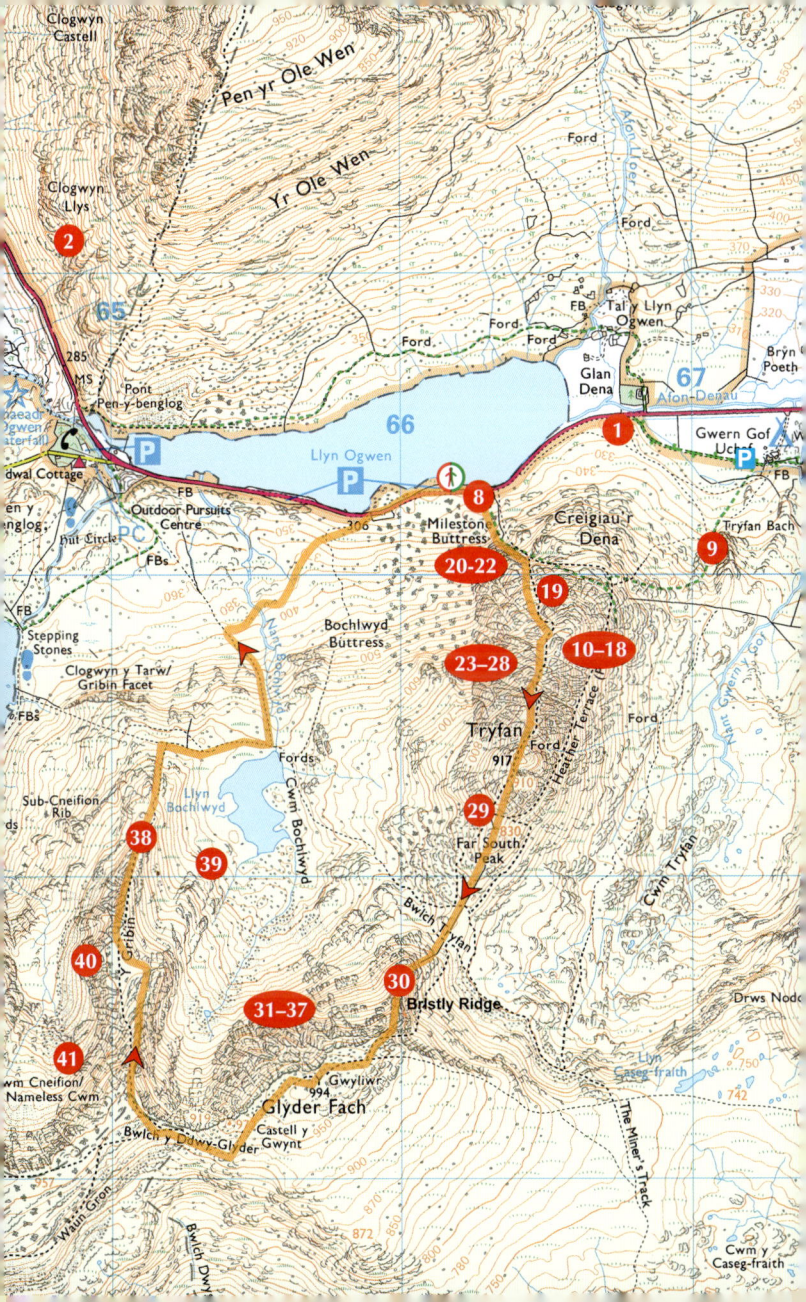

Scrambles in Snowdonia

The Glyderau

The finest scrambling in North Wales is to be found in the Glyderau, either within rock-walled cwms or along the crests of intervening ridges. Hence the large number of routes described in this section.

The medium is almost always reliable – rotten rock and treacherous vegetation being limited to a small number of notorious cliffs ignored by this guide.

The mountains described in this section – the two Glyderau and neighbouring Tryfan, Y Garn, Foel Goch and Carnedd y Filiast – occupy most of the high ground between the Llanberis and Ogwen valleys. In simplified terms the range consists of a string of summits lying parallel to the A5 between Bethesda and Capel Curig.

Route 8
Cwm Bochlwyd Horseshoe 1 ✪ ✪ ✪

A classic horseshoe ridge traverse incorporating some of the greatest scrambling in the Glyderau.

Location	Glyderau, Ogwen
Grade	1 ✪ ✪ ✪
Circuit time	5hr
Route length	9km
Conditions	Extremely popular during fine summer weekends. The highly polished rock – unpleasant but not especially difficult to climb when wet – soon dries after rain during warm or breezy weather. Bristly Ridge is exposed to strong crosswinds.
Topo	Also see Routes 19, 29, 38 and 39

This exhilarating ridge traverse is similar in quality and difficulty to the Snowdon Horseshoe. In circling Cwm Bochlwyd it visits the summits of Tryfan and Glyder Fach; ascends two classic ridges – the North Ridge of Tryfan and Bristly Ridge on Glyder Fach; and descends two lesser ones – the South Ridge of Tryfan and the Gribin Ridge. All these components of the traverse are described separately later, but for convenience links are described here.

Route 8 – Cwm Bochlwyd Horseshoe

Scrambles in Snowdonia

Approach
From Capel Curig or Bethesda along the A5. Park in the lay-by (SH 663 603) below the Milestone Buttress, a prominent feature on the lower west side of the North Ridge of Tryfan.

Ascent/Descent
Ascent of Tryfan via the North Ridge: See Route 19.

Descent from Tryfan via the South Ridge (Route 29): Traverse to the South Summit then descend the South Ridge, generally by its gentler west side, to the broad col between South and Far South summits. Again avoid difficulties by flanking the Far South Summit on the west side (although the adventurous may prefer to stay roughly with the crest for additional challenge) and then descend to **Bwlch Tryfan** (SH 662 588).

Ascent of Glyder Fach via Bristly Ridge: See Route 30.

Descent from Glyder Fach via the Gribin Ridge (Route 38): From the summit, continue south west for 300m to the fairytale **Castell y Gwynt** (Castle of the Wind). For added interest this can be scrambled over directly or, much faster, is passed on the left by a path to **Bwlch y Ddwy Glyder** (SH 652 582). Ignore the continuation of the path to Glyder Fawr and instead circle the rim of Cwm Bochlwyd for a further 200m onto the promontory above the Gribin Ridge. Descend the ridge by scrambling on the well-travelled crest to a broad level grassy section (alternatively the scrappier scree and scramble path to the left can be used). Continue along the east side of the ridge until a grassy path curves right and descends to the **Llyn Bochlwyd** outflow. Descend the path on the west bank of the stream then, after the angle eases, cross the stream and pick a rightward diagonal descent over boggy ground with occasional paths to gain the A5 at a large car park (SH 659 601) less than 500m from the start.

Scramblers finding a route up Tryfan's North Ridge on the Cwm Bochlwyd Horseshoe

'Adam and Eve': the twin monoliths on the summit of Tryfan

Tryfan (917M)

Tryfan's distinctive shape dominates the view when approaching Llyn Ogwen from either direction along the A5 road. Pundits say you can't climb the mountain without at some point using your hands for support. Two erect monoliths, Adam and Eve, tip the spectacular summit; daring extroverts will entertain the gathering by attempting the traditional leap from one to the other.

Pausing for the mandatory Cannon Stone shot (Route 19)

The backbone of Tryfan is composed of two ridges: the more prominent North Ridge descends towards the A5 road and east shore of Llyn Ogwen, while the shorter and less dramatic South Ridge provides a link to Glyder Fach. The faces that support this spine – east and west – are both impressively rocky. The ascent route most used by walkers approaches from Ogwen Cottage via Cwm Bochlwyd then takes the South Ridge by its west side.

Above the prominent ramp of the Heather Terrace, which slants across the East Face, stands a series of high buttresses separated by deep gullies. These are the lines of the best-known rock climbs and scrambles on the mountain. Apart from the accessible Milestone Buttress, the huge but heather-choked West Face is largely ignored by both rock climbers and scramblers and is a good choice for the misanthropic.

On the expansive clean rock of Tryfan Bach

TRYFAN EAST FACE

Route 9
Tryfan Bach Approach   3 ✪✪✪

Exposed and sustained scrambling on the large, polished holds of a slabby face followed by a blunt ridge.

Location	Ogwen (SH 672 602)
Grade	3 ✪✪✪
Approach time	10min
Altitude and aspect	360m, west
Route length	A brief burst of sustained scrambling with plenty of hands-on interest. Height gain approximately 90m.
Conditions	The slab faces west and so catches the sun from midday onwards. The clean rock soon dries out after rain, although the difficult step on the upper ridge could remain greasy for some time. The slab section swarms with novice rock climbers throughout the summer.

Thousands of would-be climbers first clutch at ropes and rock on the slabby wedge of Tryfan Bach. There are good reasons for including an ascent as a prelude to a day on the East Face of Tryfan. First, the line of deep cracks up the left side of the slabs is the ideal route on which to practise rope techniques that might be required on more serious grade 3 scrambles. Second, it enlivens the approach to the Heather Terrace.

The ascent is split into two stages: a climb of 60m or so up the left side of the 45-degree main slab, followed by a ridge scramble with one very tricky step to the crag summit. Most parties will want to climb the route in roped pitches and although sometimes described as Diff grade climbing, it is a sustained traditional Moderate grade and nowhere technically difficult (although its scale and exposure can be surprising). The route is based on a series of deep cracks near the left side of the face, although numerous variations of line at the same grade are possible. While gaining the arête and climbing it outright looks aesthetically appealing from the ground, the better scrambling is found following the line described here. The best belay ledges are about 25m apart, although intermediate stances can be found if necessary.

Scrambles in Snowdonia

9 Tryfan Bach Approach

Route 9 – Tryfan Bach Approach

Approach
From the A5 between Capel Curig and Bethesda. Roadside parking on the long straight east of Llyn Ogwen. From the farm and campsite of Gwern Gof Uchaf (SH 673 604), follow the signed path (stile) south west to the obvious slab-fronted crag.

Ascent
Start 10m right of the left edge of the slabs and follow an obvious break slanting diagonally left to a large ledge with sling and nut belay (10m). Resume the leftward diagonal to gain a smaller ledge with sling and nut belay (5m). The rock steepens above and there's a tricky step-up rightwards 3m right of the slab edge to gain a pronounced crack line. A sentry box stance with good belays arrives soon (10m).

Continue in the same line, trending right where the slab curves across so as to maintain a 3m separation from its edge, to reach a broken area near the crest (15m).

Scramble up a 5m chimney to gain the broad ridge crest and ascend it without great difficulty by polished grooves to a spacious grass shoulder. (There is an easy descent to the foot of the slabs via the grass furrow on the west side here, or an easy way to the top of the crag by a flanking route on the left.)

Scramble up to below the final nose of the ridge and enter a steepening groove (many will find this the hardest part of the route). Both direct and leftward exits are too difficult so, just below the steepening (nut runner), use a crack and large foothold on the right wall to effect a rightwards balance across to a blunt spike. Block belay above.

Easy scrambling soon leads to the top of Tryfan Bach with a good view of the approach to Tryfan's East Face.

Descents and combinations
Descend by a path on the grassy east side to return direct to the road, or by a rocky path below the slabs of the west side to return to the start. Tryfan Bach can be used as an approach to any of the scrambles on Tryfan's East Face (Routes 10–18).

Approach and orientation for the Heather Terrace, East Face of Tryfan (ROUTES 10-18)

Approach

From the A5 between Capel Curig and Bethesda. Roadside parking east of Llyn Ogwen near the farm and campsite of Gwern Gof Uchaf (SH 673 604). From here follow the signed path left of the farm (stile) and round its back before branching off the track on a path south west to the obvious glaciated slab of Tryfan Bach. (The path to the left (east) of Tryfan Bach is an excellent one and can be followed to Bwlch Tryfan and Bristly Ridge.) Ascend to the right of Tryfan Bach, trending slightly rightwards at its upper buttress on a good path to meet a fence and stile erected across the often muddy lower lip of Cwm Tryfan.

Do not cross the stile; instead pick up a distinct path running parallel to the fence. This eventually passes steeply up an unmistakable rift with steps. Ignore a scrappy exposed path leading left at its top. Instead venture 18m further above the rift to pick up a better path initially over blocks heading left (right leads to the North Ridge). This gives a well-travelled rising traverse line with some boulders and occasional scree but mostly on excellent ground to meet the well-defined Heather Terrace. Beyond a rise the main buttresses come into view, and soon afterwards the terrace assumes its true character. Cross the first water course (a shallow runnel of heather, grass and stones) and continue below crags to the first proper gully: a deep one between rock walls, floored with large stones. This is Bastow Gully (1+), a poor route consisting mainly of scree-plodding with one rise at two-thirds height (70min).

> **Note**
>
> It was previously possible to undertake a more direct and arduous, although potentially slightly faster, approach to the East Face by crossing the stile after Tryfan Bach and heading up rightwards. This traditional climbers' approach has fallen into disuse and is now best avoided.

The Heather Terrace can also be easily accessed from the Milestone Buttress area by using the main path to the North Ridge that passes the north side of Milestone Buttress. As this path turns to head more directly up the line of the north ridge, continue over the shoulder and round on well-walked terrain to join the Gwern Gof Uchaf approach at a jumble of polished boulders near the top of the unmistakable rift with steps in it. A well-walked rising line leads to the Heather Terrace (as described above).

Heather Terrace (Routes 10–18)

Orientation

From Bastow Buttress on the far right of the terrace where it becomes a distinct wide gangway it is best to keep an eye on the deepest gullies. The next gully after Bastow is Nor' Nor' Gully. The 'GA' scratched into the rock up the terrace from Nor' Nor' Gully is 'Grooved Arête' (VD) on the North Tower. After this North Gully is deep, slimy and green – no one would logically choose to climb its lower section. A distinct prow-like block dominates the path at a rise between the lower part of North Gully and the less pronounced Little Gully. The Central Buttress that follows has 'FPR' (First Pinnacle Rib – VD) confusingly scratched into the rock in two different places: the first one encountered is actually Second Pinnacle Rib, an alternative start, and the next one appears just before South Gully is reached. (Adding to the confusion, the FPR routes have since been renamed in the latest Climbers' Club guide as Pinnacle Rib and Overlapping Rib Routes.) Their distinct 'Pinnacle' can be seen on the face 100m above and is reached by Route 16. Beyond South Gully, the Heather Terrace continues below the jumbled sprawl of the South Buttress to meet the dreaded scree path that connects the excellent path in the valley floor with the col between the South and Far South Summits (avoid the scree path if looking for a pleasant descent and opt for the slower but less punishing path down from Bwlch Tryfan to the valley floor).

Overcoming the chockstone at the start of Bastow Buttress (Route 10)

Tryfan East Face

- ⑩ Bastow Buttress Variant
- ⑪ Nor' Nor' Buttress Variant
- ⑫ Nor' Nor' Gully
- ⑬ Nor' Nor' Groove
- ⑭ North Buttress Variant
- ⑮ Little and North Gullies
- ⑯ Pinnacle Rib Variant
- ⑰ South Gully
- ⑱ South Buttress

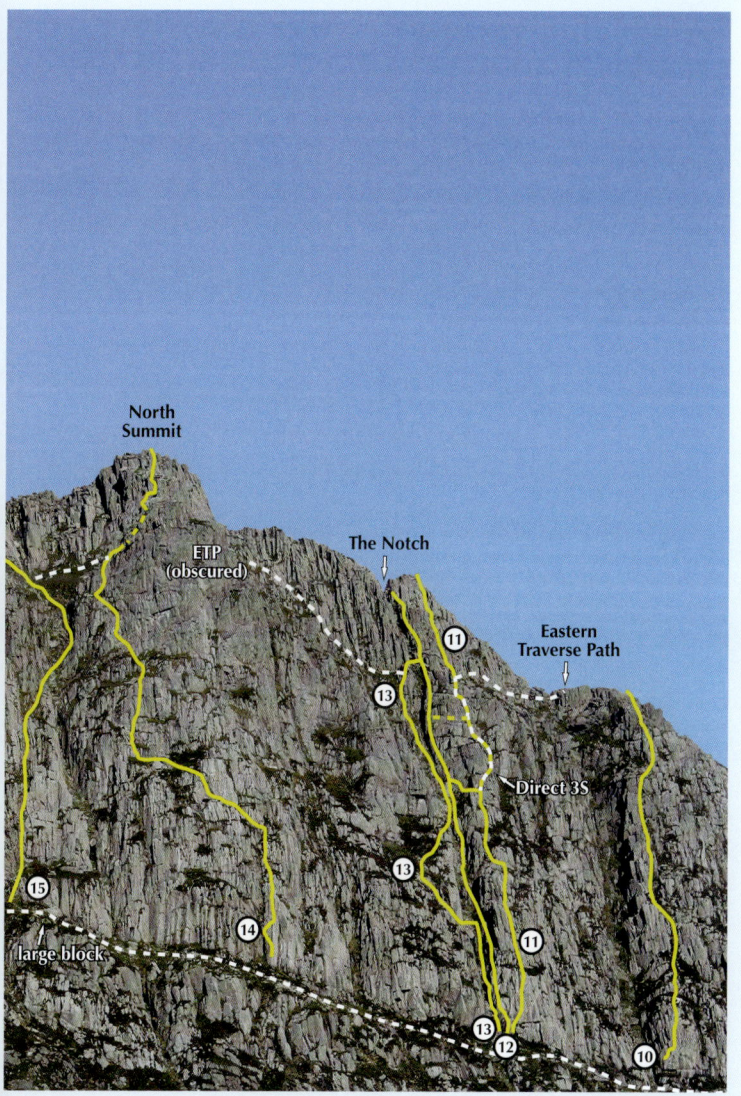

Scrambles in Snowdonia

Route 10
Bastow Buttress Variant

2+ ✪✪✪

This tremendous line is the first of the routes encountered on the Heather Terrace approach, and therefore a good choice for the impatient.

Location	Tryfan, Ogwen (SH 666 597)
Grade	2+ ✪✪✪
Approach time	1hr
Altitude and aspect	640m, east
Route length	A sustained but snappy undertaking. Height gain approximately 140m.
Conditions	The buttress dries quickly and faces the morning sun.

The route finishes far short of the summit, but arrives on the North Ridge below the best scrambling, while either Nor' Nor' Groove or Little and North Gullies could be used as a descent for the energetic wishing to combine routes on the East Face. The buttress consists of a typical East Face mix of rock ribs and heather runnels. Some of the situations, which include an airy narrow arête, are uniquely exciting.

Approach
See 'Approach and orientation for the Heather Terrace'.

Ascent
From about 10m up Bastow Gully (above its first small step), follow an obvious break slanting rightwards – with a brief struggle to get past the first chockstone – towards the ridge on the right. Continue rightwards in a superb position, soon transferring to the upper of two breaks, to gain a heather ledge on the ridge crest. Surmount a small step to a heather ledge with block belays.

Heather scrambling within view of Bastow Gully leads to the foot of the next rock feature: two ribs with a wide heather runnel between them. The rib on the left is difficult. Take the right-hand side of the left rib at a challenging 2+ (it can be tackled on its far left edge or middle at grade 3). Alternatively a mixture of the central heather runnel and right-hand rib can be taken. Now ascend the rib above, slightly on its left side (easier than it looks), to a blunt ridge.

Route 10 – Bastow Buttress Variant

The textured rock of Bastow Buttress

Trend left over heather and boulders and, when practical, regain the left-hand rib. Ascend the delightfully narrow rib with interest and some difficulty as close to the crest as possible, often overlooking Bastow Gully. (If necessary, most of these difficulties can be avoided on the right at a substantially reduced grade.) Continue to the large platform below the Nose on the North Ridge. Ascend to the summit as for Route 19.

Descents and combinations

See Route 19. Myriad combinations are possible. The Eastern Traverse Path could be used to gain Nor' Nor' Groove (Route 13) or Little and North Gullies (Route 15) to return to the Heather Terrace. Alternatively, heading over the line of the North Ridge, it is possible to reach Notch Arête (Route 27) or V Buttress (Route 25) using the faint grade 1- path that commences at the cairn below Notch Rocks (see Route 24 descents and combinations).

Scrambles in Snowdonia

Route 11
Nor' Nor' Buttress Variant

3 ✪✪ or 3S ✪✪

A delightful scramble up discontinuous cracked ridges, with one interesting gully diversion on excellent rock: exhilarating in the morning sunshine.

Location	Tryfan, Ogwen (SH 666 596)
Grade	3 ✪✪ or 3S ✪✪
Approach time	1hr
Altitude and aspect	670m, east
Route length	One of the longer East Face outings. Height gain approximately 200m.
Conditions	The buttress is quick-drying and faces the morning sun.
Topo	See Route 10

Similar to the Bastow route, although less successful in avoiding the gully it tries to escape (unless the serious direct alternative at 3S/Diff is taken – see description below). The deviation into the gully is clever, however, and offers a surprisingly satisfying escape via a through-route. Echoey blocks on the entry pitch should be treated with respect.

Approach
See 'Approach and orientation for the Heather Terrace'. Beyond Bastow the Heather Terrace appears as a distinct gangway. Follow it to the next prominent gully, Nor' Nor', which is steeper than Bastow and contains more jammed boulders.

Ascent
From the entrance to Nor' Nor' Gully, scramble diagonally right over heathery rocks for 6m or so then ascend with difficulty over echoey flaky blocks to heather ledges (21m in total).

Scramble up to the next rise, which can be avoided scruffily on the right, although is best taken by one of the two cracks near its left edge (a wobbly flake in the right-hand crack dictates that the left crack is the better option). Concentration and a helpful chockstone aid progress here.

Enter a gap behind perched blocks from the left and ascend the step that follows slightly on the right. Continue up heather and short rises to below the wrinkled rock

Tackling the harder direct alternative on Nor' Nor' Buttress

of the next step. Tackle this on the right, returning to the crest as soon as is practicable. The ridge above now rises steeply into rock climbing territory (see variation below) so escape easily left into Nor' Nor' Gully.

Ascend the right-hand side of the gully, initially over scree, then by rock ribs and a couple of steps. Stay right at a vague fork to reach a distinct slabby boulder. Scrabble awkwardly over this, ready for an immediate and easily missed rightwards exit over jammed boulders. Now for the clever bit: instead of plodding up the rest of the gully or gaining the upper ridge crest easily from further on, tackle the jumble of wedged boulders in the chimney immediately above the tricky slab and enter the deep, dark cleft. The right side of the cleft is formed by a pinnacle. This provides a through-route which brings you out above the buttress's difficult rock climbing section. Once through, avoid the temptation of easier ground by spiralling up to the top of the pinnacle. Step easily across the void through which you have just passed. Pick an appropriate line to head directly to the summit of Nor' Nor' Buttress above the Notch, passing over the Eastern Traverse Path en route.

Direct variation (3S/Diff)

This 'variant of a variant' is included only as many scramblers have sought to tackle it: it is unquestionably a serious undertaking with limited protection for the leader at a key moment. Ignoring the clever gully bypass, tackle the ridge crest directly, heading for a perched block. Gain a horizontal break on the arête 3m above (runners). Standing on the break, commit to the steep knife-edged arête (the left side offers the best, albeit tiny, footholds). A grassy ledge eventually gives a belay and recovery. Exit the ledge by means of a flared off-width crack and continue directly to reach a 10m-high buttress. Climb its wide central groove on its right to a vertical corner (runners) – a wobbly chockstone here has wobbled off and the exit up the corner is now trickier than it once was. Rejoin the main route at the top of the 'clever' through-route.

Descents and combinations

See descents and combinations for Routes 19 and 10.

Route 12
Nor' Nor' Gully 2+ ✪

Surprisingly good gully scrambling enlivened by several tricky obstacles.

Location	Tryfan, Ogwen (SH 666 596)
Grade	2+ ✪
Approach time	1hr
Altitude and aspect	670m, east
Route length	Would go quickly if not for its obstacles! Height gain approximately 200m.
Conditions	Often completely dry, in which conditions it is best tackled. Flooded by morning sunlight. Be cautious with loose material.
Topo	See Route 10

Despite being tightly sandwiched between two sister routes, with which it momentarily shares terrain, the gully nonetheless has a distinctive character. On a dry day this direct line from the Heather Terrace to the North Ridge is a more pleasing outing than might be expected. Its evil third rise is, however, quite stiff and needs care.

Approach
See 'Approach and orientation for the Heather Terrace'. Beyond Bastow the Heather Terrace appears as a distinct gangway. Follow it to the next prominent gully, Nor' Nor', which is steeper than Bastow and contains more jammed boulders.

Ascent
Clamber over short steps and ascend the first main obstacle – a boulder blockage – by compact rock on the left. Note the quartz slab belonging to Route 13 on your left at the top (an escape if needed). Take the second rise by rock and a vegetated groove on the right. Overcome the 'evil' third rise on the left by means of a steepening ramp of compact rock to gain a chockstone at its top. With the aid of the chockstone, step awkwardly left in an **exposed and serious position** to avoid a scree exit and gain the path of Nor' Nor' Grooves.

Reaching the top of Nor' Nor' Gully

Route 13 – Nor' Nor' Groove

The gully now eases into a scree runnel with a few short steps. Where it curves right at a vague fork, scramble up rightwards to tackle a tilted slabby boulder (if all else fails, try facing out slightly to make best use of footholds). Scramble more easily up the gully continuation, emerging on the North Ridge at the prominent Notch. Continue as for Route 19 to the summit.

Descents and combinations
See descents and combinations for Routes 19 and 10.

Route 13
Nor' Nor' Groove

1+ ✪

Quality scrambling up the rock grooves of a gully within a gully.

Location	Tryfan, Ogwen (SH 666 596)
Grade	1+ ✪
Approach time	1hr
Altitude and aspect	670m, east
Route length	Long but straightforward. Height gain approximately 200m.
Conditions	The grooves are on the shady side of the gully and may remain greasy for a while after rain.
Topo	See Route 10

This devious scramble cleverly avoids the harder obstacles in the true gully line by a series of leftward variants. It is a viable means of descent for the competent scrambler.

Approach
See 'Approach and orientation for the Heather Terrace'. Beyond Bastow the Heather Terrace appears as a distinct gangway. Follow it to the next prominent gully, Nor' Nor', which is steeper than Bastow and contains more jammed boulders.

Ascent
From the entrance to Nor' Nor' Gully, ascend in five stages a natural line of tiers above the gully bed on the left flank (with one awkward move – jammed right foot

Getting into the Groove

helps – that starts the topmost shallow groove) to enter a recess above the first major obstacle in the gully proper.

Ascend a hidden quartz slab on the left and follow a path up through an open area of heather until crags loom above. Dodge craftily back right – taking care with scree – to re-enter the gully above its 'evil' third rise. Ascend the gully, to a vague fork within 15m of the difficult slabby leaning boulder on Nor' Nor' Gully (refer to previous route if in doubt). Now either go 3m left and ascend a stepped break, or avoid this section completely by taking a broad branch farther left, traversing back right at the Eastern Traverse Path to regain the gully. Scramble up the gully continuation, over an initial step, to emerge on the North Ridge at the prominent Notch. Continue along the North Ridge to the summit.

Descent by this route
An excellent means of descent, only marginally harder than in ascent. Reverse the ascent description, being careful not to miss the path that escapes rightwards (looking out) above the gully's 'evil' third rise. Follow the path rightwards through heather until it leads back left to the quartz slab, which is best gained from its gully side rather than directly. At the foot of the slab, avoid being drawn into the gully bed and take care to locate a worn but narrow and exposed passage over two flakes which access the natural ramp system leading to the foot of the gully.

Descents and combinations
See descents and combinations for Routes 19 and 10.

Route 14
North Buttress Variant
2 ✪✪

A rising right-to-left line across the face of a large, broken buttress, using runnels, ledges and rock grooves to avoid difficulties.

Location	Tryfan, Ogwen (SH 666 595)
Grade	2 ✪✪
Approach time	1hr 5min
Altitude and aspect	690m, east
Route length	A long, meandering line. Height gain approximately 220m.
Conditions	Most of the easier-angled sections are covered in heather, although the protruding rock is clean and reliable. Worth waiting for dry weather. Faces the morning sun.
Topo	See Route 10

Grass shelves and discontinuous rock ribs break up any continuity of line on the lower two-thirds of North Buttress. The upper third rears up in the compact crag of Terrace Wall, towering above the middle pastures. North Buttress rock climbs seek out difficulties in the lower ribs and then tackle Terrace Wall direct, whereas this route exploits the lower weaknesses and flanks Terrace Wall altogether. The line is devious but logical, winding through difficult terrain with surprising ease. A direct finish above the Eastern Traverse Path leads satisfyingly to Tryfan's North Summit.

Approach
See 'Approach and orientation for the Heather Terrace'. Beyond Bastow the Heather Terrace appears as a distinct gangway. Follow it to the next prominent gully, Nor' Nor', which is steeper than Bastow and contains more jammed boulders. Continue to the entrance of Green Gully, which has a grassy bed and no obvious continuation below the Heather Terrace. It defines the right-hand side of North Buttress. About 30m beyond Green Gully, and therefore 25m beyond the scratched 'G.A.' of the classic rock climb 'Grooved Arête', is a V-shaped recess backed by a runnel, with a small amount of scree at its base and a flake chimney on its right wall. This is the start of the route. (The preceding V-groove 5m to the right has a 3m-high distinct narrow fin of rock protruding from it.)

Ascent

The runnel behaves itself for 20m or so and then becomes a path. Escape right here onto a broken rib and follow it, and its heather-covered continuation, to regain the runnel. A couple of metres higher, exit left onto the main face by a steady travelled ramp of heather and rock which terminates at a grass recess below a 10m bay wall. Ascend the centre of the easy angled but awkward wall, exiting leftwards from mid-height to access easier ground and an expansive terrace.

Tandem scrambling on North Buttress

A slabby buttress at the rear of the terrace is best overcome on its far left edge, overlooking North Gully. A corner provides easy access onto the wall. Return right and avoid a second low wall by a ramp of slabs leading up left. Easy ground above the slabby buttress again allows a return rightwards and leads to another wide grassy terrace.

The Terrace Wall – 50m of smooth and compact vertical rock – now rises above. Avoid it by flanking it on the left: follow a clean runnel which curves diagonally left beneath the wall and continues beyond as a series of steps. An avoidable final steep corner groove is accessed by moving rightwards and leads – challengingly – to the scree amphitheatre above North Gully and the Eastern Traverse Path.

To reach the North Summit, head up rightwards to the notch through which the traverse path passes. From the notch, steep rock appears to bar the way. Negotiate this by a brief venture onto terraces on the left (amphitheatre) side of the ridge, moving upwards and rightwards to gain the crest of the North Buttress at the first opportunity within easy reach of its summit.

Descents and combinations

See descents and combinations for Routes 19 and 10.

Route 15
Little and North Gullies 1 ✪ ✪

A pleasant introduction to gully scrambling via the bed of a dry, shallow trough and the easing upper part of a major fault line in majestic surroundings.

Location	Tryfan, Ogwen (SH 665 594)
Grade	1 ✪ ✪
Approach time	1hr 10min
Altitude and aspect	740m, east
Route length	Long but straightforward. Height gain approximately 175m.
Conditions	The rock is sound throughout with only a little scree debris, and that limited to the unimportant sections.
Topo	See Route 10

Central Buttress is the most massive of the three on the East Face and supports the summit blocks. Its base, furrowed by heather runnels and buttressed by rock ribs, presents a complicated structure on which potential lines are difficult to trace. This route uses the deep runnel of Little Gully to break through this lower barrier and thus gains the upper section of North Gully with few complications. A viable means of descent.

Approach
See 'Approach and orientation for the Heather Terrace'.

Ascent
Use a rock ramp on the outer left wall of the gully to avoid the mossy interior of the first step. Now ascend the trough – with occasional rises of pleasant scrambling – to gain a notch overlooking North Gully.

Continue up the trough a little on the left until it finally expires some distance short of North Gully. Follow a ledge that leads conveniently across to the right and, beyond a final rise, enter the scree bed of the main gully below unpleasant, moss-covered boulders.

A zig-zag on the right avoids the worst of the boulders and gains the scree terraces of the upper amphitheatre, where the Eastern Traverse Path will be found. This

Commencing one of the steeper sections midway up Little Gully with North Buttress in the sun

heads up left to access the Central Summit finally by a polished ramp at the rear of Adam and Eve. Alternatively, continue to the top of North Gully to gain the North Ridge just below the summit.

Descent by this route
From the back east side of Adam and Eve, head right (facing out) down a smooth ramp, until able to walk back left to gain a shoulder above a cairn. From here numerous scrambly paths lead north down into the amphitheatre between the Central and North summits. (The amphitheatre can also be gained from the notch between the North and Central summits.) From the amphitheatre follow North Gully down, taking care with scree paths, until a clear path on the right (looking out) exits North Gully above its treacherous step by means of a shoulder. This leads to the top of Little Gully. A reassuringly polished chimney commences the scramble down Little Gully and the Heather Terrace is soon reached.

Descents and combinations
See descents and combinations for Routes 19 and 10.

Route 16

Pinnacle Rib Variant　　　　　　　　　　　　　　　　3 ✪✪

A scrambler's version of a vaunted classic rock climb.

Location	Tryfan, Ogwen (SH 665 593)
Grade	3 ✪✪
Approach time	1hr 15min
Altitude and aspect	750m, east
Route length	Sustained throughout its length, allow plenty of time if pitching. Height gain approximately 165m.
Conditions	Solid rock with ample belays. Wait for dry conditions for the first pitch in particular, as it will be very tough in anything but the driest conditions.
Topo	See Route 10

A pleasant scramble with a stiff entry pitch that weaves much of the line shared by the classic rock climb, First Pinnacle Rib – to which it is inferior. The scramble offers an alternative, albeit sustained, first pitch and avoids the tricky and famous parts of the parent route – notably the often-dodged Yellow Slabs and Thompson's Chimney pitches. As such, the scramble has value for those looking for a marginally easier variant of a popular classic (although you could of course just climb the rock climb). **Note:** FPR is now known as Overlapping Ridge Route, while its sister route, Second Pinnacle Rib, is now known as Pinnacle Rib Route. All these itineraries meet at the Pinnacle, so expect climbing traffic on summer weekends.

Approach
See 'Approach and orientation for the Heather Terrace'.

Ascent
Five metres right of South Gully and 10m left of the FPR scratched into the rock that marks First Pinnacle Rib is a clear, and steep, V-groove system. (Confusingly, there is another FPR scratched into the rock a farther 50m or so lower down the Heather Terrace; it marks the start of Second Pinnacle Rib and has led hundreds astray over the years.) Tackle the sustained and challenging steep V-groove system directly until a precarious rise at half-height makes its right-hand rib the better option; this

Approaching easier ground above the Pinnacle

is followed until an obvious easy ledge enables the direct groove to be regained and followed to a belay at the top. From the belay, trend right a little and follow well-climbed rock to the left of a large suspended block. Continue until the famous Pinnacle is reached.

From behind the Pinnacle move right for 5m to below an obvious open-book V-groove. Climb the V-groove, easiest from the right, and at its top trend leftwards to find the easiest line. Here the gradient eases. The formidable obstacle of the final buttress, traditionally overcome by Thompson's Chimney, is too difficult. Instead, pass the buttress on the right-hand side, moving back left before meeting the Eastern Traverse Path. A lovely polished 2m hand-jam crack enables the ledge system leading to Adam and Eve to be gained.

Descents and combinations
See descents and combinations for Routes 19 and 10.

Route 17
South Gully   3- ✪

High retaining walls lend an impressive atmosphere on a direct route to Tryfan's summit.

Location	Tryfan, Ogwen (SH 665 593)
Grade	3- ✪
Approach time	1hr 15min
Altitude and aspect	750m, east
Route length	A direct and generally rapid ascent. Height gain approximately 160m.
Conditions	The route dries surprisingly quickly; however, the rock may remain greasy for a long time after wet weather and the slab start is exceedingly difficult if damp.
Topo	See Route 10

The looming gully walls restore a proper sense of enclosure to the wide recess of South Gully, the couloir that separates Central and South buttresses. There are no easy escapes once the initial barrier has been overcome.

The route gives interesting scrambling over short steps – some of which are difficult – to the summit.

Approach
See 'Approach and orientation for the Heather Terrace'.

Ascent
The first step in the gully can be taken by a series of smooth slabs and difficult grooves on the right, which are **treacherous if wet** (the less exposed furthest right slab in the corner above the square recess gives a tough technical challenge best left to climbers). It is far simpler to avoid the slabs altogether and head up the gully a short way, then make a devious rightward traverse from a spike below a chockstone towards easy ground above the slabs. The gully bed now widens into a broad slope.

South Gully Rib splits the gully. The left side gradually narrows into a scree chute then becomes rocky and is eventually barred; step left here and scramble up to easy ground. Beyond the scree, avoid what appears to be a square block (but is another dividing rib) by the short gully and steep slab just to its right.

Return to the main bed and surmount the final obstacle – a 10m dividing rib – by grooves on the right. An easy slope and short wall at the back of the amphitheatre lead to broken rocks between the Central and South summits.

Descent by this route
Feasible with prior knowledge. Take care to avoid the corner grooves near the foot of the gully: it is tempting to slide down the top groove, only to become trapped between a horribly insecure lower groove and an extremely difficult re-ascent – reverse the chockstone entry instead.

Descents and combinations
See descents and combinations for Routes 19 and 10.

Accessing the starting slabs of South Gully via the chockstone

Route 18
South Buttress

A varied and pleasant route that shares many of the characteristics of the East Face rock climbs – spiky ribs, heather runnels and spacious ledges – yet receives comparatively little traffic.

Location	Tryfan, Ogwen (SH 665 593)
Grade	3 ✪✪
Approach time	1hr 15min
Altitude and aspect	750m, east
Route length	A moderately long line with some thought-provoking sections. Height gain approximately 160m.
Conditions	Dries quickly and catches the sun from morning through mid-afternoon. Avoid in damp conditions.
Topo	See Route 10

This route, based on an intermittent rib line, takes the gentler left flank of South Buttress (when climbed direct throughout it is known in rock climbing guides as South Rib). The difficulties, although short and not excessive, are often exposed and therefore demand steadiness. A chimney through-route adds character.

Approach
See 'Approach and orientation for the Heather Terrace'. A short distance beyond South Gully (Route 17), a shoulder is passed from which the stile in the col between Tryfan and the Far South summit can be seen. The terrace path divides just after here. Take the upper and fainter path for roughly 40m until an area of cracked slabs on the path floor is reached. Two broken ribs rise above the path, with a tiny grass bay between them. A small diagonal plinth of rock bridges the grass between the two ribs.

Ascent
Tackle the crest of the left-hand rib, resorting to its right flank and bridging into the recess where necessary. Follow the rib for 50m until it degenerates into a pile of boulders at its last gendarme. A gangway that slants easily rightwards towards the crest of a second rib is on your right, with a similar but hard-to-access gangway found a few metres below it. Following either gangway to the rib crest and continuing directly offers a very stiff 3S challenge, so instead move 2m along the upper gangway

On the initial rib of South Buttress

to reach a shallow split chimney. Climb the left side of this (easier than it looks) for 6m to exit onto another short, sloping gangway rising up from a grassy area and leading rightwards to the rib crest. Use the gangway to gain the rib and then follow its exposed crest to a notch.

The direct continuation of the rib above the notch is difficult, so walk left for 15m to a cave/chimney formed by huge perched blocks. Thrutch up the chimney: the highest and most direct exit is by means of a 40cm hole and can be attempted if slim and covered in oil. Most will exit leftwards onto a ledge. Ignore the direct continuation and instead, facing out from the mountain, head right then scramble up past the top of the 40cm hole in an excellent position to regain the rib at a broad, flat area.

Move right and follow a broken rock rib a short distance. Above a jumble of rocks over on the right is yet another clean, pronounced rib. Tackle this directly with a slightly undercut start (the holds come). Turn a blocking pillar via a short chimney on the right side or by an open groove next to the chimney. Continue up the rib to a grass ledge below the final wall. Climb the wall directly by a short groove towards its left side (technical, hard to start, but safe), stepping easily left after 2.5m to avoid a vegetated crack. Alternatively, to dodge the groove, traverse scenically left to a platform near the South Ridge. Either way, easy rock then leads to the South Summit.

Descents and combinations
See descents and combinations for Routes 19 and 10.

TRYFAN WEST FACE

Route 19
North Ridge

1 ✪✪✪

Tryfan's North Ridge is justifiably the most popular scramble in the Glyderau. An absolute classic with sustained interest, it passes through impressive rock scenery and should not be missed.

Location	Tryfan, Ogwen (SH 664 601)
Grade	1 ✪✪✪
Approach time	20min
Altitude and aspect	420m, north
Route length	With approximately 530m height gain, this is a long route with considerable hands-on scrambling. Most parties make relatively fast progress.
Conditions	Extreme popularity means that holds are polished, although this does not detract from the enjoyment. Start early or late on fine weekend days to avoid crowds. Not especially difficult under wet or windy conditions, although it would be wise then to opt for its easier alternatives.

The jagged crest of the North Ridge rises without deviation to the summit and can be seen from almost anywhere in the Ogwen Valley. The ridge is broader than it seems from a distance and is more of a rocky shoulder than a true crest; as such, an endless number of equally enjoyable variations are possible. The scrambling among its stunning terrain is always interesting, and when extended into a horseshoe ridge traverse (Route 8) provides one of the finest outings in British mountains. Typically, short rises well-furnished with holds punctuate leisurely walking sections from where the unfolding view can be enjoyed to the full. Of the numerous alternative lines, by far the best is to stay as close to the crest as possible. **The route is also an excellent means of descent.**

Scrambles in Snowdonia

Tryfan West Face
- ⑲ North Ridge
- ⑳ Milestone Buttress Approach
- ㉑ Milestone Gully Approach
- ㉒ Milestone Continuation
- ㉓ Wrinkled Tower
- ㉔ West Face Route
- ㉕ V Buttress
- ㉖ V Arete
- ㉗ Notch Arete
- ㉘ Y Gully

Route 19 – North Ridge

Scrambles in Snowdonia

Approach

From Capel Curig or Bethesda along the A5. Park at a lay-by (SH 663 603) below the Milestone Buttress, a prominent feature on the lower west side of the North Ridge. From the lay-by, ascend near to and on the left side of a stone wall. Do not cross the stile to Milestone Buttress but trend left on a fairly wide scree path to gain a shoulder on the North Ridge (although the impatient can start scrambling more directly).

Ascent

This is a very popular route; if you find yourself on anything but well-travelled rock you've probably gone wrong and should check your line. Staying as close to the ridge centre as possible, continue up and keep your eyes peeled for a quartz platform where you'll find the surprisingly easy-to-miss famous Cannon Stone and its classic photo opportunity. (A direct grade 2 scramble can be found up the buttress almost directly behind the Cannon.) Most will surmount the high barrier behind the Cannon Stone around its left side in order to return to the crest (be careful not to go too far left over easy terrain). Continue to another large platform below a prominent high nose

Corralling the troops into the Notch

Route 19 – North Ridge

of rock – Notch Rocks (many parties, intimidated by their steepness, are pushed left and unwittingly wind up on the Eastern Traverse Path at this point). Notch Rocks are overcome with more ease than first appears. Take time to inspect the best line up their front (just left of centre) then follow this on polished rock to a minor summit, descending on the far side to the Notch.

Escape the Notch by polished holds – not difficult – and ascend a gully to the North Summit. Descend from this and continue easily up over boulders to reach the twin standing stones of Adam and Eve on the Central Summit.

Descent by this route

In descent the best description is simply to stay roughly with the crest and look out for polish. At the quartz platform above the Cannon Stone trend right to find the descent, while on the quartz platform below the Cannon Stone trend left. Avoid heading too directly to the Milestone parking area; it is better to bear right and east away from the Milestone to pick up the easiest access to the scree-covered approach path. An alternative to the upper scrambling is provided by the Eastern Traverse Path, which flanks the North Ridge on its east side. This can be gained from the summit via a prominent slab on the east side of Adam and Eve. The path skirts the amphitheatres of the upper East Face, although it rarely drops more than 30m or so below the crest.

Descents and combinations

- Via Cwm Bochlwyd: traverse to the South Summit then either follow Route 29 down the crest, or avoid most difficulties by flanking the Far South Summit on the west side and then descend to Bwlch Tryfan (SH 662 588). Turn right and follow an improving path down to Llyn Bochlwyd. Descend the path on the west bank of the stream then cross it for a rightward diagonal descent over boggy ground to gain the A5 at a large car park (SH 659 601) less than 500m from the start, or stay on the path back to Ogwen Cottage.
- From Bwlch Tryfan head east to reach an excellent path back to the Gwern Gof Uchaf campsite.
- See Route 8 to continue on the classic Cwm Bochlwyd Horseshoe.

Coping with wet rock on Milestone Buttress as a party retreats above

Route 20

Milestone Buttress Approach 3 ✪✪

A rising diagonal line – occasionally difficult and exposed – across an open, slabby buttress.

Location	Tryfan, Ogwen (SH 663 602)
Grade	3 ✪✪
Approach time	20min
Altitude and aspect	380m, west
Route length	Easily accessed and fairly short. A good option where time is limited. Height gain approximately 80m.
Conditions	The rock is reliable but badly polished where the line crosses rock climbs. It becomes slippery when wet, especially on the entry section, and the route is then best avoided.
Topo	Also see Route 19

The Milestone Buttress is the most prominent and accessible crag on the West Face. Facing the afternoon sun, its blocky front – free of vegetation and shaped by cracks, chimneys and slabs – makes an exciting approach to the North Ridge or the first of a chain of scrambles on the West Face.

Because this is the easiest way up the buttress, careful route-finding is essential. Roped protection should be considered for some of the more awkward and exposed obstacles and is essential in less than ideal conditions.

Approach

From Capel Curig or Bethesda along the A5. Park at a lay-by (SH 663 603) below the Milestone Buttress, a prominent feature on the lower west side of the North Ridge. From the lay-by, ascend near a stone wall – soon crossing it at a stile – then clamber across boulders trending right to below the slabby west face of the buttress.

Ascent

A protruding narrow slab defines the right-hand side of the main slab frontage, beyond which is an open scree couloir (Milestone Gully – Route 21). Climb the slab in two stages of 8m on good but polished and occasionally spaced holds. (Alternatively,

Tryfan – Milestone Buttress
- ⓴ Milestone Buttress Approach
- ㉑ Milestone Gully Approach
- ㉒ Milestone Continuation

avoid the slab by traversing in from the gully at one of several points.) Now scramble more easily for 10m to a recess beneath the huge tilted block of the Pulpit.

Crouch left beneath the Pulpit and follow a diagonal line of flakes leftwards to a recessed ledge. Swing up to the left (exposed) and continue diagonally left, across wrinkled slabs, to another recess. Go up over blocks to enter a large, rock-walled bay (belay).

The corner chimney is too difficult, so ascend an easier one 4m to the right on spiky holds to grass in 7m. Move left to enter a rock trough and ascend this to open heather slopes. Finally, trend right to arrive at boulders at the top of Milestone Gully.

Descent by this route
Not as difficult as you might expect, although certainly not recommended without thorough knowledge of the route in ascent.

Descents and combinations
To return directly to the foot of the face, descend via Route 21. Alternatively, take a vague path from the top of Route 21 that arcs due east over a rise to traverse gradually downwards – with one awkward grade 1 step – to the scree path on the North Ridge. Although it is possible to gain the North Ridge directly up heather and boulder slopes at grade 1+, it is best to maintain the character and difficulty of this approach by combining it with Route 22.

Route 21
Milestone Gully Approach 2- ✪✪

An entertaining if ugly-looking gully which, above a baffling step, provides 50m of excellent steep scrambling.

Location	Tryfan, Ogwen (SH 663 601)
Grade	2- ✪✪
Approach time	20min
Altitude and aspect	400m, west
Route length	A sustained scramble of moderate length. Height gain approximately 90m.
Conditions	Wet conditions are common. The heavily polished and water-worn rock is free from lichen and so loss of friction in such conditions is minimal. The rock is of better quality than that usually found in gullies and loose material is rare.
Topo	See Routes 19 and 20

In Milestone Gully the difficulties are sustained but not excessive, apart from the – avoidable – 'baffling step'. The baffling step invariably brings looks of befuddlement and consternation; gold star if you get it right first time!

Approach
As for Route 20. An open scree couloir defines the right-hand side of the buttress front.

Early morning procession of scramblers in Milestone Gully

Ascent

Ascend the couloir into the narrowing gully then trend left up rock shelves. A smooth, chin-high black shelf bars the return back right – 'the baffling step'. Use whatever means you have at your disposal to overcome it (or avoid it by taking a rightward line from below the wet shelves to gain a steep but easy little chimney). Scramble up the cracked left side of the upper rock slot and exit left at the top over blocks.

Descent by this route

Perfectly viable in exact reverse of the ascent, and a little more difficult.

Descents and combinations

See Route 21.

Route 22

Milestone Continuation   3 ✪ ✪

A worthwhile diversion providing 40m of difficult – but protectable and escapable – scrambling followed by easier exploratory terrain for those approaching the North Ridge via the Milestone Buttress.

Location	Tryfan, Ogwen (SH 663 601)
Grade	3 ✪ ✪
Altitude and aspect	500m, west
Route length	Normally incorporated into longer days. The difficult section provides a brief burst of grade 3 and is followed by roughly 100m height gain on varied terrain.
Conditions	The rock is sound and friction good. Catches the afternoon sun.
Topo	See Routes 19 and 20

The enticing starting face is a delectable piece of rock – although sadly short-lived. The step up from its left edge is reachy and may offer a momentary thrill (especially for the short). Scrambling of an exploratory nature completes the line.

Scrambles in Snowdonia

Climbing skywards on the starting face of Milestone Continuation

Approach
Initially by ascending Route 21 or 22. From the top of Milestone Gully, walk up 30m to the base of a second crag, a Milestone Buttress in miniature.

Ascent
Start at the toe of the buttress and climb a hand-width dog-leg crack for 10m to a ledge on the left edge of the slab (possible escape down to the left). Make a long reach or mantelshelf from the left onto a second ledge and scramble awkwardly up a series of easing ribs until they are swallowed by the heather slope. Continue on rock near the left edge or, more easily, up heather on the right. Exploratory easy scrambling directly ahead gains the North Ridge well below the Cannon Stone.

Descents and combinations
See descents and combinations for Routes 19 and 10.

Route 23

Wrinkled Tower
(aka Wrinkled Slabs and Castle Chimney) 3S ✪ ✪ ✪

Varied and difficult scrambling up a series of intimidating steps and towers on the huge West Face of Tryfan.

Location	Tryfan, Ogwen (SH 663 599)
Grade	3S ✪ ✪ ✪
Approach time	30min
Altitude and aspect	510m, west
Route length	A relatively long route with sustained interest. The lower section in good conditions can go by quickly enough despite its technicalities, but most parties will be slowed significantly by Castle Chimney and its exposed escape. Height gain approximately 250m.
Conditions	The rock offers good friction when dry but can be hopelessly greasy when wet. The exposed crux dries quickly after rain, however. Faces the afternoon sun.
Topo	See Route 19

Beyond the busy Milestone Buttress, the West Face promises a great scrambling adventure – provided a route can be contrived among the clinging heather, cascading runnels and impossible towers. This is the route. The notorious exposed solution to the Faulty Tower (Castle Chimney on Castle Rocks) lies at the upper limit of scrambling difficulty; this unmissable pitch and other obstacles can be adequately protected with a rope and a few runners.

Approach

Initially as for Route 20. Beyond Milestone Gully a second, vegetated buttress is bounded on the right by a watercourse, to the right of which are acres of heather-covered slabs. Walk beneath the slabs and enter the scree couloir that defines their right-hand side, below a bristling rib.

Ascent

From the couloir entrance, ascend leftwards on heather and rough slabs. Gain piled blocks several metres above either by a rarely used through-route on the left or,

Scrambles in Snowdonia

Wet rock increasing the difficulty at the piled blocks of Wrinkled Tower

better, by a slabby corner on the right. Continue more easily then move left to piled rocks on the rib crest below a smooth nose of rock.

Gain a small ledge at 2m then use a perfect flake to go out left, high or low, to a useful spike (runner). Climb straight above the spike on good holds, finishing with a difficult move – avoidable by a step left to grass – to huge blocks (10m).

Scramble over the blocks and pull through a gap on the left to gain a large ledge at the left side of a 4m pinnacle flake. A broad, slabby rib rises above; ascend it slightly on the left via blocks until the angle relents. Scramble easily up a gently angled shallow rib of blocks until beneath the left side of the imposing Faulty Tower, set above distinctive daubs of quartz.

From the top of the rib, traverse right across the grass gully for 10m or so and gain the foot of the improbable Faulty Tower above the quartz. The chimney fault, partially choked by a 5m flake, offers a slim chance. Struggle up the chimney (thread runner) to a recess in its upper part. The slimy continuation is appallingly insecure, so, unlikely as it may seem, get onto a ledge on the left (small nut) and follow a narrowing, sloping ramp leftwards into a position of stomach-turning exposure. Keep your nerve and reach for a flake on the very edge (sling protection). Now have faith and stretch high above the flake to a superb edge and pull over onto a ledge with a block belay a little higher. (The ledge is steady enough to reverse, but the chimney less so.) If all this sounds too exciting it can be avoided on the left by scrambling easily above the shallow rib then traversing rightwards to the block belay – considerably reducing the route's overall grade.

The next task is to regain the crest of the tower. Either gain it directly above the block with difficult long reaches to flakes, or, better, sidle a few metres left and climb the deep rift behind a flake pinnacle, stepping out (exposed) to easy ground above.

Ten metres of easy scrambling lead to the base of a clean slab split by a boot-wide crack. Ascend the crack and flake slivers to the slab top in 10m (avoidable, but it's a pity to miss this). Continue on easing rock and scramble up a final rib via shattered blocks and a slab near the left edge. Ascend over heather and boulders to gain the North Ridge about 100m above the Cannon. Continue to the summit as for Route 19.

Descents and combinations
See descents and combinations for Routes 19, 10 and 24.

Route 24
West Face Route 3 ✪

One of the less-frequented Tryfan scrambles, it is varied – good to start and finish – and works up a large, broken face.

Location	Tryfan, Ogwen (SH 663 597)
Grade	3 ✪
Approach time	30min
Altitude and aspect	550m, west
Route length	A moderately long route. Height gain approximately 250m.
Conditions	The start is water-washed in bad weather and requires care after periods of heavy rain, so dry conditions are particularly desirable. Some large rocks in the middle are precariously balanced and a judicious, experienced approach is required. Faces the afternoon sun.
Topo	See Route 19

An easier alternative to Wrinkled Tower, following an interrupted line of slabs, ribs and towers on the huge West Face: the route can be adapted to include the sublime Notch Arête.

Approach

There are two approaches:

- Much the easiest approach as it avoids the worst of the scree, but it seems indirect and counterintuitive: from the metal gate at the Milestone lay-by (SH 663 603) that gives normal access to the eponymous buttress and North Ridge, head 150m west along the road to the next metal gate. Pass through this and follow grassy tongues and faint paths running parallel to, but 100m away from, the steeper terrain of the West Face. When high enough, move over scree chutes to join the scree and heather runnel that leads up and round to the rib at the foot of the route.
- Initially as for Route 23. Right of the scree couloir is a less prominent rib, and to the right of this is a scree tongue leading into a runnel of heather and rock – both of which are followed round to the right towards a broad rock rib, below which is a platform of grass and scree (very small cairn).

Considering the options at the poised blocks on West Face Route

Route 24 – West Face Route

Ascent
The left side of the rib is uninviting so start at the right side of the ledge, almost in the corner formed by a protruding rib. Scramble up a water-washed staircase of clean rock, slightly left at first then straight up (easier than it looks). After 50m or so, ignore easy ground on the right and trend left below a dihedral (corner) formed by a protruding rib. Continue steeply but on good holds until barred by a smooth slab interspersed with cracks.

Ascend the slab by a central heather trough until it ends abruptly after 7m, then escape diagonally left via spikes to heather.

The next buttress is characterised by gravity-defying blocks and impressive cannon stones on its left side. It may be overcome in one of three ways, all of them rather precarious:
- It is best to access the jumble of rocks above its most tottering section by a traverse in from the right. Ascend a narrowing grass tongue for a few metres, ignoring a vertical grass-filled slot to the right and a v-cleft centre. Spot a logical line leftwards. Pull convincingly across on good holds to reach the left edge, where a surprising ledge round the corner on the wall bounding the jumble of rocks brings salvation to a momentarily precarious position. An easy step down onto the middle of the jumble above its worst material is now possible.
- With great delicacy, climb over all the poised blocks next to the cannons. If this does not appeal (and it may well not), try:
- Sneaking round the cannons to climb their left side and enter the jumble high up.

Exit the jumble at the top (best on the left) to a platform and continue to an – avoidable – 6m barrier, climbed centrally. Now take any route to the terminal Sunset Rib and climb it on superb rock with a difficult finale to arrive on the North Ridge at the large platform below the nose formed by the Notch Rocks, and continue to the summit as for Route 19. Alternatively, before ascending Sunset Rib identify a detached tower/spike at the lower right edge of Notch Rocks on the west face and take a rightwards rising line towards it (occasional scramblers' and goat paths) to gain the start of Notch Arête (Route 27).

Descents and combinations
- See Route 19.
- It is possible to descend the couloir on the left of the route (looking out): begin at a large cairn on the level ground below Notch Rocks. Follow the open couloir down, eventually joining a faint path – this must be followed to the left (looking out) of a small dividing rib (**right is treacherous**). The path curves down, with some minor steps on the left side of the couloir (looking out) and to the right of Buzzard Buttress and the V Buttress (Route 25).
- It is not difficult to finish the route then return down part of the couloir to pick up the line to Notch Arête (Route 27).

Topping up the tan on the right arête of V Buttress

Route 25

V Buttress

3 ✪✪

An unfrequented route that follows a spiky arête to a knife-edge finish.

Location	Tryfan, Ogwen (SH 663 597)
Grade	3 ✪✪
Approach time	40min
Altitude and aspect	580m, west
Route length	A short line with sustained interest. Easily incorporated into longer outings. Height gain approximately 90m.
Conditions	The rock is quick-drying and offers excellent friction, although it is a trickier proposition immediately after rain. Best in the afternoon when it is often bathed in sunshine throughout. If following the described line, the rock is sound. However, loose material can be found off-route. There are ample gear placements and good belays.
Topo	See Route 19

This short line is best combined with Notch Arête to form a tremendous West Face link-up. It can be ascended in its own right and proves a good, shorter excursion lower down the mountain if the weather is looking unpredictable.

Approach

As for Route 24 (using the first option) but continue up beyond that route, passing the grassy couloir where a steep descent path (grade 1-) is worth noting, as is a prominent sharp cannon stone that thrusts out from the bottom left of a buttress – the Flat Iron. Continue to the right edge of the buttress until below the gully that accesses the giant V Cleft.

Ascent

From the right-hand toe of the buttress, head up the gully for no more than 15m. Just below the narrowing gates of the giant V Cleft, access the buttress on the left by heathery rock ramps which lead to an open-book V-corner below a huge rectangular flake. The corner is hard to start but the holds do come. Exit right at its top. Move along the short ledge to its very end and a small perch overlooking the V Cleft. Pull onto the ledge above – exposed but easy – and clamber up a slot between the rectangular flake and another steep pinnacle. (If the V-corner proves too perplexing, a traverse left from its mouth above a slab can be made to reach easier ground that allows the large leaning rectangular flake to be passed behind to reach the ledge and small perch.)

A slab draws you back to the right arête, which is then followed more or less directly. As the angle of the buttress eases, trend left onto the crest for the best rock and weave through flaky pinnacles until confronted by a stubborn 5m buttress. This is overcome by an airy move from the top of an obvious 2m-high detached thin flake – finish direct. The North Ridge can be gained easily enough below Notch Rocks by a faint path up the couloir above.

Descents and combinations

Descent of the route is not recommended without prior knowledge. Use the climbers' descent path on the right of the buttress when looking out (grade 1-). Most parties will want to connect this route to Notch Arête (Route 27). Notch Rocks are the continuous rocks above to the right. The smooth face of Notch Arête is not visible from here, but heading up and rightwards towards a large pinnacle at the right foot of Notch Rocks will get you there (faint climbers' paths). Remember to traverse round right below the pinnacle to locate the right-bounding gully and the start of the route. Alternatively, the varied scrambling of Sunset Rib at the top of West Face Route (Route 24) left and across the couloir can be followed entertainingly to the North Ridge.

Route 26

V Arête 3 ✪

An exposed and bold scramble high on the quiet side of Tryfan.

Location	Tryfan, Ogwen (SH 663 597)
Grade	3 ✪
Approach time	40min
Altitude and aspect	580m, west
Route length	Sustained and fairly steep. Easily incorporated into longer outings. Height gain approximately 120m.
Conditions	Quick-drying on clean rock, although not well-travelled and some blocks, especially high up, should be treated with respect. Catches any afternoon sun.
Topo	See Route 19

Route 26 – V Arête

The giant V Cleft is an unmistakeable feature of Tryfan's west face. If V Buttress forms its left-bounding edge, then V Arête is the right-bounding edge of the V. Although it lacks the distinctiveness of its sister route across the cleft, V Arête is nonetheless a worthy companion that proves marginally harder in being longer, steeper and more sustained. (The cleft in between the two routes offers poor quality scrambling with dubious grassy holds and should be avoided.)

The narrow rib on V Arête

Approach
As for V Buttress (Route 25).

Ascent
At the toe of the arête just below the narrow mouth of the V Cleft there is a massive flake. Come in from the left and scramble easily up behind the flake. Head rightwards for a few metres then move back left over relatively steep and exposed terrain to gain the crest of the arête and a perch less exposed than it looks from below. Weave the easiest line closest to the crest, moving right when necessary, until a steep tower coming up from the cleft bars the way. To the tower's right is a clean and narrow slabby rib set at an amenable angle. Protection is hard to place on the rib but good holds come when needed. Above the rib, move back onto the airy arête and continue up a series of ribs to the top, taking care with occasional suspect blocks.

Descents and combinations
- From the top, it is easy to link up to the visible and sublime Notch Arête (Route 27) directly above.
- To descend at grade 1, join a faint traversing path about 20m above the end of the route and follow this rightwards (facing in). This dips across Y Gully, crossing a rib on the other side by an easily seen prominent triangular tooth about 1m tall. Thereafter, follow an exposed natural descending traverse line to join the well-used scree path down the side of the West Face cliffs.
- Descend Y Gully (Route 28) at grade 2 from the point where the traverse path enters it.

Route 27

Notch Arête 2 ✪✪✪

A joyful bound up a distinctive wide slabby ramp.

Location	Tryfan, Ogwen (SH 664 596)
Grade	2 ✪✪✪
Altitude and aspect	780m, west
Route length	Sustained but free-flowing and always seems to be over too quickly. Normally a component of longer outings. Height gain approximately 150m.
Conditions	Quick-drying on solid slabby rock that takes no drainage. More precarious in the wet. Perfect on a sunny afternoon when it is bathed in light and feels closer to Yosemite than North Wales.
Topo	See Route 19

When seen from the Gribin Ridge, Y Garn or Pen yr Ole Wen, the Notch Arête that bounds the right-hand side of Notch Rocks is an unmistakable feature high up on Tryfan's West Face. It is not actually an arête at all, but rather a wide slabby ramp leading to the summit of Notch Rocks, set at the perfect amenable angle for sustained but never strenuous grade 2 scrambling. The route consistently delights and every move seems to offer the perfect hold. Its only drawback is that it will almost certainly leave you wanting more... you could always descend and do it again.

Approach

A large tower can be seen at the bottom of Notch Rocks on their West Face side; Notch Arête begins on a platform above the tower. The platform is gained by traversing rightwards beneath the tower then moving up boulders and scree. A number of approaches are possible:

- Notch Arête is best approached by one of the lower routes on the West Face (Routes 24–26 and 28). See the combination sections at the end of those routes.
- The route can be accessed directly from the valley floor by following the V Buttress (Route 25) approach but bypassing that route by means of the grade 1- path to its left – thereafter refer to the initial approach description above.

Route 27 – Notch Arête

North Wales or Yosemite? Superb conditions on Notch Arête

- A descent can be made from the large cairn below Notch Rocks on the North Ridge. Follow the couloir down until able to move round beneath the tower described above (see Route 24 descents).
- From the Notch in the North Ridge – a point reached from the East Face by Nor' Nor' Gully or Nor' Nor' Groove (Routes 12 and 13) – a 150m path of fairly steep scree runs down parallel to Notch Arête and leads to the start of the route, which is on the right looking out. Any continuation of this descent is hazardous unless already familiar with the topography and orientation of the West Face.

Ascent
Getting onto the slabby face proves the trickiest part of the route. At a point where the scree in the gully bed becomes smaller, walk onto a nearly-level slanting platform above the tower. A stubborn buttress bars access to the slabby ramp of Notch Arête. On the right is a tempting wide corner crack – tougher than it looks (3S). The middle of the buttress is far too hard, so move to the left side of the platform and identify a very clear 3m chimney just wide enough to fit in. (This could be fought up directly if you wish to shed skin and test your range of vocabulary.) By coming in from slightly left of the chimney and moving onto its left-bounding edge, a clean white slanting platform above can be accessed (a little technical, but not exposed). Standing – fore-shortened – before you is the beginning of a 150m-long stretch of pure gold; head up its middle and enjoy.

Descent by this route
Possible with prior knowledge, but a considerably more daunting prospect.

Descents and combinations
See Routes 19, 10 and 24.

Route 28
Y Gully

2 ✪

An open and easily spotted gully gives good if short-lived scrambling over enormous boulders.

Location	Tryfan, Ogwen (SH 663 595)
Grade	2 ✪
Approach time	40min
Altitude and aspect	640m, west
Route length	Moderate length gully scramble. Height gain approximately 90m.
Conditions	Quick-drying on clean rock. The gully catches the afternoon sun.
Topo	See Route 19

Dating from 1894, Y Gully is one of the oldest recorded routes in the Ogwen Valley and the first on Tryfan's West Face. Surprisingly for a gully route of its vintage, the line is almost wholly clean and free of vegetation. A short through-route is possible for troglodytes, although an airier line to its left proves a highlight that shouldn't be missed. Best followed by Notch Arête or added to an itinerary with ascents of other West Face routes.

Approach
See Route 26. Y Gully is the next pronounced gully up from the V Cleft and is shaped as its name suggests. The route takes its straight left branch.

Ascent
Scramble easily over several obstacles before reaching a giant boulder perched above several others. Start in the centre and move rightwards until beneath the giant boulder. This can now be passed via ledges and ramps on the left

Taking the pleasant and airy ramp option in Y Gully

(pleasant and airy) or by a strenuous – better remove your rucksack and push it forward – squirm on the right (unpleasant, but funnier). Further up, a jutting prow is best passed on the left. Stay with the left side of the gully above until finally moving onto a steep left-bounding rib of clean rock, which is followed delicately to its top.

Descent by this route
Descent of Y Gully is perfectly feasible at grade 2, although it is best to flank the upper rib. Remember to pass the jutting prow – the first major obstacle in descent – on the right looking out.

Descents and combinations
- The excellent and similarly graded, although more sustained, Notch Arête (Route 27) is about 20m up to the left of you.
- An exposed grade 1 descent from the start of the left-bounding rib is described at the end of Route 26.

Route 29
South Ridge Direct

1 ✪

Easy scrambling on avoidable steps to a magnificent rocky summit.

Location	Tryfan, Ogwen (SH 663 590)
Grade	1 ✪
Approach time	1hr 30min
Altitude and aspect	750m, south
Route length	Lack of an obvious line can slow parties down, but this is part of its appeal. Height gain approximately 170m.
Conditions	Exposed to bad weather and strong crosswinds, although not dangerously so. Dries very quickly after rain.

A shorter version of the North Ridge, with just as much scope for variation. It barely warrants a description, with any number of equally satisfying lines being possible – including the potential of some amusing through-routes. It is a suitable introduction to scrambling as the path to the left (west), which itself has bits of scrambling, is always within easy reach.

Route 29 – South Ridge Direct

Approach
As for Route 30 to Bwlch Tryfan.

Ascent
Ignore the path on the left, and instead ascend the broad-backed ridge directly over the Far South and South summits to the twin standing stones of Adam and Eve on the Central Summit, seeking or avoiding difficulties at will.

Descent by this route
A suitable descent. It is most commonly followed in descent by those looking for an alternative to the path – although some steps are difficult to see from above; be prepared to search around for a feasible line.

Descents and combinations
See Routes 19 and 8.

Testing the tipping point of the Cantilever Stone on top of Glyder Fach (Routes 30–37)

Glyder Fach (994M)

Glyder Fach's summit plateau may not match the fairytale loftiness of Tryfan, but it lacks nothing in dramatic setting and outlook. Some 100m east of the summit, where huge monoliths lay scattered like giant matchsticks spilled from a box, you will find the Cantilever, improbably balanced on its supporting rock, tempting you to pose photogenically at its tip; and 300m south west, the stockade of massive splinters known as Castell y Gwynt – Castle of the Winds.

    The north west face hangs in a complex mural of crags and boulder slopes above Cwm Bochlwyd, cold and unfriendly on grim winter days, warm and welcoming on bright summer afternoons. Concentrated on these crudely sculptured rocks are some of the best scrambles in North Wales. The face is bounded to the east by Bristly Ridge and to the west by the Gribin Ridge. Both are good: Bristly Ridge is described in this section, while the Gribin Ridge is more logically described with the Glyder Fawr routes.

Route 30
Bristly Ridge   1 ✪✪✪

Top-class scrambling on this famous and aptly named pinnacled ridge.

Location	Glyder Fach, Ogwen (SH 661 587)
Grade	1 ✪✪✪
Approach time	1hr 30min
Altitude and aspect	750m, north
Route length	A moderately long outing sustained at the grade throughout. Height gain of over 300m.
Conditions	The polished rock is mostly sound, but take care with poor material near the start. Dries quickly after rain during warm or breezy weather. Unpleasant but not especially difficult when wet. Vulnerable to strong crosswinds. Extremely popular during fine summer weekends; start early or late to avoid crowds.

This famous and aptly named ridge defines the left side of the north west face and links Bwlch Tryfan with the Glyder Fach summit plateau. Although worthwhile in its own right, an ascent of this remotely situated and exhilarating scramble makes a natural and logical continuation to a traverse of Tryfan by its North and South ridges (Route 8). It is marginally harder than Tryfan's North Ridge.

Of many alternative lines on the flanks of the broad ridge, a direct route is nowhere excessively difficult and proves to be the most satisfying.

Approach
From Capel Curig or Bethesda along the A5 to a car park at Ogwen Cottage (SH 649 604) – approximately 150m east of YHA Idwal Cottage – or use overspill parking in lay-bys farther east. Take the path left of the toilet block, fork left after a few metres, and cross a footbridge onto the stone track. Where the track curves rightwards towards Cwm Idwal, bear left and ascend a steep path on the west bank of a stream to Llyn Bochlwyd. Cross the stream outflow and follow the path to Bwlch Tryfan (SH 662 588).

Ascent
Follow the stone wall to the base of Bristly Ridge, the obvious pinnacled buttress leading up towards the summit of Glyder Fach. Ten metres to the right of where the

Glyder Fach
(30) Bristly Ridge

Route 30 – Bristly Ridge

Great Pinnacle Gap, Bristly Ridge

wall meets the crag there is a short gully. Ascend the short gully, exiting left over a tiny and hard-to-spot man-made wall to the foot of the more imposing Sinister Gully with its overhanging prow higher up. Scramble carefully up its bed, detouring onto the left wall where it steepens to reach easier ground, or following the gully to its top (slightly harder).

Continue up a slabby shoulder to a narrowing of the ridge. Scramble over a small pinnacle onto a larger one then descend into the prominent notch of Great Pinnacle Gap. Escape by a short wall just right of the slender Great Pinnacle, then pass through a gap between a squat pinnacle (on the right) and the main body of the ridge to reach easier ground. An elevated boulder pavement finally leads onto the summit plateau.

Walk south west to join the normal ascent path and follow it (with a slight detour left to see the Cantilever) to the summit rock pile.

Descent by this route

The ridge makes an interesting and commonly used descent to Bwlch Tryfan, although prior knowledge of the route will help in avoiding false lines – particularly in the lower reaches where trending right (looking out) and aiming for the line of the dry stone wall will aid access to Sinister Gully. The ridge is a little tricky to identify from above – look for some spiky fingers 5m to the left of a cairn. If the terrain steepens but the route is not well-travelled, you've probably gone wrong.

Descents and combinations
- The eroded scree couloir east of Bristly Ridge provides a fast if scruffy descent to Bwlch Tryfan.
- From the summit, descend the east shoulder over boulders then grass to within a few hundred metres of Llyn y Caseg-fraith, then turn sharp left to follow the mostly contouring Miners' Track north west to Bwlch Tryfan or continue north to Gwern Gof Uchaf.
- See Route 8.

Route 31
The Chasm Face

3 ✪✪✪

Excellent varied scrambling up walls and ramps into a trap escaped by an entertaining and highly constricting through-route.

Location	Glyder Fach, Ogwen (SH 656 586)
Grade	3 ✪✪✪
Approach time	1hr 15min
Altitude and aspect	760m, north west
Route length	Not as time-consuming as might be expected given its technical sections. Height gain approximately 300m, although the upper half is on grade 1 terrain.
Conditions	Clean, sound rock. Dries quickly on breezy summer days, but not otherwise. Best enjoyed in the afternoon sun in summer. Parts of the route are shared with The Chasm rock climb.

The most impressive of the sharp-edged columns of rock that protrude from the north west face of Glyder Fach are clustered above and to the left of the Alphabet Slab, a distinctive feature at the foot of the cliffs. It is through these sentinels that the Chasm Face route finds its way.

Uniquely improbable in the lower part, where it weaves and tunnels through vertical rock, its upper slope entertains with open scrambling on superb rock.

Route 31 – The Chasm Face

Approach
There are two options:
- As for Route 30 to Llyn Bochlwyd. From the far side of the lake, a vague path leads up heather and scree slopes to the lowest point of the cliffs. Ascend a gully on the left side of the Alphabet Slab to a ledge above. The blunt base of Main Gully Ridge rises above, and to its left is the shallow depression of Main Gully.
- From Bwlch Tryfan head down the main path west for 150m or so to some large stepping-stones. Leave the path and head left on a path over a rise, then contour towards the crag on an intermittent grassy path that joins a clear well-travelled line traversing the upper scree with surprising ease.

Entering the bowels of Glyder Fach

Ascent
Scramble up Main Gully for about 40m, until above the challenging chockstone step, then trend left over grass ledges. Pass above the wide chimney of the Chasm itself and struggle over piled blocks (protectable) to gain a triangular ledge below a loathsome corner.

The corner looks hopeless, so climb up the steep wall just to its left for 3m then make a series of diagonal ape-like swings leftwards on flakes and spikes to a belay in a notch on the left edge of the catwalk ledge – challenging!

From the notch, creep up a half-metre-wide catwalk – exposed but not difficult – to enter the upper chasm. Overcome a smooth step and go up to beneath an arch formed by a fallen block (claustrophobic, overclad or over-breakfasted scramblers will use this arch – the Arch Tempter – to escape rightwards into Main Gully). Above the arch the dreaded Vertical Vice – crux of The Chasm rock climb – threatens all sorts of unspeakable torture, so avoid this insecure chimney/crack by squirming leftwards through an improbable narrow cleft to enter the bowels of the mountain via belly-laughs and swear words! A superb vertical chimney completes this subterranean exit to daylight and salvation.

Glyder Fach

- ㉛ The Chasm Face
- ㉜ Main Gully
- ㉝ Main Gully Ridge
- ㉞ East Gully Ridge
- ㉟ East Gully
- ㊱ Shark Buttress
- ㊲ Dolmen Ridge

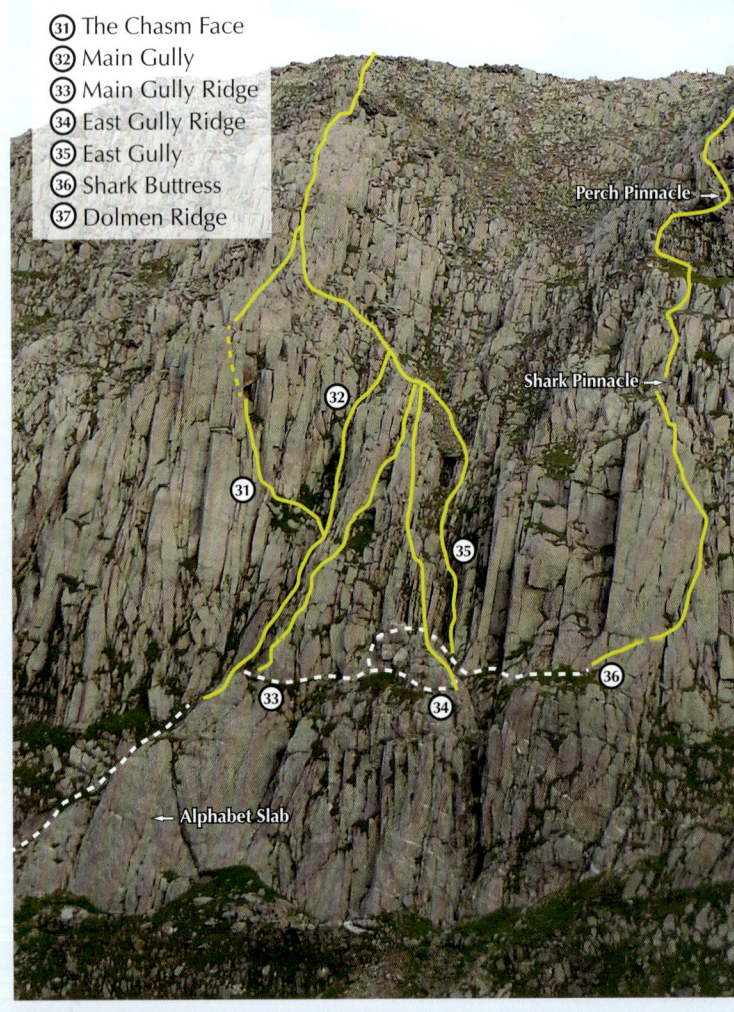

Route 31 – The Chasm Face

The main difficulties are now over, so find your own way up or around the outcrops of the upper slope. Depending on the line chosen, you will arrive on the summit plateau somewhere between the Cantilever Stone and the summit rock pile.

Descents and combinations
As for or by using Route 30. For those wishing to return directly to the foot of the face after exiting the through-route, descend either Route 32 or 35 to the top of the Alphabet Slab.

Route 32
Main Gully 2- ✪✪

A scramble of surprising quality, with a notorious tricky chockstone move.

Location	Glyder Fach, Ogwen (SH 656 586)
Grade	2- ✪✪
Approach time	1hr 15min
Altitude and aspect	760m, north west
Route length	The awkward chockstone slows many parties down. Height gain approximately 300m.
Conditions	The rock is unexpectedly clean and sound. Neither grass nor rock debris intrudes. Dries more quickly than most gullies, especially on breezy summer days, but remains damp and greasy otherwise.
Topo	See Route 31

Main Gully is not really a gully at all, but a rocky depression between the columns of the Chasm Face area and the protruding bulk of Main Gully Ridge. With the exception of a troublesome chockstone, it provides simple scrambling up a rocky depression followed by avoidable problems on the short steps of the upper face.

Approach
As for Route 31.

Practising ropework at the start of Main Gully

Ascent
Move left from the top of the Alphabet Slab to enter the depression, and ascend to a narrowing at a slot until beneath an awkward chockstone. Many find this difficult to fathom and even fewer overcome it gracefully (easiest facing left). Should it prove an impasse, then a retreat and ascent of the more conventional East Gully offers the best alternative.

Ascend more easily up the upper section, to emerge near the top of Main Gully Ridge and its junction with the top of East Gully Ridge.

The upper gully and couloir can be ascended but scree and loose blocks prove unappealing. Instead, trend left to gain the slope above the Chasm Face and scramble over or around short steps to the summit plateau.

Descent by this route
A practical means of descent from neighbouring scrambles – provided it can be found. Hardest at the chockstone near the bottom. East Gully (Route 35) is an easier descent.

Descents and combinations
As for Route 31.

Route 33
Main Gully Ridge

3 ✪✪✪ or 2 ✪✪✪

An airy route climbing the walls and ribs of Glyder Fach's upper face.

Location	Glyder Fach, Ogwen (SH 656 586)
Grade	3 ✪✪✪ or 2 ✪✪✪
Approach time	1hr 15min
Altitude and aspect	760m, north west
Route length	The technical lower part of the route has roughly 100m of height gain. This is followed by 200m or so height gain on grade 1 terrain to the top of the mountain.
Conditions	Takes little drainage. Excellent rock.
Topo	See Route 31

A delightful blunt ridge above the Alphabet Slab provides the most direct means of ascending the Main Cliff. The scrambling is fluid, although the exposed and technical hard start can be avoided if necessary. Spike belays will be found at intervals.

Approach
As for Route 31.

Ascent
From spikes at the foot of the ridge, balance diagonally right high or low (the latter being easier and more secure) to gain easier rock and hence a block on the ridge crest (9m). Alternatively (reducing the overall grade to 2), ascend Main Gully for 6m or so then traverse right past three spikes and pull into a position of sudden exposure at the block on the ridge crest.

Pull awkwardly onto a higher block and go up to a grass recess below a corner. Ignore the corner and step right onto a rib, ascending this to another ledge (7m).

Balancing across the technical start of Main Gully Ridge

Follow a natural line of stepped blocks to a level section on the crest, about 40m above the top of the Alphabet Slab.

The ridge above is too difficult, so scramble up the wide rift to its right with a nice chimney exit at the top and gain the easing rocks of East Gully Ridge.

Continue up easing rock above the merged ridges then trend left to finish up the pleasant upper section of the Chasm Face, or descend Route 32 or Route 35.

Descents and combinations
As for Route 31.

Route 34
East Gully Ridge   3 ✪✪✪

The ridge overlooking East Gully makes for a thrilling scramble.

Location	Glyder Fach, Ogwen (SH 655 586)
Grade	3 ✪✪✪
Approach time	1hr 15min
Altitude and aspect	760m, north west
Route length	Height gain roughly 100m, followed by 200m on grade 1 terrain to the top of the mountain.
Conditions	Dries quickly. Excellent rock although friction is important so not recommended in damp weather or after rain. If even marginally damp or misty the grade becomes 3S.
Topo	See Route 31

This difficult scramble follows a series of ribs leading to easier ground on the upper face. The steep lower section is completely avoided by a long traverse from above the Alphabet Slab, while the grade 3 intricacies of the middle section can, if necessary, be flanked on the gully side – although none too easily. Belays can be found at regular intervals.

Approach
Initially as for Route 31. From the top of the Alphabet Slab, follow a narrow path rightwards, ignoring the worn climb that leads over a rib to East Gully in favour of crossing

Surmounting the exposed spike on East Gully Ridge with Tryfan beyond

the quartz slabs of the protruding rib, then gradually descending rightwards to a sloping rock ledge at the foot of the left-bounding ridge of East Gully. This is about 50m from the top of the Alphabet Slab.

Ascent

Take the initial tricky rise on the right edge to a prominent notch below a narrower rib (where the transverse path from East Gully passes). Follow excellent holds for 30m to a level area, then scramble over blocks for 10m to a notch of piled blocks below a more compact section of the ridge.

Scramble up a few metres then climb a 2m hand-width jamming crack. Mantelshelf onto a spike at its top (runner). Now step delicately up to the left and continue to a narrow rock ledge. Continue up easing rock to block belays in 5m, just short of another notch. (Alternatively, go 3m right from the notch to a bilberry ledge, up a slab for 3m to blocks, pull strenuously up a crack on the left to a ledge, and then gain the narrow ledge of the direct route by a simple corner – significantly reducing the overall grade.)

The Main and East Gully ridges merge above; ascend the right-hand edge, easing, until it narrows and curves left. Continue trending left to gain pleasant scrambling on the upper part of the Chasm Face, or descend either East Gully or Main Gully.

Descents and combinations

As for Route 31.

Route 35
East Gully

1+ ✪

Atmospheric gully climbing through impressive surroundings.

Location	Glyder Fach, Ogwen (SH 655 586)
Grade	1+ ✪
Approach time	1hr 15min
Altitude and aspect	760m, north west
Route length	Height gain roughly 100m before the 200m or so at grade 1 to reach the top of the mountain.
Conditions	Narrower and better defined than Main Gully, East Gully takes a little more drainage and is therefore best in dry periods. The boulders and scree above the steps require the usual caution necessary in gullies, although they are not as loose as might be expected.
Topo	See Route 31

Many will find East Gully offers considerably more interest than its more popular neighbour, Main Gully. East Gully also provides an excellent means of descent if doing a number of scrambles at the crag – although the exit that avoids a Severe grade bottom section needs to be clearly identified.

Approach
As for Route 31. This route accesses East Gully above its bottom section (a rock climb at Severe). From the top of Alphabet Slabs, follow an exposed grassy path for 20m or so and traverse across a moderately angled slab with quartz ledges until it is possible to scamper easily upwards and pass over the notch in East Gully Arête. Descend easily for 4m into the gully bed.

Ascent
Simply scramble up the gully by the most direct and amenable route, with the capstones at the top of the steep sections passed on the right. As the gully fans out into a jumble of scree and boulders, bear left to pick up the junction of East Gully Ridge and Main Gully and continue up to the summit of Glyder Fach as for Route 31.

On the first capstone of East Gully

Route 36 – Shark Buttress

Descents and combinations
In descent East Gully is not appreciably harder and proves easier and safer than Main Gully. Remember to pass the capstones on the left (looking out) and ensure the well-used 4m clamber out of the gully (on the right looking out) is taken in order to avoid the Severe lower section of the gully. As for Route 31.

Route 36
Shark Buttress

3S ✪✪✪

Varied and complex scrambling that incorporates an ascent into the very jaws of the Shark – a startling thrust of twin pinnacles uncannily reminiscent of a great white.

Location	Glyder Fach, Ogwen (SH 655 586)
Grade	3S ✪✪✪
Approach time	1hr 15min
Altitude and aspect	760m, north west
Route length	A long outing with considerable time on rock and technical challenges throughout. Height gain over 300m.
Conditions	Wait for dry conditions. Much the least popular part of the Main Cliff; generally excellent rock.
Topo	See Route 31

This challenging line seeks out the best from the central area of terraced buttresses. The route contains one particularly committing and difficult-to-back-out-of move at the very limits of scrambling – a rope is advised.

Approach
As for Route 31 to a sloping rock ledge at the foot of the left-bounding ridge of East Gully. Cross the gully to a grassy shoulder below a compact, vertical skyscraper tower supported on wrinkly slabs (Hawk's Nest Buttress).

Evading the jaws of the shark

Route 36 – Shark Buttress

Ascent
Ascend diagonally right across the lowest part of the lower slabs (not difficult but exposed and unprotected), passing above a narrow chimney and following ledges at the right-hand side of the buttress to gain a notch behind a large flake (30m).

Step from the flake onto a smooth, slabby wall and climb it to grass ledges in 3m – challenging. Ascend the left side of the obvious recess into a shallow slot. After a few metres this steepens and becomes vegetated, so pull out left onto a tiny ledge below a wide crack in the back of a V-groove with a protruding block at its top. Ascend the crack to a block on the right then reach left on a good flake-edged block to pull out onto the buttress front.

Ascend left over piled blocks until below a huge pinnacle with a chockstone jammed near its top. To the right is a smooth-cornered recess: home of the 'committing move'. Ascend the wide left-hand crack for 2m to a spike, fix thread protection on a chockstone, then pull acrobatically left onto the lower part of the left edge (difficult). Continue more easily up wrinkly slabs for 3m or so to block belays.

Shark Pinnacle stands 10m above, its summit an idyllic viewpoint in the evening sunlight. It will not be gained easily. Climb delicately up its 5m back (on the side that faces the mountain). Alternatively, fighting your way up via the boulder wedged in its jaws is also possible. Descend carefully by a controlled slither.

The impending buttress beyond is overcome with surprising ease: continue almost directly behind the pinnacle – coming in 1m or so from the left but trending slightly rightwards. From the grass belvedere above, continue for a few metres over slabs and a rock glacis then go left up a grass terrace to below Perch Pinnacle – more a large pulpit block than a pinnacle. The variegated loose and slimy rock band that tops out on nearly always wet grass below the Perch Pinnacle is best avoided. Therefore clamber up easier terrain on the far left, overlooking East Gully, to access the top of the Pinnacle. (Harder alternatives at a Difficult rock climbing grade on clean rock can be found for roped parties on the right-hand side.) Excellent, easier scrambling above leads onto Dolmen Ridge just before it dips to the col and merges into the main bulk of the mountain.

Descents and combinations
As for Route 31.

Scrambles in Snowdonia

Route 37
Dolmen Ridge

3 ✪✪✪

A long, classic and much-loved scramble with a memorable steep section. Interest and challenges are sustained throughout.

Location	Glyder Fach, Ogwen (SH 654 585)
Grade	3 ✪✪✪
Approach time	1hr 15min
Altitude and aspect	760m, north west
Route length	A long outing with considerable time on rock. The steep recessed groove will slow most parties. Height gain over 300m.
Conditions	The rock is generally rough and sound. Dries quickly and catches the late afternoon sun in summer.
Topo	See Route 31

The curving line of West Gully defines the right-hand side of the main face. On the left side of the gully, at about half-height, stands the compact, triangular crag of Dolmen Buttress. This excellent scramble crosses West Gully to ascend the upper right edge of Dolmen Buttress, then uses the left-bounding ridge of the gully to gain the Glyder Fach plateau just a few metres from the summit rock pile

Approach
As for Route 30 to Llyn Bochlwyd. From the far side of the lake, ascend south west towards the back of the cwm (heading for Bwlch y Ddwy Glyder, the col between Castell y Gwynt and the Gribin Ridge) to a tiny pool – marked only on 1:25,000 maps. A winding path direct to the bottom of West Gully and start of the route can be picked up to the left of the boulder-strewn watercourse running down from the hidden pool.

Ascent
From a few metres right of the gully opening pick a worn line, intially rightwards, between two distinct quartz seams. After 20m or so, bear back leftwards over ledges to ascend a steady line on the ribs and ledges that bound the right side of the gully, keeping its bed in sight. A narrowing in the gully bed signals the need to identify the ramp that accesses Dolmen Buttress at half-height. Cross the bed of the gully

Route 37 – Dolmen Ridge

25m above the narrowing to gain a clear ramp sloping easily upwards to the left. (Alternative means of approaching this point include: using the gully itself – unpleasant; less satisfying lines on the rocks to the left of the gully; or wandering lines moving further rightwards from the starting quartz seams before returning to the gully.)

From the end of the ramp, tackle the delightful well-scratched recessed groove system steeply and directly with much exposure to gain the main ridge crest.

The ridge now eases, but continues to give interesting scrambling in exposed positions overlooking West Gully. Eventually it curves to the right, dips to a small col and shares its course with Shark Buttress (Route 36), merging into the main bulk of the mountain. The summit lies directly ahead.

Descents and combinations
As for Route 31.

Starting the steeper section above the sloping ramp

Spiky rock fingers near the summit of Glyder Fawr with Snowdon in the distance

Glyder Fawr (1001M)

Glyder Fawr occupies a commanding position at the bend in the centre of the 15km main Glyderau ridge. Its Cwm Idwal face rises in a series of slabs and walls almost from lakeside to summit – a vertical height difference of nearly 500m. This is the most interesting and best-known face of the mountain, not least because of its supporting plinth known as the Idwal Slabs, a traditional rock climbing venue and the most distinctive landmark in Cwm Idwal. Less obvious challenges await in Cwm Cneifion, a hanging valley enclosed by Glyder Fawr and its subsidiary ridge of the Gribin, and on the southern flank which rises dramatically out of the Llanberis Pass defile.

The most popular walking route to the summit begins from Ogwen Cottage and ascends via Cwm Idwal and the Devil's Kitchen path, culminating in a demoralising slog up the scree paths above Llyn y Cwn (the lake can also be reached from the west by a good path from Gwastadnant in the Llanberis Pass). The summit can also be gained via the south spur, starting from Pen y Pass. Otherwise the peak is generally combined with an ascent of Glyder Fach in a circular walk from Pen y Pass or Ogwen Cottage.

Scrambling interest focuses on the northern side; on the north west (Idwal) face, and on the ridges that bound or lie within Cwm Cneifion, the high and remote cwm that nestles between Glyder Fawr and the upper part of the Gribin. Clogwyn Du looms impressively from the shady side of the cwm yet offers the scrambler nothing more than inferior possibilities on flanking rocks. In contrast, the sunnier Gribin side of the cwm appears to provide limitless opportunities. Unfortunately, a large part of this face consists of scree-littered and nondescript slabby rock. For this reason the selected scrambles follow only the more continuous ribbons of rock, of which the Cneifion Arête is by far the most distinct.

The last two routes in this section ascend out of the Llanberis Pass via Esgair Felen, the south west spur.

Route 38
Gribin Ridge 1 ✪

Enjoyable walking along a prominent, easy-angled ridge enlivened by pleasant scrambling on a final rock crest.

Location	Glyderau, Ogwen (SH 651 592)
Grade	1 ✪
Approach time	40min
Altitude and aspect	700m, north
Route length	Mainly hiking with some scrambling to gain over 250m of height.
Conditions	Not greatly affected by wet rock, although exposed to crosswinds. In either case it may be best to follow the easier and more sheltered scrambly path slightly on the Cwm Cneifion flank of the upper rock crest.

The Gribin rises between Cwm Bochlwyd and Cwm Cneifion to join the main Glyderau ridge midway between Glyder Fach and Glyder Fawr. A popular, scrambly walk, it provides an enjoyable route up to, or down from, either of the two summits. Impressive views into the bordering cwms compensate for the trifling amount of genuine scrambling.

The usual route on the upper rockier section flanks the crest on the Cneifion side, so take this section direct to avoid other parties, increase scrambling interest, and restore concentration with the sobering exposure of a drop into Cwm Bochlwyd.

Approach

Via the A5 from Capel Curig or Bethesda. Park at Ogwen Cottage (SH 649 604) – approximately 150m east of YHA Idwal Cottage – or at overspill parking areas to the east. Follow the Cwm Idwal path until it curves right. Bear left here, using the stepping-stone path to cross a boggy area, then ascend the stream bank to Llyn Bochlwyd. Turn right and follow a grassy path onto the right-bounding ridge of Cwm Bochlwyd.

Scrambles in Snowdonia

Glyder Fawr
㊳ Gribin Ridge (upper section)

Ascent

Once gained, the ridge path is well worn and obvious. Apart from an occasional short step it involves nothing more than pleasant walking to a large grass shoulder below the upper rock crest. (The False Gribin, Route 39, and Cneifion Arête, Route 40, emerge near here from east and west respectively.)

Above, the ridge rears up, narrows and turns to rock. The normal path zig-zags up this section on the Cneifion (west) side, although for maximum interest it should

Route 38 – Gribin Ridge

be taken direct. The crest soon falls back into a stone-studded slope with the paths east to Glyder Fach and west to Glyder Fawr nearby.

Descent by this route
A descent of the Gribin is common. When approaching from Glyder Fawr in mist, contour the rim of Cwm Cneifion to be certain of locating the promontory at the top of the upper rock crest. On the lower section, stay on the right (east) flank to be sure of finding the path that leads across to the Llyn Bochlwyd outflow.

Descents and combinations
Best used as part of Route 8. In descent Route 39 can be incorporated. From the summit of Glyder Fawr, descend on or as for Route 42. Refer to the previous section for descents from Glyder Fach.

High above the Ogwen Valley on Gribin Ridge

Scrambles in Snowdonia

Route 39
False Gribin 1 ✪

Uncomplicated scrambling up a broad-backed subsidiary ridge to the final rock crest of the Gribin.

Location	Glyderau, Ogwen (SH 653 591)
Grade	1 ✪
Approach time	40min
Altitude and aspect	550m, north east
Route length	A straightforward enough way to gain approximately 180m of height, usually elongated by continuing up Route 38.
Conditions	As for Route 38, although less used.
Topo	See Route 38

A variant on the Gribin which, by judicious choice of line, can treble the amount of scrambling. The name is a little unfair because, although the ridge is a subsidiary one, it is the true continuation of the upper rock crest. A combination of the two scrambles is a fantastic route to the Glyderau summit ridge.

False Gribin with Tryfan looming

Route 39 – False Gribin

Approach
Initially as for Route 38 to Llyn Bochlwyd. Circle the lake to its south west shore and ascend to the indistinct foot of the ridge.

Ascent
Ascend first over rock and heather on the broad-backed lower ridge. String together short rocky steps until the ridge steepens to give good, easy scrambling with a wide choice of line, usually best on the left.

The route joins the Gribin Ridge just above the grass shoulder. Continue as for Route 38.

Descent by this route
The route is not significantly more difficult in descent.

Descents and combinations
Usually followed by an ascent of Route 38. See Route 42 for descents.

Scrambles in Snowdonia

Cwm Idwal

140

Route 39 – False Gribin

- ㊵ Cneifion Arête
- ㊶ Maybe Tower Rib
- ㊷ Seniors' Ridge
- ㊸ Seniors' Gully
- ㊹ Direct Approach to Seniors' Ridge
- ㊺ Idwal Staircase and Continuation
- ㊻ North West Face Route

Route 40
Cneifion Arête 3 ✪✪✪

A well-loved classic scrambling line up a beautiful crescent-shaped rib.

Location	Cwm Cneifion, Glyderau (SH 648 588)
Grade	3 ✪✪✪
Approach time	1hr
Altitude and aspect	650m, west
Route length	For some a fast route, for others a big undertaking: experienced solo parties will fly up the upper section, while roped parties pitching the whole route will take much longer. Height gain approximately 120m.
Conditions	Quick-drying. Rock quality is excellent. Square-cut holds allow an ascent in wet conditions, although the increase in difficulty soon becomes unacceptable if rain is combined with strong winds.

When seen from the shoulder of Seniors' Ridge, the line of the Cneifion Arête is simply breathtaking. A brilliant route, the arête is unsurprisingly popular, although it is sufficiently remote to be spared overcrowding. Its initial 30m rise should be viewed as sustained Moderate. In dry conditions it is technically straightforward and, although most will want a rope here, it is easily protected.

The steadier upper part provides scrambling of a sustained and exposed nature which can be climbed in pitches, 'moving together' or solo according to conditions and the experience of the party.

Approach

Via the A5 from Capel Curig or Bethesda. Park at Ogwen Cottage (SH 649 604) – approximately 150m east of YHA Idwal Cottage – and follow the path into Cwm Idwal, from where there are several options:

- From about halfway along the lakeside path, strike diagonally up the hillside to gain the floor of lower Cwm Cneifion. The arête now appears above on the left, knife-edged and obvious.
- Much better, use Route 43 to reach Cwm Cneifion.
- Alternatively, use either Route 44, 45 or 46 to gain a shoulder on Seniors' Ridge 50m above Cwm Cneifion, which can then be accessed easily.

On the upper curving crest of Cneifion Arête

Ascent
A slabby and vegetated front is bounded on the right by a near-vertical side wall; the route ascends the easier lower part of this wall to gain the crest between wall and slab, which it then follows as closely as possible.

A scree path rises steeply to a small bay just right of the foot of the arête proper. From the bay, 10m of steep climbing on good holds leads to an optional belay just below the crest. Traverse awkwardly right for a few metres then ascend leftwards to gain the crest below a short chimney (belay). The chimney leads to easier ground within a few metres.

Now that the major difficulties are over, the best line follows the exposed crest as closely as possible. This can become a little too exciting during windy conditions, although numerous spike belays are available if required.

The arête finally falls back into the Gribin Ridge at the large grass shoulder below its final rock nose. Continue as for Route 38.

Descents and combinations
A descent of Route 38 is the fastest means of returning to Ogwen Cottage, although the summit of Glyder Fawr will beckon most. A descent of Seniors' Ridge (Route 42) and Seniors' Gully (Route 43) maintains interest back to Lyn Idwal. Maybe Tower Rib (Route 41) can also be added to the itinerary by the indefatigable.

Scrambles in Snowdonia

Route 41
Maybe Tower Rib 3 ✪

*Definitely! Good-quality steep scrambling to escape a
remote upper cwm via a protruding rib and tower.*

Location	Cwm Cneifion, Glyderau (SH 649 585)
Grade	3 ✪
Approach time	1hr 30min (or 20min from the top of Route 42)
Altitude and aspect	790m, west
Route length	A route of moderate length. Height gain approximately 120m.
Conditions	The rib is often damp and cold due to its location and high altitude. Wet lichen adds to the insecurity in all but perfectly dry conditions. The rock is reasonably sound, although the piled blocks near the top should be handled with care.
Topo	See Route 40

To the right of Cneifion Arête the Gribin flank of Cwm Cneifion curves round in a shattered headwall containing much rock but few distinctive features. Although it is scruffy compared to the Cneifion Arête, the rib has its moments – not to mention its tower – and the solitude will be appreciated by seasoned scramblers. The route is longer and better than might be expected and is easily added to longer itineraries.

Difficulties on the lower part are short but appreciable; belays and protection are available at intervals throughout this section.

Approach
- Maybe Tower Rib is best used as an additional scramble and approached from a descent of Seniors' Ridge (42). Identifying the route is easy in clear visibility: on the west face of the Gribin Ridge the collection of indistinct crags right of the Cneifion Arête have a shallow gully towards their right-hand end which nonetheless proves easily the deepest gully on the face. The gully is bounded on its left by Maybe Tower Rib; at its top is a distinct block tower (most easily identified from above). Descend Seniors' Ridge to a broad flat grassy area roughly level with the base of the aforementioned gully and contour the cwm directly to it (no path, but pleasant usually dry walking) – 20min from the top of Seniors' Ridge.

Definitely on the tower of Maybe Tower Rib

- Alternatively, ascend directly as for Route 40 to lower Cwm Cneifion then continue over scree into the upper cwm.

Ascent
The lower part of the right-bounding gully is not particularly well defined. Ascend a shallow rib right of the true watercourse then, where the gully becomes more distinct, gain the ridge to its left. Interest increases as the ridge narrows and leads to a gap behind a squat 2m pinnacle at the foot of the main steep buttress (10m up to the left is another small diamond pinnacle).

Start up the little corner behind the squat pinnacle, then make an awkward swing left after a couple of metres before it becomes particularly greasy, grassy and difficult. Cross back rightwards above the corner and bear right to gain the edge overlooking the gully. Trend back left and up a tricky steep section before moving back right to regain the edge. Now carefully ascend blocks on the exposed right edge and continue up the spiky remains of the rib to gain the top of the tower directly. Pass over the top of the tower, which is descended easily by a natural ladder. At the top turn right to find the path leading to the summit of Glyder Fawr.

Descents and combinations
As for Route 40.

Scrambles in Snowdonia

Route 42
Seniors' Ridge

1 ✪

A broad ridge with frequent scrambling opportunities.
Steady – as its name suggests.

Location	Glyder Fawr, Ogwen (SH 646 587)
Grade	1 ✪
Approach time	1hr
Altitude and aspect	640m, north
Route length	Over 300m of height gain on easy enough terrain that is quickly covered.
Conditions	A suitable ascent for most conditions
Topo	See Route 40

Seniors' Ridge, the blunt north ridge of Glyder Fawr, separates the high and remote hanging valley of Cwm Cneifion from the deeper and much larger hollow of Cwm Idwal. Its Cneifion flank is short and unremarkable, whereas the Idwal flank – a succession of rock slabs 400m high – is one of the most dramatic sights in Snowdonia. The ridge crest itself is broad and its path often ignores good scrambling possibilities. By keeping well right (west) of the path, a surprisingly sustained and enjoyable scramble can be found.

Approach
Via the A5 from Capel Curig or Bethesda. Park at Ogwen Cottage (SH 649 604) – approximately 150m east of YHA Idwal Cottage – and follow the path into Cwm Idwal. Best approached using Route 43.

Ascent
Once on the broad back of the ridge, leave the path at a steep wall of continuous rock overcome by a steadier-than-it-looks rightwards curving groove. Continue mostly on the west side of the ridge, seeking or avoiding difficulties at will, to the rock-littered summit slopes of Glyder Fawr.

Descent by this route
A good scrambling descent but it is hard to follow the best line in descent and most will end up using the path, which has some limited scrambling. The path

Route 42 – Senior's Ridge

Making the most of the good scrambling on the west side of Seniors' Ridge

accesses Cwm Cneifion from a shoulder 50m above its floor, where Route 43 is best descended.

Descents and combinations
- Descend north west from the summit via unpleasant scree paths (cairned) to Llyn y Cwn, and then via the Devil's Kitchen path into Cwm Idwal.
- Alternatively, from the summit of Glyder Fawr, circle the head of Cwm Cneifion and descend via the Gribin Ridge (Route 38).

Scrambles in Snowdonia

Route 43
Seniors' Gully

1- ✪

Useful for quick access to and from Cwm Cneifion, and a decent wet-weather alternative or introductory scramble.

Location	Cwm Idwal, Ogwen (SH 645 589)
Grade	1- ✪
Approach time	35min
Altitude and aspect	440m, north
Route length	A quick enough outing involving over 170m of height gain, roughly half of which is in the gully proper.
Conditions	A straightforward scramble in wet conditions
Topo	See Route 40

Linking the ever-popular Cwm Idwal with the more secluded Cwm Cneifion, Seniors' Gully gives an eastern border to the Idwal Slabs. It provides some easy scrambling steps on water-worn rock with little exposure until emerging abruptly at the floor of the upper cwm, where it links with the similarly graded Seniors' Ridge.

Approach

From Ogwen Cottage (SH 649 604) – approximately 150m east of YHA Idwal Cottage – follow the path in Cwm Idwal and onwards on the left of the lake to the foot of the Idwal Slabs, a huge expanse of gently angled rock (SH 644 589).

Ascent

Begin up the path immediately left of the starting slabs of the Direct Approach to Seniors' Ridge (Route 44). The path has some good well-travelled steps and corners on it. The gully proper can be found straight ahead just after passing the steep section of Route 44 that breaches the East Wall (also a climbers' descent from Idwal Slabs). Follow the gully up, clambering over rock steps to a small waterfall and dank

Descending Seniors' Gully

slimy cave. Climb the stepped channel to the left and head up more continuous rock without difficulty to emerge in Cwm Cneifion.

Descent by this route
Simple to find and follow in descent: identify the top of the route where a small stream exits the north west side of the cwm.

Descents and combinations
- To continue at roughly the same grade, pick up a path on the right to ascend Seniors' Ridge (Route 42) and eventually reach the top of Glyder Fawr.
- Seniors' Gully can also be used as a fast scrambling approach to the Cneifion Arête (40) or Maybe Tower Rib (41).

Route 44
Direct Approach to Seniors' Ridge 2 ✪

An exciting breach of the East Wall of Idwal via a series of open gullies and grooves.

Location	Cwm Idwal, Ogwen (SH 645 589)
Grade	2 ✪
Approach time	30min
Altitude and aspect	440m, north west
Route length	A fairly lengthy meandering route. Approximately 200m height gain.
Conditions	Water from the East Wall affects the lower grooves after prolonged bad weather. Parts of the route are often used by climbers descending from the Idwal Slabs and consequently the rock is highly polished.
Topo	See Route 40

A good scramble in its own right, although it is most often used to access Cwm Cneifion or as a precursor to Seniors' Ridge. The route takes a series of open gullies/grooves and short chimneys, culminating in an exposed breach of the retaining wall and some awkward short steps beyond.

Breaching the East Wall of the Idwal Slabs on Route 44

Route 44 – Direct Approach to Seniors' Ridge

Approach
As for Route 43.

Ascent
The left side of the Idwal Slabs curls over to form the retaining East Wall. In general the route ascends cracks and shallow grooves in the vegetated, slabby rock overshadowed by this wall.

A 20m-high rectangular slab lies recessed to the left of the main sweep of slabs. Ascend a cracked minor slab to its left then trend left up a polished ramp. Continue more easily to a grassy bay then ascend a gully/groove between quartz slabs on the right and a vegetated area on the left.

The line now continues next to the East Wall (avoid paths and worn rock that pull you leftwards); the route includes a short, awkward chimney. Above a minor final obstacle – a shallow and reclining wide crack close under the fearsome Suicide Wall – trending left take the path to enter a couloir. To the right you will now see a vegetated break leading to a grass ledge and saplings with smooth walls above and below: this is a false line. Instead, continue up the rock bed of the couloir for 20m or so and hence locate the correct breach line – a series of highly polished footholds rising rightwards above the smooth walls. This is the normal climber's descent from Idwal Slabs. The scrambling here is exposed but no more difficult than anything encountered below. Many climbers abseil the steep section on the right, but they and their ropes are avoided by a rising traverse from the left.

Above the breach, follow the two polished grooves leading rightwards; thereafter head up via short walls, with one distinct polished groove proving particularly awkward, and avoid the temptation to head left towards Seniors' Gully or Cwm Cneifion too early. A junction with Seniors' Ridge on a level shoulder about 50m above the floor of Cwm Cneifion is the end of the route. To gain the summit of Glyder Fawr, continue as for Route 42.

Descent by this route
A common climber's descent, although not recommended without prior knowledge. It is absolutely vital to locate the platform above the two grooves before attempting to find the breach in the East Wall. The breach itself can be unnerving in descent, and the lower gully/grooves disproportionately awkward.

Descents and combinations
A viable approach to Route 40 or 41: descend from the level shoulder at the foot of Seniors' Ridge by a path into the cwm for the former, or ascend half of Seniors' Ridge to approach the latter. To return easily to Llyn Idwal use Seniors' Gully (Route 43) or the nearby hiker's path.

Route 45

Idwal Staircase and Continuation 2+ ✪✪✪

A route of two contrasting halves: an atmospheric dark cleft followed by long open scrambling on slabby rock.

Location	Cwm Idwal, Ogwen (SH 645 589)
Grade	2+ ✪✪✪
Approach time	30min
Altitude and aspect	460m, north west
Route length	A sustained and satisfyingly long route. Height gain approximately 200m.
Conditions	After rainy periods a stream sluices down Idwal Staircase. Spray feeds lichen on the surrounding rocks and so, paradoxically, the most water-worn areas prove to be the least slippery – although recent popularity has cleaned the rock somewhat. The upper slabs dry quickly after rain, but should be avoided on damp or misty days as visibility and friction prove assets on this long, open and adventurous terrain.
Topo	See Route 40

The north west face of Glyder Fawr rises from lakeside to summit in a discontinuous series of slabs and reclining buttresses. This route exploits an uncharacteristic fault line in the lower section to gain rough slabs above the rock climbing territory on the lower left side of the face. Thus it gains Seniors' Ridge with more style and only slightly more difficulty than either of its two neighbours.

The Staircase section can be hideous after rainy periods and at such times will delight only gully freaks! In dry periods, when the stream is but a trickle, the staircase is an atmospheric romp on excellent rock.

Approach

From Ogwen Cottage – approximately 150m east of YHA Idwal Cottage – to the lakeside path in Cwm Idwal. Continue to the foot of the Idwal Slabs, a huge expanse of gently angled rock beyond the lake (SH 644 589).

Route 45 – Idwal Staircase and Continuation

Ascent
An overhung gully, black and water-washed, defines the far right-hand side of the Idwal Slabs. Ascend for 8m on narrow ledges to where the Staircase darkens beneath the curling roof. Thankfully the angle eases a little here and rock spikes begin to appear. Continue in this comforting manner until within a couple of metres of large, jammed boulders where the slit curves left towards the waterfall. Water levels will dictate the line taken. In dry periods follow the true gully to its conclusion. However, if wet, traverse narrow ledges leftwards to drier, spiky rock beyond the watercourse.

From the top of the gully head left over grass towards orange-tinted slabs of rough rock to commence the contrasting second half (actually two-thirds) of the scramble. Beginning with a rising leftwards line, ascend at will on good holds, relishing the open freedom and endless possible variations of line all at the same grade (roped parties will find belays at regular intervals but few intermediate runners). If you have ventured leftward and are faced by a difficult large recess of steep rock, locate a rib on its outer right edge to overcome it. Continue more or less directly to the ever-out-of-reach highest visible point, passing over a quartz ledge en route, until finally emerging on Seniors' Ridge a short distance above Cwm Cneifion.

Descent by this route
Difficult to locate and even more difficult to execute. Not recommended.

Descents and combinations
See Routes 40–44.

In the dark cleft commencing the Idwal Staircase

Route 46
North West Face Route (aka Idwal Buttress)

2 ✪✪

Open, slabby scrambling followed by a higher section of rocky shelves.

Location	Cwm Idwal, Ogwen (SH 644 588)
Grade	2 ✪✪
Approach time	30min
Altitude and aspect	470m, north west
Route length	A moderately long route, but not as sustained as its predecessor. Height gain approximately 220m.
Conditions	Does not suffer the drainage that affects the previous two routes and so dries quickly on breezy summer days. Catches the afternoon sun.
Topo	See Route 40.

Provides an approach to Seniors' Ridge that is more open than either of the two previous routes. It takes the buttress right of the Idwal Staircase then finds a way up rocky slopes in the centre of the face before joining Seniors' Ridge below its final rise.

The rock is excellent throughout and, despite a lack of traffic, heather does not intrude. Requires some astute route-finding in the upper part to avoid excessive difficulties.

Approach
From Ogwen Cottage – approximately 150m east of YHA Idwal Cottage – to the lakeside path in Cwm Idwal. Continue to the foot of the Idwal Slabs, the huge expanse of gently angled rock beyond the lake (SH 644 589). Follow the path to where, at a stream, it touches the lowest rocks of the right-bounding buttress of the main sweep of the Idwal Slabs (the wet, black and overhung gully of Idwal Staircase, Route 45, bounds the left side of this buttress).

Ascent
A blunt rib and grass furrow on the buttress front are bounded on the right by blank slabs. Ascend the rock in the furrow and then the vague rib between furrow and slabs, curving right, to where the line is broken by a gully coming up from below.

Tackling the left edge beyond the distinct quartz seam

Scramble straight up to gain the top of this introductory buttress. (A worthwhile variation at 2+ can be made by leaving the furrow 7m or so below a distinct quartz seam and following a rising line on good, stepped holds across orange-tinted slabs to gain the left side of the buttress, which is followed to the top.)

To the right a rock spur protrudes from grass slopes: climb the spur.

Above is a clear gully descending from a notch in Seniors' Ridge. The route weaves a line up the clean rock to the right of this, with the option of either passing up through or traversing leftwards slightly above a distinct quartz band to emerge on Seniors' Ridge just above the gully top. Pick out the line and enjoy pleasant scrambling on the large, satisfying holds of the buttress right of the gully to a 15m smooth section which guards the obvious horizontal quartz band. Trend right below the smooth section to gain the quartz band at a large and sloping quartz-covered ledge, then head back left above the quartz using a terrace system to eventually gain the broad back of Seniors' Ridge.

Descent by this route
Impractical and unappealing.

Descents and combinations
See Routes 40–44.

The dry upper reaches of Bryant's Gully (Route 47)

Route 47
Bryant's Gully

2+ ✪✪✪

An excellent line amid impressive rock scenery provides the longest and one of the finest continuous scrambles in Snowdonia.

Location	Esgair Felen, Llanberis Pass (SH 626 569)
Grade	2+ ✪✪✪
Approach time	10min
Altitude and aspect	220m, south
Route length	Despite its short approach, it is the longest route in this guide and a big undertaking in anyone's book! Allow plenty of time. Height gain approximately 520m.
Conditions	The route is ideal on a warm spring or summer's day after a prolonged period of dry weather – wait for these conditions to fully appreciate it. In or following wet weather expect a long and slippery epic struggle; and in such circumstances ensure a rope is packed.

Esgair Felen, the south west spur of Glyder Fawr, presents itself to the lower Llanberis Pass as a huge triangular face of outcrop-studded scree slopes. Those outcrops closest to the road are frequented by rock climbers, although few venture onto the tottering cliffs above. Bryant's Gully follows a gully line extending from the valley floor almost to the crest of the Esgair. Some obstacles are difficult – especially if wet – although for the most part they are not too serious and exposure is limited. The gully ascends in three distinct stages: water-worn steps, an open trough, and a defined upper section between photogenic rock walls. The route is exceedingly long and plenty of time should be afforded to it. Grade 2 obstacles – often of a 'traditional' nature – occur throughout its length and should not be underestimated. **Note:** Refer to the updates page on the Cicerone website for Bryant's Gully naming conventions.

Approach
Leave the Llanberis Pass road at SH 625 568 below Carreg Wastad and above the buildings of Ynys Ettws (several lay-bys for parking nearby) and ascend grass and scree near the stream course. The stream issues from a gully, tree-filled at its base, which splits an area of broken crags to the right of Carreg Wastad (a 60m-high

Glyder Fawr – Esgair Felen
47 Bryant's Gully
48 Esgair Felen Direct

Route 47 – Bryant's Gully

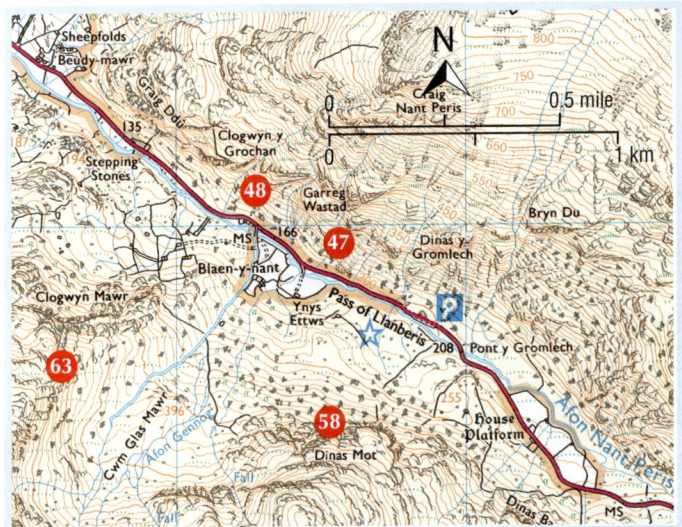

rectangular crag situated a few hundred metres up the hillside). It is 400m down the road from the more distinctive giant open-book crag of Dinas Cromlech.

Ascent

Narrow and well defined from the outset, the gully leads to the trees up several steps. A smooth boulder in the tree area is hopelessly slippery; it can be overcome with a struggle and a good soaking: duck under a little roof and slither leftwards on a tilted slab being thankful – as there are no footholds – for positive handholds including a quartz chock. (Alternatively, an unsurprisingly well-travelled dry option at 2- can be found on the left.) After a small bay a variety of steps and chockstones follow. An imposing jammed boulder is passed on its left side by steep scrambling on large juggy holds (the tempting right-hand side is 3S and not recommended). A final difficult step leads onto the open hillside at the end of the first section.

The gully opens out as a trough in heather slopes but soon narrows between walls. Cunningly climb a step with a jammed boulder to enter an alcove. The trap is now sprung. However, the right wall is not quite so difficult as it first seems: from its middle, take a rising rightwards line – steep but with positive holds – before returning back left. A second recess below a magnificent array of black basalt columns is also exited on the right.

The array of black basalt columns in Bryant's Gully

The gully now begins to curve rightwards (an enticing variant rising leftwards from here involves difficult scrambling on loose rock – avoid). Once gained, the groove to the right of a dividing riblet in the gully offers pleasant scrambling. A final imposing chockstone above red scree is passed with surprising ease on its right. The whole gully line loses identity in a bowl of red scree as you emerge at a spectacular viewpoint on a grassy shoulder. To avoid the worst of the scree, follow a long rib to the right – taking care with suspect spikes and blocks – until a headwall pushes you rightwards into a scree-filled gully. The sharp grassy crest of Esgair Felen is soon reached and followed to the summit of Glyder Fawr.

Descent by this route
A descent is feasible but strongly discouraged without prior knowledge gained during an ascent.

Descents and combinations
From the summit of Glyder Fawr descend steeply north west by a cairned scree path to Llyn y Cwn. Ignoring the drier path to the right, cross boggy ground westwards to a stile and find the well-defined path which descends to Gwastadnant about a mile farther down the Llanberis Pass from the starting point.

Either the Gribin Ridge (Route 38) or Seniors' Ridge and Gully (Routes 42 and 43) would make an appropriate easy scramble for those wishing to descend into the Ogwen Valley.

Route 48
Esgair Felen Direct

2+ ✪

Intermittent scrambling up the impressive south west ridges of Esgair Felen.

Location	Esgair Felen leading to Glyder Fawr, Llanberis Pass (SH 623 572)
Grade	2+ ✪
Approach time	5min
Altitude and aspect	180m, south west
Route length	A long route with a short approach; the terrain is mixed and the technicalities not sustained. Progress is likely to be much faster than might be expected for such a long route. Nonetheless, it remains a substantial outing. Height gain approximately 520m.
Conditions	Quick drying, especially in its upper half. Catches any sunlight from dawn till dusk. The rock is generally sound although some loose material may be encountered as the route has been newly devised for this update; as such it is one best tackled with a cautious approach.
Topo	See Route 47

If searching for a line on continuous rock at a consistent grade, look elsewhere. Nonetheless, the route is long and although hiking is required to link some of its sections, it has considerable merit in offering a dry alternative to Bryant's Gully and as an interesting means of connecting the Pass of Llanberis and Ogwen Valley. The surroundings are impressive; and if the upper reaches offer a sense of remoteness and isolation, relatively straightforward escapes and easier alternatives in the event of inclement weather ensure this is an amenable scramble.

For map, see Route 47.

Approach
Park at the lay-by beneath Clogwyn y Grochan (SH 622 571). The route commences up ribs to the right of the watercourse bounding Clogwyn y Grochan on its east side just above a collection of hawthorns.

Ascent

Head up the hillside to the right of Clogwyn y Grochan, crossing the watercourse. Connect a series of short ribs on the right edge of the watercourse until the steep and intimidating crags of Ysgar Fewr are met at a flat area. At the first steep wall creep round a metre beyond its left edge and ascend steep but easy steps leading up through a sentry box to reach the crest of Ysgar Fewr at its first pinnacle. Follow the crest to yet another intimidating wall. Although more promising than the first, it remains too hard so pass the steepening on the left before trending back right to reach a saddle 4m below the easily accessed pinnacle summit of the Ysgar Fewr spur.

The way onwards is barred by an imposing headwall too difficult for the scrambler. A deviation left into the watercourse would not be wished on your worst enemy, so instead descend slightly rightwards and follow a faint sheep path for 40m to cross the couloir and reach the right-hand end of an obvious small quartz buttress. Climb this towards its right edge in the direction of the lowest of the sharp pinnacles on the crest above. Above the quartz, move onto water-washed slabs for some short-lived intricate padding if dry (if wet the slabs are best avoided by heather on the right). A direct line that passes up behind the first pinnacle looks amenable – it isn't, and proves **a dangerous grade 3S on friable rock**. Instead, follow a natural line diagonally leftwards up heather and ferns to exit the amphitheatre on the left of a small and often dry watercourse.

The angle now changes and the mountain opens out. Above is a short, wide wall with a large rowan tree in the middle. Coming in from the right and passing through the rowan provides fun of sorts, although most will dodge easily up the wall on the left end. Continue hiking up grass and heather slopes to reach an interesting short rib in 80m. Start up the rib at the left end and work up on good in-cut holds.

The main watercourse crossed on the approach is nearby to your left and a large buttress lies in wait ahead. Trend leftwards to meet the buttress at its left edge, 15m left of a rowan tree and at a point where a vague rib with a boulder at its bottom draws very close to the stream. The white spiky vague rib above the boulder begins a long stretch of good scrambling. This is the crux of the route so much caution is needed to check holds. Head up the rib, passing a steepening after 5m slightly on the left side. As height is gained the rib becomes easier until the gradient suddenly shifts and the main difficulties have been overcome. (Should this section prove too difficult, cross the stream and head up an easy-angled grassy runnel to meet grass slopes and trend up the hillside to rejoin the route at the 'great tower'.)

The best scrambling and positions are now found by following the rock on the right. On reaching the 'great tower' of Esgair Felen its lower-bounding section of greener rock is friable, so trend rightwards to pass this and head up a scree bed to locate a shallow gully cutting in from right to left. Follow the shallow gully, passing over a short difficult step at mid-height, to reach the crest of the great tower. Pick a

Above dramatic cliffs high on Esgair Felen Direct

line up the crest to suit. The summit of Esgair Felen is soon reached. Its parent mountain, Glyder Fawr, can be seen 1km to the west and will beckon most.

Descents and combinations
As for Route 47.

Y Garn (947M)

Y Garn is the highest of several summits on the northern limb of the dog-leg Glyderau ridge. When viewed from Llyn Ogwen its shape has been likened to that of an armchair, with the abrupt North East Ridge (normal ascent and descent route) on the right, pinnacled East Ridge (Route 50) on the left, and tiny Llyn Clyd nestling on the seat between. The south east flank, which is also used as a normal route of ascent and descent, slopes gently down to Llyn y Cwn in its marshy saddle. The north east side of this saddle drops sharply into Cwm Idwal as the Devil's Kitchen cliffs, up which Route 49 finds a way.

Before going any further we need to sort out some terminology. In this book 'Devil's Kitchen cliffs' refers to the entire group of buttresses, otherwise known as Clogwyn y Geifr, which stands at the head of Cwm Idwal; 'Devil's Kitchen' is the central deep rift in these cliffs, out of which there is no easy exit; 'Devil's Kitchen path' is the normal ascent/descent route on the ramp that slants up leftwards from the Devil's Kitchen entrance towards Llyn y Cwn.

Route 49
Devil's Kitchen and the Sheep Walk ⠀⠀⠀⠀⠀⠀ 3S ✪✪✪ or 1- ✪

A unique and unforgettable exploratory excursion into a dark, stream-flushed cleft followed by easy scrambling up a scenic terrace, described here in two parts.

Location	Cwm Idwal, Glyderau (SH 638 588)
Grade	3S ✪✪✪ (to reach the foot of the final waterfall) or 2 ✪ (to reach the foot of the infamous boulder waterfall). The Sheep Walk is 1- ✪ if done independently.
Approach time	45min
Altitude and aspect	600m, north east
Route length	In the Devil's Kitchen, with only 100m of height gain – and 100m of height loss on the return – how long could the full 3S route possibly take? Allow plenty of time and find out. The Sheep Walk has a height gain of 130m.
Conditions	The Devil's Kitchen is always wet but it is worth allowing as much time as you can for the stream to subside after heavy rain. In rare periods of drought the route may offer marginally easier ascent options but will be less atmospheric. The grass of the Sheep Walk needs care in wet weather.

The excursion into the pounding cacophony and dramatic scenery of the Devil's Kitchen will not be to everyone's taste. Although the days of the tweed-clad masochists who relished this kind of sport are long gone, following in their footsteps offers an amusing assault on the senses that will be remembered long after the glow of other classic climbs has dimmed. Anyone who loves spending time in the Welsh hills should do this at least once in a lifetime.

The normal path to Llyn y Cwn ascends a widening terrace to the left of the Devil's Kitchen; the narrower and more exposed Sheep Walk is its near mirror-image on the cliffs to the right. There is not much scrambling on the Sheep Walk, which explains the detour into the Devil's Kitchen, although it offers a novel little outing not without merit in itself.

Note

The Devil's Kitchen is the only route in this book that must be reversed when its end is reached, and therefore should not be attempted unless you are willing to downclimb what you have ascended. **An abseil is required** to reverse the boulder waterfall pitch, so only competent parties equipped with the skills and equipment necessary should venture above here (there are no fixed anchors, but good natural features – pack a 30m+ rope). The easiest upwards escape from the Devil's Kitchen is by a serious V-Diff climb that will feel many grades harder when wet (as it almost always is) and requires considerable rock climbing experience.

Approach

From Capel Curig or Bethesda along the A5 to a car park at Ogwen Cottage (SH 649 604) – approximately 150m east of YHA Idwal Cottage – or use overspill parking in lay-bys farther east. Take the path behind the toilet block, fork right after a few metres, then ascend through a quarried rift, exiting on the right at its end. Follow a less obvious path, crossing a stile, to a mound overlooking Llyn Idwal. Take the path on the west shore of the lake and ascend among boulders to the Devil's Kitchen entrance – the central dark cleft in cliffs at the head of the cwm.

Ascent – Devil's Kitchen

Scramble up the stream bed over assorted slippery obstacles to the main test-piece: the huge boulder of the Waterfall Pitch. You have four alternatives from which to choose: an immediate retreat; a 4m struggle up the left side of the boulder with good thread protection that can be pre-placed (recommended); a slippery and hard-to-protect 6m climb up the right-hand corner over which flows the waterfall; and an exit up the gap under the boulder often occupied by a subsidiary waterfall.

Having used all means at your disposal to overcome the Waterfall Pitch, more wet scrambling over short rises leads past a giant blade of rock (the Leaning Pillar) to where the

At the Leaning Pillar in the evil depths of the Devil's Kitchen

Route 49 – Devil's Kitchen and the Sheep Walk

Socks over shoes aid the pool traverse to reach the final waterfall

stream plunges 20m into a basin at the back of the cleft. Scary. Traverse above a pool by its left wall to reach the absolute back of the cleft and stand in the cave behind the waterfall. Needless to say, this is as far as we can go without resorting to serious rock climbing.

Descent by this route
The descent is made in exact reverse, with an **abseil** at the boulder waterfall pitch.

> **Note** There is no descent into the Devil's Kitchen itself.

Ascent – The Sheep Walk
From the entrance to the Devil's Kitchen, the Sheep Walk terrace curves out rightwards – narrow at first but with a small path – between the main cliff face and a shorter supporting wall. Most of it is exposed walking, with some scrambling on ribs to be found on the right as the ramp widens. The route emerges on the south east slope with a path nearby leading rightwards to the summit of Y Garn or left towards Glyder Fawr.

Descent by this route
A descent of the Sheep Walk is a reasonable prospect provided it can be located from above. The reddish scree at its top is a good indicator.

Descents and combinations
- Via the giant stone steps of the Devil's Kitchen path: from the emergence of the Sheep Walk (or the summit of Y Garn), descend gentle slopes south east to Llyn y Cwn and pick up the path heading north east to return to Lyn Idwal.
- From the summit of Y Garn, descend the blunt ridge north for a few hundred metres then fork right to descend the narrow and steeply angled north east ridge by a good path.

Route 50
East Ridge   2 ✪✪

A heathery introductory rib followed by a more sustained, narrowing rock ridge.

Location	Cwm Idwal, Glyderau (SH 642 597)
Grade	2 ✪✪
Approach time	20min
Altitude and aspect	450m, east
Route length	A route of moderate length interspersed with passages of hiking. Height gain approximately 350m.
Conditions	Quick drying.
Topo	See Route 49

A popular route with an intermittent beginning but a satisfying and panoramic end which, when coupled with a descent from the summit of Y Garn via the north east ridge, provides a tremendous horseshoe of Cwm Clyd.

Approach
As for Route 49 to the mound overlooking Llyn Idwal.

Ascent
Gain the introductory ridge, left of the stream that descends from Cwm Clyd, and pick initial lines to suit on the rock's strange golf-ball holds. A path soon leads to a

Learning the ropes on the East Ridge of Y Garn

steeper buttress; traverse to its centre by means of a rising line from the left with a move in an airy position that proves harder than any found on the upper ridge (this buttress is a highlight of the lower ridge, although it can be circumvented on the left if needs must). Continue until the ridge levels out at Cwm Clyd. Follow a path left to the base of the large buttress that guards the East Ridge.

Avoid a difficult direct ascent of the buttress by sneaking round the corner and scrambling up on the left side of the ridge, returning to the crest as soon as possible. (Alternatively, the main ridge crest can be gained from the right of the truncating crag by means of a well-used muddy-stepped scrappy recess.) Thereafter take the ridge direct – exposed in places – until it narrows delightfully and levels out below a final rise.

Short cracks and a corner lead directly to the top's easy slopes. Walk around the rim of Cwm Clyd to the summit.

Descent by this route

A feasible descent, with a slight increase in difficulty. In descent the harder parts of the lower ridge are best passed by devious paths.

Descents and combinations

As for Route 49.

Foel Goch (831M)

Foel Goch is rarely climbed in its own right – this being the unfashionable end of the Glyderau – but more often in combination with a walk over Y Garn or Carnedd y Filiast. When viewed from Llyn Ogwen the formidable skyline ridge of Yr Esgair dramatises an otherwise unremarkable mountain.

Cwm Coch bites deep into the eastern side of the mountain. It is bounded on the left by a broad-backed shoulder supported by the bristling crags of Creigiau Gleision, and on the right by Yr Esgair, the north east ridge.

Route 51

South Arête 1+ ✪

Pleasant and straightforward scrambling on the easiest of Foel Goch's routes.

Location	Creigiau Gleision, Foel Goch (SH 635 611)
Grade	1+ ✪
Approach time	40min
Altitude and aspect	560m, north east
Route length	A route of moderate length that provides plenty of time on rock. Height gain approximately 120m.
Conditions	A much more serious outing when wet, as the rough rock surprisingly becomes slippery.
Topo	Also see Route 53

Finding the start of the scramble provides the biggest challenge on this easy but adventurous ridge route. The rock is not continuous but interest increases as height is gained and the route proves a worthy companion to the adjacent Needle's Eye Arête, it being perfectly feasible to climb both routes on the same outing to this unfrequented crag.

Approach

From Capel Curig or Bethesda along the A5. At Ogwen Cottage, take the old road past YHA Idwal Cottage onto the west side of the Nant Ffrancon valley. There are three possible approaches:

Route 51 – South Arête

Foel Goch – Creigiau Gleision
- ⓢ₁ South Arête
- ⓢ₂ Needle's Eye Arête

- From between the farms of Blaen-y-nant (SH 642 608) and Pentre (SH 639 615): after the road drops steeply, cross a cattle grid and park on the left (limited space). From the gate strike directly up the hillside following the fence on its left towards Yr Esgair. At a bend in the fence a faint rising leftwards path joins the well-defined traverse path from Idwal. Follow the traverse path but stop 110m before the sheepfolds on the shoulder.
- From the bridge just before the road drops steeply down to Blaen-y-nant, take a rising traverse right (faint path) to join a main path above a rock bluff. Follow this rightwards, with a short descent below an outcrop, to a scree slope. Ascend diagonally right up a grass couloir and continue in the same line with some easy scrambling to emerge in Cwm Coch a short distance below the cliff. Follow the path west from the sheepfolds for 110m.
- Cwm Coch can also be reached by a path running parallel to the wall that connects Llyn Idwal and Cwm Coch.

Directly above you is a large square buttress with a dusting of quartz on its top left. Across the couloir to its left is a cave. Head up between the two. A face behind the square buttress has an unmistakable 2m left-to-right rising diagonal quartz stripe. Grass cols appear on the right and left skylines here. From the basin topped by the quartz-striped face (marking the start of Needle's Eye Arête, Route 52) follow a path 20m left (east) over a shoulder into a lesser branch of Eastern Gully. Continue

Poised on the airy blocks at the top of South Arête

traversing for 30m to a higher shoulder at a notch with a square-topped rock tower on the left. This notch is the start of South Arête, which is ill-defined initially.

Ascent
Pick a line up the easy rock steps of the lower ridge, not veering too far from Eastern Gully to the right. The ridge becomes more defined and the scrambling more interesting as height is gained. Where a steep tower bars access to the ridge crest, look for a very small and bizarrely situated stone wall to the left of the tower. Step over this, skirting the tower to reach a nick where a chockstone forms a small window in the ridge crest. Regain the crest here to reach a final difficult buttress, which is overcome via a 3m corner on its left (some parties move into Eastern Gully to avoid this). The route finishes along airy ridgetop blocks to meet a path heading up to Foel Goch's summit.

Descent by this route
Despite the grade, this route is not recommended in descent.

Descents and combinations
There are a few options:
- To return to Nant Ffrancon or Llyn Idwal from the summit of Foel Goch, head initially south east along the cliff-top path, passing over the top of Routes 51 and

52, in order to access Cwm Cywion below the tiny Llyn Cywion. Follow the main watercourse down to a wall and the transverse path that connects Llyn Idwal and Cwm Coch. (This transverse path can be followed roughly south east to Llyn Idwal or north to reach Cwm Coch which can then be descended.) Continue to follow the path down beside the watercourse, emerging on the Nant Ffrancon road at SH 642 606.

- With care, it is possible to descend directly to the foot of the route: descend the scree gully that begins with a path to the right looking out (east) of the South Arête until a blind step becomes apparent below – this must be avoided. Head left (looking out) over a grassy shoulder to access another grassy gully; descend this until it is possible to move back right to the original line below the blind step. Grass and scree lead without complication to the foot of the crag.

Route 52
Needle's Eye Arête 3 ✪

Adventurous scrambling up a pinnacled arête on an unfrequented crag.

Location	Creigiau Gleision, Foel Goch (SH 634 611)
Grade	3 ✪
Approach time	40min
Altitude and aspect	560m, north
Route length	A route of moderate length that provides plenty of time on rock. Height gain approximately 120m.
Conditions	Although the rock is intrinsically sound, some of the blocks are precariously balanced and demand care. The cliff is not well visited and the rock can be lichenous; the route offers excellent friction in the dry, but after wet weather is best avoided.
Topo	See Routes 51 and 53

The left-hand side of Creigiau Gleision crumples into a series of saw-toothed arêtes interspersed with scree chutes. The Needle's Eye Arête is merely one among many, and its purity of line is apparent only in retrospect. The route has a distinctly alpine flavour, with continuous and often exposed scrambling on which rope protection may be desirable.

Fast progress up Needle's Eye Arête

Approach
As for Route 51 to below the 2m quartz stripe.

Ascent
A scree couloir issues from a gully – Eastern Gully – that winds up into the heart of the cliff; Needle's Eye Arête bounds this on its right. Although it is possible to access Needle's Eye Arête from Eastern Gully by means of a heather ledge part way up, the gully is often greasy and it is better to move round to the right of the 2m quartz stripe and then follow a scrappy vegetated couloir back left to gain the arête below an uncompromising step. Creep rightwards awkwardly beneath a bulge and go up a heather runnel to regain the arête at a notch overlooking Eastern Gully. Ascend a slab on the edge, and the subsequent exposed arête, to a hole in the rock – the Needle's Eye. Now either surmount the step above direct on perched blocks of doubtful stability, or dodge it on the left by an awkward heather traverse, regaining the arête via a short wall.

Continue more easily up the exposed arête to another step, which is taken direct to pinnacles. Beyond several more short rises, all of which can be taken direct, the arête emerges onto the east shoulder a little to the right of Eastern Gully.

Ascend the shoulder over a slight col onto grass slopes leading north to the summit.

Descents and combinations
As for Route 51.

Route 53
Yr Esgair

3S ✪

A tempting-looking ridge line ascended with loose scrambling above a dangerous start.

Location	Cwm Coch, Foel Goch (SH 633 614)
Grade	3S ✪
Approach time	40min
Altitude and aspect	580m, north east
Route length	Allow plenty of time for second thoughts! A fairly long route. Height gain approximately 270m.
Conditions	Attempting this route in all but perfect conditions would be reckless. Wait for a period of prolonged dry weather and turn back if the grass is wet – you have been warned.

This thoroughly nasty scramble has been included only for completeness. The route follows the north east ridge, obvious and direct. A prominent notch separates the low-angled lower ridge from its steeply angled continuation. Absence of belay anchors and difficult scrambling ensure that escape from the notch is a hazardous affair. Technical difficulties ease thereafter, yet the terrain remains treacherous and a lack of easy escape is the strongest motive for continuing. **Only those experienced in dangerous terrain should consider an ascent**, and they would be wise not to bother.

Note

The updaters survived checking this route. With gear to protect the crux, a 50m rope (with which it is *just* possible to reach a good belay at the top of the heather shoulder), excellent conditions and understandably low expectations, Yr Esgair can prove perversely enjoyable.

Approach

As for Route 51 into Cwm Coch. Trend rightwards to gain the ridge, broad and indistinct at first.

Are looks deceiving? On the tempting-looking line of Yr Esgair before the notch

Ascent
After a heathery approach ridge there is some interesting and exposed easy scrambling along the sharp end of the lower ridge leading to a pronounced notch below

Foel Goch
51 South Arête
52 Needle's Eye Arête
53 Yr Esgair

the main ridge. The difficulties that lie ahead are now bleakly obvious. This is a good place for second thoughts and escape is possible left into Cwm Coch.

Above the notch a knife-edged arête leads to a heather shoulder at 15m. The hardest moves are at the top, not helped by the appalling prospect of a fall into the gully on the right. There is an unearthed nut runner placement on the shoulder, ideal for protecting the second but **not suitable as a belay anchor** – continue to the rock ahead, which is reached on exactly 50m of rope from the notch.

Beyond the heather shoulder the ridge rears up in a continuous line to the summit: ascend it, technically straightforward but insecure, making the best use of shattered leaves on the left and vegetated furrows on the right. The ridge ends abruptly a few metres from the summit and thus almost redeems itself.

Descent by this route
Forget it.

Descents and combinations
As for Route 51.

Carnedd y Filiast

Route 54
The Ridge (aka Atlantic Ridge) 2+ ✪✪

Excellent scrambling on quality rock straight up the edge of enormous slabs.

Location	Carnedd y Filiast (SH 624 627)
Grade	2+ ✪✪
Approach time	45min
Altitude and aspect	570m, south east
Route length	A route of moderate length with sustained hands-on activity throughout. Height gain approximately 200m.
Conditions	The ridge dries fairly quickly but can be greasy after prolonged rainy periods.

The expansive slabs of Carnedd y Filiast lie at too gentle an angle to interest many rock climbers – although the unique Waved Slab is an exception. Scramblers, however, will relish the quietly impressive surroundings and the chance to pad up nearly 300 metres of rough rock along the ridge at the right edge of Atlantic Slab. The route is committing but never daunting and provides ample belays and runners should they be required.

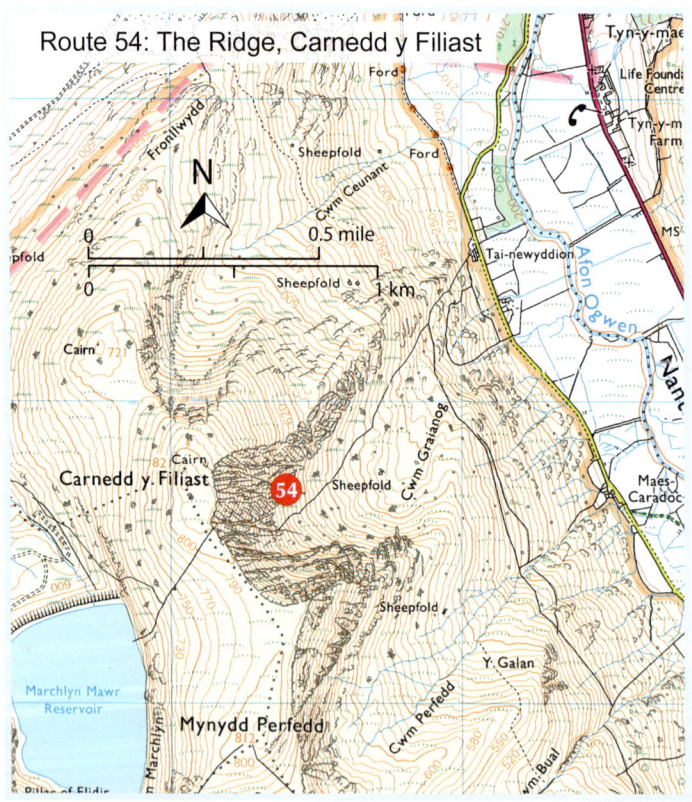

Route 54 – The Ridge (aka Atlantic Ridge)

Approach
From Ogwen Cottage on the A5 take the old Nant Ffrancon road past Idwal Cottage youth hostel for 3.5km to a small lay-by parking area 100m south of the outdoor centre Tai-newyddion. From the parking area the best option is to walk back south along the road for 100m to a cattle grid. Here strike directly up the demanding hillside on very faint paths to the visible Cwm Graianog, pass a heart-shaped sheep pen and eventually reach a large stone wall. Cross this where large boulders abut the wall below the base of the furthest left slab (Atlantic Slab) and pick a line up a wide scree tongue to reach the route.

Ascent
The route starts at the lowest point of the Atlantic Slab at its right edge. Follow the broken ridge up strips and small slabs of rock, then move right onto an overlap. Stay with the best rock on the ridge crest, gaining exposure and fantastic views of the vast Waved Slab. The ridge peters out near the top of the slab and the summit of Carnedd y Filiast is just a couple of minutes' walk to the west.

Descents and combinations
- To return to Nant Ffrancon, head up to the summit and take the intermittent path north east from the summit to eventually join the road north of Tai-newyddion.
- To descend directly to Nant Ffrancon by the approach route or return for more scrambling in Cwm Graianog is more awkward than would be hoped. Follow

An ocean of rock at Atlantic Slabs

the top-out spur north east down boulders and mounds of heather until clearly beyond the cliffs, then struggle down heather to the wall.
- The south spur of Cwm Graianog can be descended, with care, by staying on its right side, until the cwm is easily accessed.
- An excellent ridge walk over Mynydd Perfedd, Foel Goch and Y Garn allows straightforward access to Llyn Idwal.

Note

The bizarre upturned seabed formation of the 180m Waved Slab will undoubtedly catch the eye of passing scramblers because of its angle. Although presently graded Moderate, it is too sustained for a scramble; it is steeper than it looks and VDiff might be a more appropriate grade as runners and belays are exceptionally sparse. Climbed anywhere up its dead centre it is an excellent outing for experienced rock climbing parties. Bone-dry conditions are essential.

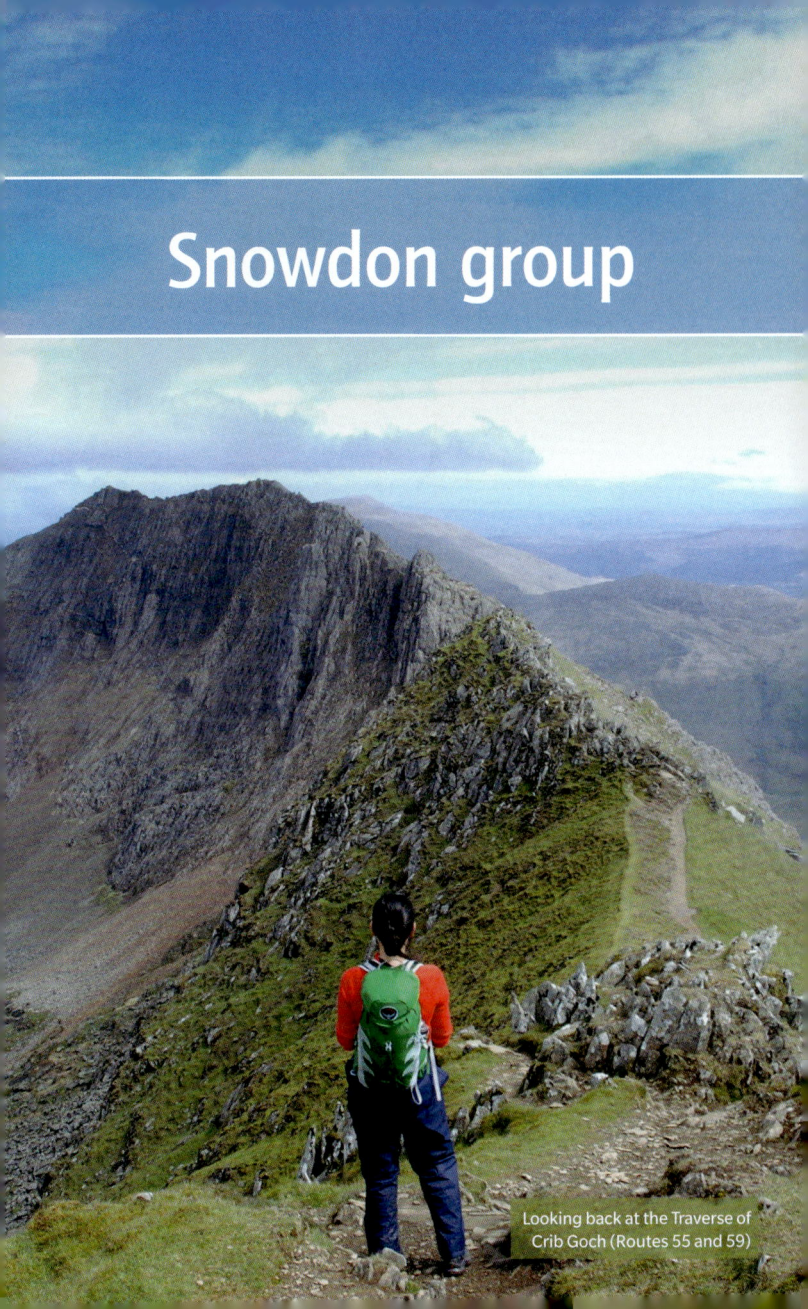

Snowdon group

Looking back at the Traverse of Crib Goch (Routes 55 and 59)

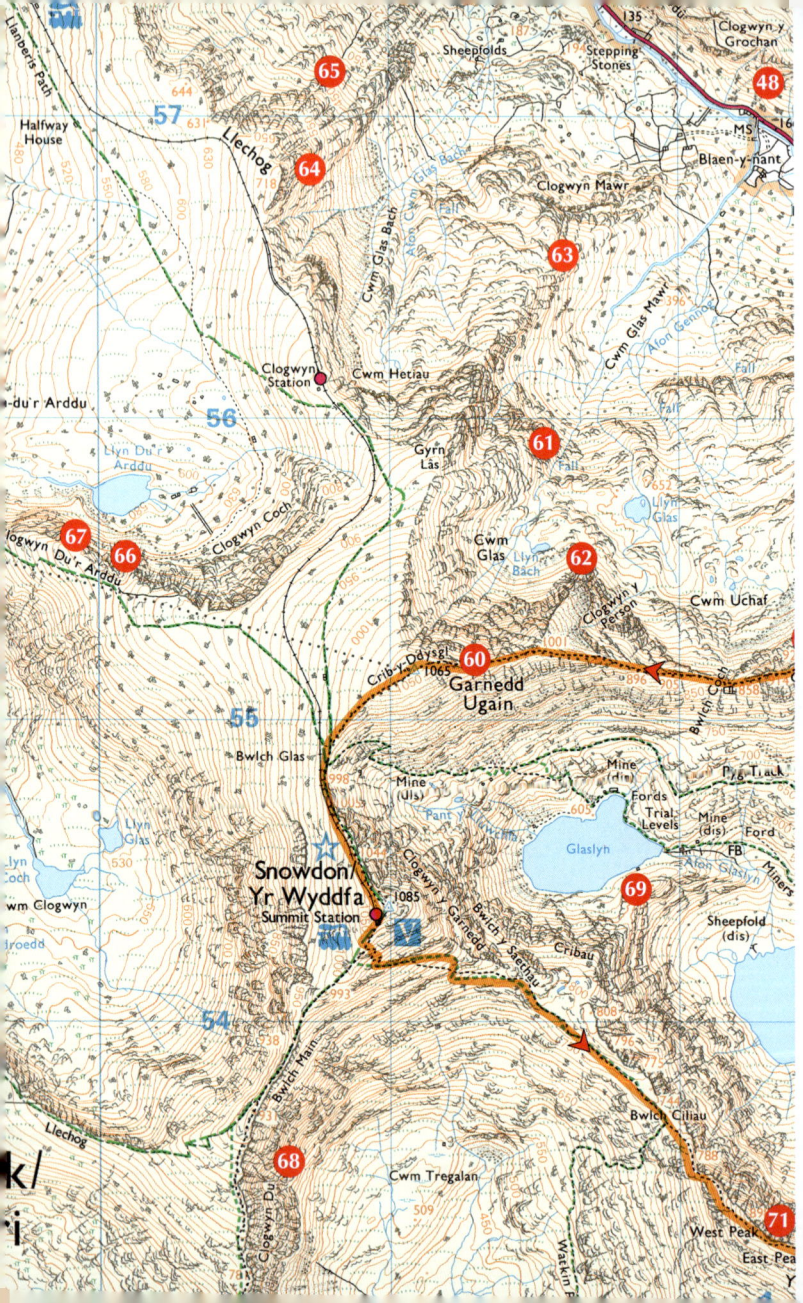

A Brocken spectre between Crib y Ddysgl and Crib Goch (Route 55)

Snowdon Group

Snowdon and its satellites form the southernmost of the three highest mountain groups in North Wales, combining the scale of the Carneddau with the ruggedness of the Glyderau. The impressions are of open valleys and bulky summits, yet also of rocky cwms and knife-edged ridges.

Normal walking routes to Snowdon's summit continue to inspire with grand scenery, despite heavy traffic and clinically reconstructed paths. Reclusive walkers will find more subtle pleasures on the unworn paths of neglected lower hills. For rock climbers the scope is enormous, with a choice ranging from pseudo-alpinism on Lliwedd to technical intricacy on Dinas Mot. The potential for the scrambler is equally diverse, if not as extensive.

The group is contained by the triangle of roads linking Beddgelert, Caernarfon and Pen y Gwryd. Concentrated at the eastern end are the most important peaks – Snowdon, Crib y Ddysgl, Lliwedd and Crib Goch. Close neighbours Snowdon and Crib y Ddysgl dominate the group. Six major ridges radiate from their summits, delineating the corresponding six cwms.

Route 55

The Snowdon Horseshoe 1 ✪✪✪

One of the finest ridge traverses south of Scotland.

Location	Snowdon group
Grade	1 ✪✪✪
Circuit time	6hr
Route length	12km
Conditions	Avoid wet or blustery weather, conditions that can make the crossing of Crib Goch nerve-wracking and treacherous. Excessively popular on fine summer weekends.
Topo	See Route 69

This is a truly classic ridge traverse, including the horizontal knife-edged section on Crib Goch. It compares in both quality and difficulty with the Cwm Bochlwyd Horseshoe. Given the length of the undertaking, rope protection is impractical. Three sections require special care: the initial rock barrier and scoop on the East Ridge; the traverse of the Pinnacles on Crib Goch itself; and the first step on Crib y Ddysgl.

For convenience the route is described in full here, although its constituent parts, worthy scrambles in their own right, are also listed separately: East Ridge of Crib Goch (Route 56); Traverse of Crib Goch (Route 59); Crib y Ddysgl (Route 60); Traverse of Lliwedd (Route 70).

Second thoughts and escapes

There are few Snowdon Horseshoe regulars who have not had to come to the aid of individuals that have either become 'cragfast' from exposure or that have panicked when faced with tougher-than-expected conditions on the Crib Goch traverse. Often this is the fault of party leaders overestimating their team's head for heights, although sometimes parties have unwittingly followed other groups. To save helicopter fuel it might be worth pointing out to anyone in difficulty that the East Ridge (assuming that is what has brought them there) is not especially harder in descent, while the traverse itself never becomes particularly any more difficult.

If conditions deteriorate badly while on Crib Goch then complete its traverse. A descent can then be made north west from Bwlch Coch towards Llyn Glas, or south towards Glaslyn. In either case take care in mist to avoid outcrops and steep scree. If bad weather or darkness approaches while on Snowdon, consider descending via the Pyg Track or Miners' Track rather than being forced to abandon the route at Bwlch y Saethau between Snowdon and Lliwedd with no easy descent to Pen y Pass.

Approach

From Llanberis or Capel Curig along the A4086 to a car park (hefty fee) at **Pen y Pass** (SH 647 556). When full, as is frequently the case during weekends and holiday periods, park opposite the Pen y Gwryd Hotel (SH 661 558) and walk up a footpath just south of the road that is not marked on OS maps to reach Pen y Pass in 20 minutes. Alternatively, an excellent regular Sherpa bus service running from various points including Llanberis can deliver you to this spot (a day rover ticket is often included in car park fees).

On the classic Snowdon Horseshoe

Ascent/Descent

East Ridge of Crib Goch: From the upper car park follow a well-marked path westwards for 1.5km to the prominent col of **Bwlch y Moch**.

Turn right and approach the blunt East Ridge. The first difficulties arise above a cairned shoulder. An obvious solution is to take a well-scratched, right-slanting line across fluted rock. A cunning alternative slants up left before returning to the right (above the steep part) along an exposed ledge. Seventy metres of sustained scrambling up a shallow depression above the barrier completes the difficult lower part of the ridge.

Flanking paths tempt you left or right away from the shattered rock steps that characterise the upper part of the ridge. Nevertheless it is best to stay on the crest, where the rock is firmest.

The East and North ridges converge at the east end of **Crib Goch** (literally 'Red Comb'). Although this is not the highest point on the ridge, nor even a prominent top, it is generally referred to as Crib Goch summit.

Traverse of Crib Goch: The first section, across a rock table, is simple enough, then the ridge narrows to a ragged knife-edge. Some walk along this section no-hands, while others find footholds on the left side and use the crest like a handrail.

Eventually the ridge eases and dips to the base of the first of the three Pinnacles. Flank the first on the left, easily, then traverse the left side of the second by a ledge and short scramble to a draughty notch. Now follow a series of exposed ledges slanting from left to right across the right side of the third pinnacle and so gain its summit. Descend a simple gully and scree path to **Bwlch Coch**.

Crib y Ddysgl: The ridge traverse resumes under the name Crib y Ddysgl; easy at first, then more testing where the rocks coalesce at the far side of an uncharacteristic plateau. Ignore the temptation of a flanking path on the left and tackle the initial obstacle direct. Surmount the succeeding barrier by a series of zig-zags up little chimneys and over blocks on the left side (always within 10 or 15 metres of the crest). The ridge reclines above into a shattered crest of short problems separated by longer stretches of walking. A trig point identifies the summit of **Crib y Ddysgl**.

Traverse of Snowdon: Circle the rim of the Glaslyn cwm, passing the 3m marker stone at the exit of the Pyg Track zig-zags after 300m or so, and continue to the summit of **Snowdon**.

Resist an unpleasant direct descent to Bwlch y Saethau and instead go down the south west ridge for about 200m to a 2m-high marker stone. Leave the ridge here and descend a scree path (the upper section of the Watkin Path) diagonally across the south face to **Bwlch y Saethau**. Continue along the path for 600m (or better take the circuitous ridge to its left) to a large cairn at **Bwlch Cilau** below the north west ridge of Lliwedd.

Traverse of Lliwedd: The ascent to Lliwedd, which looked so daunting from Snowdon, unfolds without complication. Stay near the left edge for the best scrambling and for tremendous views across the huge north east face.

Circle over the two summits and a minor top, then fork left and scramble down ledges on the path. Continue by an improving path to the shore of **Llyn Llydaw** and a junction with the **Miners' Track**. Follow the track for more than 2km back to **Pen y Pass**.

Crib Goch (923M)

Crib Goch is the closest of the four Horseshoe peaks to Pen y Pass, from where it appears as a ruddy pyramid rising above the green hummocks of the neglected first nails. From here the East Ridge appears on the left and the North Ridge on the right, whereas the knife-edged and pinnacled Crib Goch itself is hidden on the far side. The flanks of the mountain are largely composed of an unappealing mixture of rock and scree; only the three ridges and their supporting buttresses are at all sound. There are no easy walking routes to the summit.

Usually an ascent is made by the East Ridge, followed by a traverse of Crib Goch and finishing with an ascent to Snowdon via Crib y Ddysgl. This is what is meant by 'doing Crib Goch', as opposed to 'doing the Horseshoe' which implies continuing beyond Snowdon by traversing Lliwedd.

For convenience these elements of the Snowdon Horseshoe have been described together as Route 55. Those wishing to vary the route, for instance by an approach via the North Ridge, or a descent from Bwlch Coch, can extract the relevant bits of description from there.

Route 56
East Ridge

1 ✪

Mostly straightforward scrambling up a blunt, narrowing ridge after overcoming a tricky lower barrier.

Location	Crib Goch, Llanberis Pass (SH 628 553)
Grade	1 ✪
Approach time	20min
Altitude and aspect	700m, east
Route length	A moderately short preliminary to greater things. Some sections of hands-on interest, but with variations that ensure slower parties can be easily passed.
Conditions	Avoid wet or blustery weather, conditions that can make the crossing of Crib Goch nerve-wracking and treacherous. Excessively popular on fine summer weekends.

This is the normal route up Crib Goch and is used as a preliminary to a traverse of Crib Goch on the first leg of the Snowdon Horseshoe.

Picking a way up the East Ridge of Crib Goch

Approach
From the upper car park follow a well-marked path westwards for 1.5km to the prominent col of **Bwlch y Moch**.

Ascent
Turn right and approach the blunt East Ridge. The first difficulties arise above a cairned shoulder. An obvious solution is to take a well-scratched, right-slanting line across fluted rock. A cunning alternative slants

Descending Crib Goch's North Ridge after having climbed the Clogwyn y Person Arête

Route 57 – North Ridge

up left before returning to the right (above the steep part) along an exposed ledge. Seventy metres of sustained scrambling up a shallow depression above the barrier completes the difficult lower part of the ridge.

Flanking paths tempt you left or right away from the shattered rock steps that characterise the upper part of the ridge. Nevertheless it is best to stay on the crest, where the rock is firmest.

The East and North ridges converge at the east end of **Crib Goch** (literally 'Red Comb'). Although this is not the highest point on the ridge, nor even a prominent top, it is generally referred to as Crib Goch summit.

Descent by this route

Descend in exact reverse of the ascent. Prior knowledge of the route in ascent helps when finding the best line through the lower barrier; staying with the line of the crest and not venturing onto scree on either side is essential.

Descents and combinations

Refer to Route 55. The North Ridge (Route 57) can be used in descent should crosswinds make the traverse of Crib Goch problematic.

Route 57

North Ridge 1 ✪

A ridge walk culminating in an exposed scramble along a knife-edge on the less frequented side of the mountain.

Location	Crib Goch, Llanberis Pass (SH 625 557)
Grade	1 ✪
Approach time	45–60min
Altitude and aspect	680m, north
Route length	A short burst of scrambling at the top of a high mountain.
Conditions	Avoid windy weather.
Topo	See image of Brocken Spectre in Snowdon Group intro: North Ridge is on the left.

Scrambles in Snowdonia

> The truncating cliffs of Dinas Mot bar direct access to the long, gently rising North Ridge of Crib Goch and so help preserve its relative obscurity. Although not as fine as the popular East Ridge, some may prefer the quieter surroundings.
>
> Although much of the rock is shattered, the scrambling is not technical and the tricky section is really quite short. Route-finding is simple once established on the ridge crest.

Approach

From Llanberis or Capel Curig along the A4086. There are several approaches, all of which require solid navigational skills:

- From Pen y Pass (SH 647 556) follow the Pyg Track for about 1km until after a small bridge where the land to your right is less steep. Bear right on a long and boggy traversing line – there is no obvious path and infrequent cairns – to a shoulder below the steepening of the North Ridge above the cliffs of Dinas Mot. One hour.
- Park near Pont y Gromlech (SH 629 566), cross a stile near the bridge and take the path – becoming bouldery – to the foot of the central trapezoid slab of Dinas Mot. Ascend diagonally left up tiring scree to avoid the cliffs and enter a boulder-filled canyon. Above this traverse rightwards, rising steadily with some scrambling and passing over the exit of the gully that defines the left side of Dinas Mot, to a shoulder on the North Ridge. Forty-five minutes.
- From the large lay-bys beneath Clogwyn y Grochan (SH 621 571), walk down the road to cross the bridge at Blaen-y-nant and after a second bridge turn left to follow the right side of the stream all the way into Cwm Glas Mawr and towards the looming crags of Cyrn Las. Follow a steep stony path up and left to reach Llyn Glas with its picturesque tiny island. From here follow vague paths east around the rocky lip of Cwm Uchaf to reach the steep scree path on the west flank of the North Ridge in 600m. One hour.

Ascent

Above the shoulder the broad ridge rises gently over grass and slabs. Eventually it steepens into a barren, moonscape ridge and finally narrows to a rock rib. Where the angle eases, the rib narrows further into a knife-edged arête. The side walls of the arête are shattered and so the most secure line takes the exposed crest direct. It ends abruptly at a junction with the East Ridge near the East Summit.

Descent by this route

A viable and common descent route. If reversing either of the first or second approaches (see above), care must be taken to not leave the lower part of the ridge eastwards too early. Conversely, the ridge must be left before the steep upper cliffs of Dinas Mot are met. If in doubt, reverse the third approach option – the safest and most common descent from the route.

Descents and combinations
Descend via the East Ridge (Route 56) or continue as for Route 55. A descent of the Cwm Glas Ridge (Route 63) makes for a decent horseshoe.

Route 58
Jammed Boulder Gully 3S ✪ ✪

Memorable scrambling with a curious through-route in an atmospheric gully to a shoulder on Crib Goch's North Ridge.

Location	Crib Goch, Llanberis Pass (SH 626 564)
Grade	3S ✪ ✪
Approach time	30min
Altitude and aspect	400m, north west
Route length	Conditions will dictate time spent on it; shortly after rain it can take at least twice as long as in prolonged dry spells. Height gain approximately 130m.
Conditions	The rock is generally sound but slippery in damp conditions.

Where Dinas Mot curves rightwards into Cwm Glas the cliffs break up into a series of uninviting buttresses separated by deep gullies. One of these gullies, Jammed Boulder, provides an exciting approach to the North Ridge or an excellent outing in its own right at the upper limit of scrambling technicality.

Although it is short, the difficulties are considerable. Moreover, there are no easy escapes from the gully and conditions are rarely ideal. In mitigation the route can be easily protected.

Approach
Park near Pont y Gromlech (SH 629 566). Cross the stile near the bridge and take the path to below the central, trapezoid slab of Dinas Mot. Cross the ladder stile on

the right and contour below cliffs, passing Western Gully, until beneath the first large recess in the barrier. Gullies define the left and right sides of an inset buttress; gain the base of the left-hand gully, which is further identified by the huge jammed boulder at half-height.

Ascent

Scramble easily up the gully to a steepening and overcome a tricky 3m block by its left side (slabs to the right of the block slope awkwardly and are insecure when damp).

Above is a bottomless cave formed by the huge boulder. Jammed blocks in the roof offer sling protection for moves left onto an undercut slab on which the holds, although good, are difficult to see in the gloom. The consequences of a slip from here are all too obvious. However, the first moves are the most difficult and better holds soon lead – rucksack permitting – through a hole in the roof to a large bay. Alternatively, ascend the outside route on the right side of the boulder to the bay (not recommended in damp conditions). If required, retreat from the bay is best made by abseil down the outside route using a threaded block anchor.

The gully rises in two stages above the bay. The first steps can be taken direct or by difficult, drier climbing up the rib on the right. Continue up the rock of the steepening gully bed until it is possible to step out right onto a jammed block (good thread runner), squeeze through another equally constricting gap, and so gain

Route 58 – Jammed Boulder Gully

Approaching the black hole beneath the Jammed Boulder

easier scrambling leading to the shoulder on the North Ridge below its rock section.

Descent by this route
Not recommended without prior knowledge in ascent. Not as difficult as you might expect, although it is tempting to abseil from the bay above the jammed boulder (which defeats the object).

Descents and combinations
To get back to the starting point, from the top of the route traverse leftwards (east), passing above the exit of Staircase Gully. Continue a descending traverse with some very easy scrambling to a bouldery canyon, which leads you down to screes at the edge of the cliffs of Dinas Mot. To ascend to the summit of Crib Goch use Route 57. Alternatively, for a superb grade 3 link-up it is also possible to traverse easily into Cwm Glas from a higher shoulder on the North Ridge and then ascend the Clogwyn y Person Arête (Route 62).

Route 59
Traverse of Crib Goch 1 ✪✪✪

Famously exposed but straightforward scrambling along a knife-edged and pinnacled ridge.

Location	Crib Goch, Snowdon group (SH 625 553)
Grade	1 ✪✪✪
Approach time	1hr (via Route 55)
Altitude and aspect	900m, north east to south west
Route length	A fairly lengthy scramble in its own right. Allow plenty of time on busy weekends.
Conditions	Avoid wet or blustery weather, conditions that can make the crossing of Crib Goch nerve-wracking and treacherous. Excessively popular on fine summer weekends.
Topo	See image in 'Crib Goch' intro: the route follows the skyline.

This famous traverse is the highlight of the Snowdon Horseshoe. It is a must-do route for aspiring scramblers and is fully described in Route 55 going from east to west. It can equally be enjoyed in the opposite direction at a similar level of difficulty.

Approach
Via the East Ridge (Route 56), North Ridge (Route 57), or, for a west to east traverse, from Crib y Ddysgl (Route 60).

Ascent
The first section, across a rock table, is simple enough, then the ridge narrows to a ragged knife-edge. Some walk along this section no-hands, while others find footholds on the left side and use the crest like a handrail.

Eventually the ridge eases and dips to the base of the first of the three Pinnacles. Flank the first on the left, easily, then traverse the left side of the second by a ledge and short scramble to a draughty notch. Now follow a series of exposed ledges slanting from left to right across the right side of the third pinnacle and so gain its summit. Descend a simple gully and scree path to Bwlch Coch.

Route 59 – Traverse of Crib Goch

Not another soul in sight on the knife-edged traverse of Crib Goch

Descents and combinations
The North Ridge (Route 57) can be used in descent should crosswinds make the traverse of Crib Goch problematic. See Route 55 for further details.

Scrambles in Snowdonia

Crib y Ddysgl (GARNEDD UGAIN, 1065M)

Garnedd Ugain, or Crib y Ddysgl as it is widely known (strictly, Crib y Ddysgl refers only to the continuation ridge of Crib Goch), is too often eclipsed by the grander presence of Snowdon to establish itself as a mountain worthy of ascent in its own right. Yet of the two it has much more to offer the scrambler: within the complex north eastern cirque of Cwm Glas; on the Llechog Buttress which flanks the long northern ridge; and, to a lesser extent, on the magnificent cliff of Clogwyn Du'r Arddu which darkens its north western slope.

Cwm Glas is one of the wildest and most impressive glaciated cirques in Snowdonia. The cwm rises in two stages to the remote upper bowl amid tremendous rock scenery. On the left here are red screes below the jagged profiles of Crib Goch and Crib y Ddysgl; on the right a rock-sided ridge that rises almost a thousand metres from valley floor to summit; and ahead the high crags of Clogwyn y Ddysgl, bounded on their left by the renowned Clogwyn y Person Arête.

Route 60
Crib y Ddysgl 1 ✪ ✪

Scenic and straightforward ridge scrambling that is the natural continuation to the Crib Goch traverse on the first half of the Snowdon Horseshoe.

Location	Snowdon group (SH 613 552)
Grade	1 ✪ ✪
Approach time	1hr 30min
Altitude and aspect	900m, east to west
Route length	One of the lengthier scrambling parts of the Snowdon Horseshoe with plenty of hands-on interest.
Conditions	As for Route 55

Although overshadowed by its more famous and exposed predecessor on the Snowdon Horseshoe, Crib y Ddysgl is a fine section in its own right. Sweeping majestically up to a battered trig-point, the ridge provides considerable interest and more than a few sections that will give pause for thought – especially on a windy day.

Route 60 – Crib y Ddysgl

Approach
Via the East or North ridges of Crib Goch (Route 56 or 57), followed by the traverse of Crib Goch (Route 59). A direct approach can be made from Upper Cwm Glas (refer to Route 62 approach) by walking up to Bwlch Coch, the prominent col between Crib Goch and Crib y Ddysgl.

Ascent
From Bwlch Coch, the ridge traverse is easy at first, then more testing where the rocks coalesce at the far side of an uncharacteristic plateau. Ignore the temptation of a flanking path on the left and tackle the initial obstacle direct. Surmount the succeeding barrier by a series of zig-zags up little chimneys and over blocks on the left side (always within 10 or 15 metres of the crest). The ridge reclines above into a shattered crest of short problems separated by longer stretches of walking. A trig point identifies Crib y Ddysgl's summit.

Descents and combinations
- The ridge itself provides a straightforward descent to Bwlch Coch. From here descend north into Cwm Glas and return to the Llanberis Pass as for the approach to Route 63.
- To reach the Pyg Track that leads down from the col between the summit and Snowdon, descend easily south west to a 3m marker stone (SH 608 548) then follow the constructed path east to Pen y Pass.
- Alternatively, descend Cwm Glas Ridge (Route 63).

On Crib y Ddysgl with Snowdon summit in the distance on the left

Scrambles in Snowdonia

Route 61
Cwm Glas Mawr Approach   1+ ✪ or 3S ✪

A fine scrambling approach to upper Cwm Glas.

Location	Cwm Glas Mawr, Crib y Ddysgl (SH 615 559)
Grade	1+ ✪ or 3S ✪
Approach time	40min
Altitude and aspect	580m, north east
Route length	Approximately 150m height gain.
Conditions	Clean solid rock in its lower part, although some care may be needed to check holds while picking a line higher up. The primary route can be ascended after rain, albeit with increased difficulty. However, friction is vital to an ascent of the grade 3S slabs variant. These slabs are slower to dry than one would expect, so allow two days of dry weather.

Parties aiming for the more famous Clogwyn y Person Arête (Route 62) would do well to include this approach scramble on their itinerary. It provides a logical warm-up on clean slabby rock that runs parallel to the course of the Afon Cwm Glas Mawr and its cascades. The route works a line up a shoulder just underneath the looming eastern buttress of Cyrn Las.

Approach
From Blaen-y-nant in the Llanberis Pass (SH 623 570), cross the river and almost immediately turn left uphill, following a path steeply on the right-hand side of the river. When the gradient eases, keep on the path near the right bank of the river, heading towards a shoulder at the left of the towering cliffs of Cyrn Las (Gyrn Las on the OS map). As the path heads left and crosses the river, continue straight ahead to where steepening terrain helps the Afon Cwm Glas Mawr form a series of small cascades. A short section of scree path leads to the foot of an obvious slabby orange wall just right of the stream.

Ascent
- To bypass the steepest part of the slabs, pick an easy line roughly 15m right of the watercourse and right of the contiguous section of the slabs. Climb this initially

Route 61 – Cwm Glas Mawr Approach

slightly rightwards before trending easily back left above the smooth steep slabs (grade 1+).

- The steep start to the slabs can be climbed in a number of ways, all of which are short-lived and more precarious than might be expected when standing at their foot – they are best avoided if in any way wet. If determined to tackle the steeper, smoother section of the slabs directly, start roughly 4m right of the stream and traverse rightwards on a rising foot ledge using flake handholds for a few metres. At a point where the holds cease at an orange wash, a long reach right for a handhold followed by a very precarious high step left on a steep section require considerable commitment. A couple more tricky moves leftwards are needed to gain easier ground (grade 3S).

Relishing the rock on the Cwm Glas Mawr Approach

Continue, taking a line well right of but parallel to the watercourse, tackling small slabby faces on solid rock. When the rock peters out into a grassy terrace, stay a little further right under the crags of Cyrn Las and climb a few short steps – a larger spur is best tackled by a recess on its right – maintaining a line parallel with the stream but avoiding the scree path to reach the waterfall and the lip of Cwm Glas.

Descents and combinations

From the top of the scramble, traverse left around the mouth of the cwm to reach the Clogwyn y Person Arête (Route 62). To head down to the road, pick up the path that enters upper Cwm Glas further around its mouth and take it to rejoin the approach.

Route 62

*Clogwyn y Person Arête
(including Parson's Nose options)* 3 ✪✪✪ or 3S ✪✪✪

One of the finest natural lines in the area.

Location	Cwm Glas, Crib y Ddysgl (SH 616 555)
Grade	3 ✪✪✪ or 3S ✪✪✪
Approach time	1hr 30min
Altitude and aspect	750m, north
Route length	For some a fast route, for others a big undertaking – especially if incorporating the Parson's Nose. Experienced solo parties will fly up the upper section, while roped parties pitching the whole route will take much longer. Height gain approximately 260m.
Conditions	Polished yet sound rock that nearly always provides positive holds. Dries quickly. Much trickier in the wet.
Topo	Also see Route 61

The Clogwyn y Person Arête is the impressive ridge that sweeps up from Cwm Glas above the truncating cliffs of the Parson's Nose to join the Snowdon Horseshoe on its approach to Clogwyn y Ddysgl.

Although there are no easy escapes from the arête, the main difficulties are concentrated in the lower part. The ridge is well-trodden, however numerous options are possible and a degree of threading your own way is required. An alternative start up the right edge of the Parson's Nose offers a more airy grade 3 start, while yet another line – the traditional rock climbing route up the Parson's Nose – is graded 3S/Diff for parties looking for even greater exposure.

Approach

- From the A4086 Llanberis Pass. Parking in several lay-bys. Cross the river and its tributary at Blaen y Nant (SH 623 570) then ascend the path up steep grass slopes to Cwm Glas, initially on the right bank of the stream, which is crossed higher up. Rocky slopes lead into into Upper Cwm Glas – although most will incorporate Route 61.
- The route can also be approached using Route 58.

Ascent

From the small pool beyond Llyn Glas the arête appears as a broad spur above the slabby buttress of the Parson's Nose. Gain the crest of the arête above the Nose by one of three approaches:

- The Western Gully of the Nose (i) using ledges on the right wall is the traditional route (grade 2).
- To the left of the gully, the more difficult rib on the right edge of the Nose itself (ii). This approach may be considered more in keeping with the open situations found on the arête. Many will find both the moves and texture of the rock on this rarely ascended start considerably better than the normal rock climb on the Nose – as such it is recommended. Start a few metres left of the gully. Ascend the easiest line on very coarse widely spaced ledges, always looking to trend back rightwards to overlook Western Gully. From the highest and broadest ledge, move left and up the easier section of the Nose (grade 3).
- The traditional climbing route (iii): start from the lowest point of the Nose and scramble up for about 40m, bearing slightly rightwards to a ledge which is easy to access from scree slopes on the right. Trend left on well-travelled rock to below the line of a shallow groove with a crack in it. Head up to this, stepping slightly right at the crack (this is a steep, exposed passage and most parties will be thankful of rope security here). Continue, following polished holds and the easiest line. The angle soon recedes and the route eases to the top of the Nose (grade 3S/Diff).

Descending from the Parson's Nose

From the top of the Nose a 5m downclimb leads to the flat top of the wedged boulder and the start of the arête proper (Western Gully arrives here).

Initially the arête is blunt and the line variable. Some steps are difficult when taken direct, although broad ledges add a sense of security. The easiest way, generally less interesting, takes a more devious line. A square recess shortly after the Nose with an off-width on its right and a wobbly spike in its middle is polished and has seen many a struggle; it is excellent but can be avoided easily round the right. An intimidating face with a transverse path beneath soon bars the way. This goes direct at Diff, but is best tackled round its right side by a tough little recess. An obvious tricky V-groove higher up the arête can also be avoided, but is best taken direct.

Eventually the angle eases and the arête becomes gradually more broken. As it merges into the summit slopes, most of a demoralising scree path can be avoided by sticking to the more rewarding – if very flaky – crest.

Descent by this route

A climber's descent and insofar as grade 3 descents go, not especially difficult, although route-finding is more complex and some of the steps appear intimidating from above. It is certainly best to descend the gully entry rather than the Nose.

Descents and combinations

The route tops-out at the 1001m spot height on the Crib y Ddysgl traverse (Route 60) of the Snowdon Horseshoe. Combinations are therefore abundant. Descents include the Cwm Glas Ridge (Route 63); East or North Ridge of Crib Goch (Routes 56 and 57); or east to Bwlch Coch, the grassy pass between Crib Goch and Crib y Ddysgl, where a scree path leads into Cwm Uchaf and a boggy plod leads north west to Llyn Glas.

Route 63
Cwm Glas Ridge   1- ✪

Strenuous walking up a broad ridge topped by a short section of scrambling.

Location	Cwm Glas, Crib y Ddysgl (SH 616 565)
Grade	1- ✪
Approach time	30min
Altitude and aspect	500m, north east
Route length	Despite height gain of approximately 300m, the route is mostly steep hiking, with limited scrambling to slow parties down.
Conditions	The ridge is little used so paths are barely worn.

The ridge that bounds Cwm Glas on its west side gives the most direct ascent to the summit of Crib y Ddysgl. Scrambling interest is confined to the prominent step high on the ridge – small compensation for such a laborious approach. Nevertheless, the views across Cwm Glas are tremendous. A better use for the ridge might be in descent as part of an alternative horseshoe begun over Crib Goch and Crib y Ddysgl.

Approach

Park as for Route 62 and cross the bridges at Blaen y Nant, ascending a path on the right side of the stream to a break and stile in the high stone wall reached after about 10 minutes. Follow the path into the mouth of Cwm Glas Mawr between two massive

Route 63 – Cwm Glas Ridge

boulders. Continue for about 200m and then strike rightwards (north west) on a faint path leading past a stone sheepfold to gain the broad back of the ridge.

On the spiked and grassy Cwm Glas Ridge

Ascent
Ascend the ridge crest (mostly walking) to a level grass section. The ridge now rears up as a spur of broken rock. Follow either this direct to maximise the amount of scrambling (care is needed with dirty and loose rock) or bypass this section on a path to the right. Continue up a second steepening and along a narrow pinnacled crest to a final nose, ascended by scrambling up a recess slightly on the right. Walking remains, veering slightly left to gain the summit of Crib y Ddysgl.

Descent by this route
An uncomplicated descent. Most difficulties can be flanked, usually on the west side.

Descents and combinations
As for Route 60. It is possible to descend this route after ascending via the North Ridge and Traverse of Crib Goch and Crib y Ddysgl (Routes 57, 59 and 60).

Route 64
Llechog Buttress 2 ✪✪

Intricate and interesting scrambling up a blunt-fronted buttress.

Location	Llanberis Pass (SH 607 568)
Grade	2 ✪✪
Approach time	1hr 10min
Altitude and aspect	550m, north east
Route length	The scrambling on the approach and some intricate sections on the route proper make for a fairly lengthy undertaking.
Conditions	The rock is sound but can be greasy after rain, although it is relatively quick drying.

The squat buttress of Llechog crowns the west-bounding ridge of unfrequented Cwm Glas-bach. Although the ascent finishes unfashionably low down the mountain, the solitude and quality of the scrambling more than compensate and make a perfect approach to Clogwyn Du'r Arddu.

Route-finding on the buttress itself requires care, so make an effort to positively identify the first perched block before embarking on the main face.

Route 64 – Llechog Buttress

Approach

From Nant Peris (SH 607 583) take the public footpath at the side of the Vaynol Arms. Head south to cross the river via a footbridge. Turn left. After 40m or so the path splits. Take the upper fork, pass through a wall and continue traversing the fellside. Follow a wall to a distinct rock band. After passing through this, use a stile over the next wall to pick up a path through woods. The path soon brings you out well above a house and directly below Llechog Buttress and Ridge. These routes are accessed by a long low-relief ridge, which is gained 60m up its left (east) side via a small boulder field. An initial grassy couloir gives a grade 1 step and establishes you more centrally on the low-relief ridge. Thereafter, various hiking and scrambling lines offer progress with most obstacles avoidable on the left. Paths through heather lead to a perched block jutting out leftwards from the foot of the main buttress.

Note: A more direct approach from SH 614 576 has traditionally been possible, however, recent access issues have been reported.

Ascent

A formidable step rises above the perched block. The left-slanting groove is much too difficult, as is the rock above a detached pinnacle on the right, so scramble easily up a vegetated groove on the left side of the barrier, with one slightly awkward heave to pass a chockstone on the left. Continue up grass then rock runnels beyond until it is possible to move rightwards onto a platform identified by a 3m block perched near its edge.

On the smooth left-slanting groove of Llechog Buttress

Above is a jumble of steep rocks. Go up a left-slanting break, initially by a smooth groove (technical). Above, pull energetically over a chockstone to blocks below a wall. Escape rightwards over blocks to a fine rock platform.

The wall above the platform is hopeless, and the smooth groove on its right side no better. However, the right-hand rib of the groove allows a step right into a dirtier but more amenable groove (ensure the step across isn't too high). Ascend the groove then, immediately above a steepening at wedged flakes, follow a narrow and exposed ramp diagonally left (much easier than it looks – the holds come and the exposure is short-lived) until above the initial groove.

The next step is shorter, more broken and leads directly to a platform with large and small pinnacles. Ascend the left-slanting shattered break behind the pinnacles to a grass bay. Scramble up a very short, capped chimney (or better, go 15m up to the right of the pinnacles and ascend a 5m crack in the slab). Trend right and scramble easily up the remainder of the rock spur.

Descents and combinations
- It is possible to descend directly and unpleasantly between Llechog Buttress and Llechog Ridge (Route 65), but a more satisfying return to the Llanberis Pass can be made using Route 63.
- Alternatively, a circular hike can be made by descending north west next to the fence and picking up a path to a stile at the 610m spot height. Cross the stile and descend a steep grass path into the cwm. The path surprisingly peters out.

Route 65 – Llechog Ridge

Continue down until the approach path is met by a wall. Turn left to return to Nant Peris.
- Either Route 66 or 67 on 'Cloggy' will beckon the enthusiastic. Descending only slighty, contour the slope west of Llechog, crossing the railway to gain the Llanberis path, and then pick up the clear, although indirect, approach path to Clogwyn Du'r Arddu at SH 604 563.

Route 65
Llechog Ridge

2- ✪

The shallow ridge to the right of Llechog Buttress, although playing second fiddle to its neighbour, is longer and better than it appears.

Location	Llanberis Pass (SH 607 572)
Grade	2- ✪
Approach time	1hr
Altitude and aspect	460m, north east
Route length	The scrambling on the approach and some intricate sections on the route proper make for a fairly lengthy undertaking.
Conditions	The rock is generally good but the difficult quartz break can be lichenous and slow drying.
Topo	See Route 64

A promising start is never quite lived up to by the route as a whole. Many obstacles can be avoided and the ridge at times lacks definition. Nonetheless, there is plenty here to entertain and it is not without its moments. The location is spectacular.

Approach
As for Route 64 almost to the top of the low-relief ridge. Then contour rightwards, passing beneath a rib to a compact tower of rock that terminates the west ridge and up to which runs a dry stone wall.

Ascent
The tower front is too difficult, as is the chockstone-filled crack a few metres up the left side. Left of this is a square-cut slot: scramble up slabby rocks to its left then

The exposed crest of Llechog Ridge with a dusting of snow on the tops beyond

diagonally right to its easy upper part. Gain the rib on the right and ascend it more easily to the summit of the tower. A slab stands guard above a small heather ledge; pass steadily on the left or by a tricky crack on the right.

From a grass notch beyond, ascend the difficult face slightly on the left, taking care with a fence tie (or avoid it on the right). The stone wall reappears. Get onto a rib just to its left and ascend this to a shoulder of fallen blocks.

Ascend the next step slightly on the left by a difficult quartz break, dodging a short terminal wall on the left, to where the ridge reclines.

Ascend the easier upper part of the ridge at will; the more difficult and interesting scrambling, including an excellent 10m boot-width crack up a slab, being generally found on the right side. At the top a stile over a fence brings the awesome dark cliffs of Clogwyn Du'r Arddu into view.

Descents and combinations
As for Route 64.

Route 66
Eastern Terrace of Clogwyn Du'r Arddu 1+ ✪✪

An atmospheric and historic excursion to breach the colossal dark cliffs of 'Cloggy'.

Location	Clogwyn Du'r Arddu, Snowdon group (SH 601 555)
Grade	1+ ✪✪
Approach time	1hr
Altitude and aspect	650m, north
Route length	Most parties will make relatively fast progress to the top. Approximately 150m height gain.
Conditions	If damp – as they often are – the exposed step and steep clumpy grass path that gain the terrace proper feel considerably more intimidating than in the dry; this is serious terrain and no place for the novice scrambler. Despite its fame, the cliff is rarely busy and only usually visited during prolonged dry spells in summer. The rock and holds are well-travelled and sound. Nonetheless, take care not to dislodge scree from the terrace edge as it may fall onto climbers below.

Route 66 – Eastern Terrace of Clogwyn Du'r Arddu

The gentle north western cwm abruptly ends in the dark and menacing form of Clogwyn Du'r Arddu – the finest cliff in Wales. The history of first ascents on 'Cloggy' is a long and fascinating one, beginning with that of the Eastern Terrace in 1798 by the Reverends Bingley and Williams in search of plant specimens – a climb that contends with the poet Samuel Taylor Coleridge's 'recreational' descent of Broad Stand (grade 3) on Scafell in 1802 for the honour of first recorded recreational rock climb in Britain (or indeed anywhere). The cliff provides a plethora of spectacular, although extremely serious, world-famous rock climbs. Johnny Dawes' outrageous Indian Face (E9, 1986), below and above which our route passes, reveals the extremes of a pastime that the 1798 ascent of Eastern Terrace helped to set in motion. This humble scramble is best valued more for the adventure of the excursion, its history and the incredible terrain through which it passes than for the moves it offers.

Approach
- The best approach is to make it part of a link-up by using either Route 64 or 65 on Llechog.
- Alternatively, from the east side of Llanberis on the A4086, follow the narrow surfaced road opposite the Royal Victoria Hotel to a parking place at the top of the hill after 1km (SH 582 589). Walk up the interminable Llanberis Path towards Snowdon until it rises steeply left about 700m beyond Halfway House (SH 604 563). Fork right here on a path that contours high above Llyn Du'r Arddu to the foot of the East Buttress.

Ascent
Viewed frontally, the East Buttress appears in the shape of a right-angled triangle, with the East Gully – a hopelessly loose rock climb – forming the upright and the Eastern Terrace the hypotenuse.

The terrace fails to reach the base of the cliff, so begin on the left by scrambling up a rising line of polished rock steps. At a gully with an obvious boulder wedged at its top, move out rightwards on well-climbed holds in an exposed position. Take care on the zig-zag path through clumpy grass to gain the terrace, here partially overhung by a huge buttress known, rather confusingly, as 'The Boulder'.

Scramble leftwards up a series of wet steps close under overhangs to the wider part of the terrace. Wide, easy-angled slabs appear the natural line; these offer few positive holds and can be very precarious if damp (although they are grade 2 if dry). Instead, zig-zag easily up their left side then ascend the upper slabs and scree runnel to grass slopes.

Breaching the colossal cliffs of Cloggy on the Eastern Terrace

Descent by this route
Not easy to locate from above without prior knowledge, but otherwise a viable descent for climbers used to descending such exposed terrain. Remember to quit the terrace after descending the wet steps under the overhangs and take considerable care on the exposed mud-steps of the path through the clumpy grass. Avoid descent in, or just after, rain.

Descents and combinations
The route tops out near the Snowdon Ranger path, which can be followed to the multi-path junction between the summits of Crib y Ddysgl and Snowdon.

Route 67
Western Terrace of Clogwyn Du'r Arddu 3 ✪

A dramatically situated hanging terrace offers some awkward and insecure scrambling.

Location	Clogwyn Du'r Arddu, Snowdon group (SH 599 555)
Grade	3 ✪
Approach time	1hr
Altitude and aspect	660m, north
Route length	Although not sustained, it is not a route on which to move too quickly. Approximately 150m height gain.
Conditions	Nearly always wet in parts, it suffers from drainage during and for several days after bad weather. Some friable rock low down, but this causes few problems. However, a hazardous 10m passage of jumbled small boulders above the slab that follows the pocked wall mars the route somewhat and requires good mountain sense. Consideration needs to be given to the safety of parties below.
Topo	See Route 66

The Western Terrace – more difficult and sustained than its eastern counterpart – rises diagonally rightwards beneath the overlapping slabs of the West Buttress. This is serious terrain that is often unhelpfully wet and **use of a rope is strongly recommended** until the debris section.

Approach

As for Route 66 to a path division below the East Buttress. The lower path passes below the lowest rocks of the cliff (Middle Rock) and a tall dripping recess. The terrace is now obvious, overshadowed by a band of overhangs as it slants up to the right.

Ascent

Gain the terrace a short distance beyond its start by scrambling up a clean 6m groove on good holds. Trend rightwards onto the terrace and insecurely across shattered red rock to the start of the main section below huge overhangs.

The curiously pocketed rock of the Western Terrace of Cloggy

Continue up bare rock runnels – easier than they look – until barred by a 5m wall of curiously pocketed rock. Fortunately this is covered with large holds and can be protected with a rope. Ascend the wall at an amenable point towards its right end (but before it curves round to the slippery outer edge).

Ascend rock slabs (if roped, find a belay before reaching the precarious debris above, then coil the rope before passing over the debris to guard against unwitting dislodgement). Creep through **poised rockfall debris** (more stable on the right). Continue up a pleasant easy-angled slab to reach grass and a flat shoulder above the cliff.

Descent by this route
Inconsiderate and a bad idea.

Descents and combinations
As for Route 66. It is also possible to descend Route 66 – ideally with prior knowledge.

Snowdon (1085M)

The name Snowdon might conjure up images of iron rails, pipelines, eroded paths, cafés and crowds, of a mountain abandoned to the tourist. Yet nothing can detract from the pleasure of clambering up its flank to stand on the highest summit in Wales. And it is still possible, even here on a summer bank holiday, to spend an afternoon scrambling without encountering a single other person.

Snowdon Summit (as opposed to Snowdon as a whole, which loosely describes a mountain mass that includes Crib y Ddysgl and its cwms and ridges) takes the form of a squat, three-sided pyramid. Three ridges descend from the summit: north towards Crib y Ddysgl, east towards Lliwedd, and south towards Yr Aran. Three cwms lie between these ridges: the Glaslyn cwm east of the summit, Cwm Clogwyn to the west, and Cwm Tregalan to the south.

One of the described scrambles ascends out of Cwm Tregalan onto the South Ridge; the other escapes the Glaslyn cwm by its bounding ridge to finish up the East Ridge.

Route 68
Tregalan Couloir 2 ✪

Surprisingly varied scrambling based on a remote couloir offers a memorable route up Snowdon.

Location	Cwm Tregalan, Snowdon (SH 607 535)
Grade	2 ✪
Approach time	1hr 30min
Altitude and aspect	650m, south east
Route length	A moderately long route with plenty of interest, although not sustained. Height gain approximately 260m.
Conditions	Scree litters the bed of the couloir and so much of the scrambling lies on the flanking buttresses. Drainage can affect the best line, so it is wise to avoid periods during and immediately after wet weather. Catches the morning sun in summer. Rarely ascended.

Route 68 – Tregalan Couloir

The southern approach to Snowdon via the Watkin Path initially has a picturesque quality more reminiscent of the Lake District than Snowdonia. However, on entering Cwm Tregalan the pleasant glades are left behind and the rubble slopes of Snowdon dominate the view. Below the summit, and as far as Bwlch Main on the South Ridge, the face consists of a jumbled mass of broken rock. Only beyond the Tregalan Couloir does it coalesce into definite buttresses.

Approach

Two approaches are possible:
- From Beddgelert or Pen y Gwryd along the A498 to a car park with toilets at Bethania (SH 627 506). From the west bank of the river, follow the signed Watkin Path via Cwm y Llan to quarry spoil heaps (SH 613 524). Where the Watkin Path curves up to the right, bear left to contour into Cwm Tregalan, initially by a faint path. The couloir is largely hidden from this angle so locate its entrance before approaching the cliff too closely.
- Alternatively, from Bwlch Ciliau on the Snowdon Horseshoe it is possible to descend the Watkin Path for a few hundred metres and then contour Cwm Tregalan to reach the cliff.

A trapezoid buttress, cut on the right by a slanting break, defines the left side of the cliff. A larger, more broken buttress to the right is bounded on its right side by a depression, which emerges at the cliff base as a narrow gully beneath a black cleft – the first objective (further right, beyond a smaller buttress of pink-tinted rock, the face degenerates into slopes of rubble).

Ascent

Avoid the slimy beginnings of the gully by scrambling up rough slabs with white quartz spiders on the right. Where they steepen, traverse left then ascend the gully bed to a recess beneath an evil-looking, capped chimney. From here there are two options:
- A satisfying water-worn runnel slanting up to the left should be followed – water permitting – for 30m until an easy step down can be made to cross the watercourse. Picking the line of least resistance and exposure, arc steadily rightwards over the hillside to re-enter the couloir via an easy downclimb.
- If water prevents a grade 2 ascent of the runnel, go almost to the base of the evil chimney then escape rightwards up a short chimney/break – scruffy but not too difficult. Ascend 10m rightwards over heather to where it is possible to tackle the buttress front at grade 2 on superbly rough rock (an even easier minor gully can bypass this on the right). Continue up the buttress as it narrows and eases but then, where it rears up again in a broad and indistinct mass, descend diagonally left to regain the couloir bed some distance above the evil chimney.

After 15m avoid an ugly 8m step by scrambling up clean rock on the left. Regain the bed then, after 10m, avoid another step on the left. Continue up the shallow rib just to the left of the couloir bed. There is less scree higher up, although occasional friable rock needs care. Scramble over a few small rises until the couloir fans out. Go up the left side of what is now a shallow, rocky depression on the most prominent and amenable rock rib to emerge before the most dramatic and narrowest stretch of the South Ridge at Bwlch Main. Walk up the South Ridge to Snowdon Summit.

Descents and combinations

- By the Watkin Path: descend south west from Snowdon Summit along the South Ridge for about 200m to a 2m marker stone; turn left here to descend a slanting scree path to Bwlch y Saethau. Continue to a large cairn at Bwlch Cilau below the north west ridge of Lliwedd then turn right and follow the obvious path into Cwm Tregalan.
- By the South Ridge: descend south west from Snowdon Summit, veering left at Bwlch Main onto the South Ridge proper, followed towards Yr Aran. From Bwlch Cwm Llan, at the foot of the South Ridge, turn left on a peaty path – in the lower stages following the course of a dismantled tramway for a few hundred metres – to the entrance to Cwm y Llan and a junction with the Watkin Path.

Route 69

Y Gribin and the East Ridge 1 ✪ ✪

Great scrambling up a broad ridge amid impressive surroundings.

Location	Snowdon (SH 618 544)
Grade	1 ✪ ✪
Approach time	1hr 15min
Altitude and aspect	650m, north east
Route length	The Gribin is fairly sustained, but progress is usually rapid. The scrappy section on the East Ridge can feel longer than it actually is. Height gain approximately 430m.
Conditions	Takes little drainage but is best enjoyed in dry conditions. The firm slabby rock of Y Gribin is slippery when wet. Conversely the loose material on the East Ridge is more stable when damp.

The Miners' Track from Pen y Pass contours above Llyn Teyrn, short-cuts across Llyn Llydaw by a restored causeway, then rises steadily to Llyn Glaslyn below the massive north east face of Snowdon. This route escapes the cwm by ascending the excellent left-bounding rocky spur of Y Gribin to Bwlch y Saethau. An additional easy scrambling continuation up the less exciting East Ridge to Snowdon Summit is also described.

Y Gribin compares in difficulty to the East Ridge of Crib Goch, and is much more enjoyable. Its relative unpopularity can only be attributed to the fact that it emerges at a col, not at a summit.

Approach

From Pen y Pass (SH 647 556), follow the Miners' Track to the stream exit of Llyn Glaslyn at SH 619 546.

Wintry conditions on the starting slabs of Y Gribin

Ascent

Cross boulders at the stream outflow and take the faint path up a grassy terminating hump to reach a col below the steep part of the ridge.

Ignore loose flanking routes and ascend slabs slightly right of the crest. Continue roughly in the same line, occasionally detouring to the left, to a cairned promontory above the ridge. For the East Ridge continuation, take a path trending right to gain Bwlch y Saethau and stay with the ridge crest, which becomes blunt and scrappy, to Snowdon Summit. Alternatively, to follow up Y Gribin with the Lliwedd Traverse (Route 70), walk south from the cairned promontory.

Descent by this route

An uncomplicated descent, with marginal increases in scrambling and route-finding difficulties.

Descents and combinations

See Route 55.

Lliwedd (898M)

Lliwedd is synonymous with the two massive buttresses set dramatically above Llyn Llydaw on its north east face. The East Peak can offer the scrambler nothing: all routes involve significant technical difficulties. The slightly higher West Peak is the more broken of the two and its easiest climb just qualifies as a scramble. In contrast, a traverse of its two summit crests offers a steady enough route.

Route 70
Traverse of Lliwedd 1 ✪✪

This less exposed wing of the Snowdon Horseshoe provides a worthwhile easy scramble in itself.

Location	Lliwedd, Snowdon group (SH 630 535)
Grade	1 ✪✪
Approach time	30min
Altitude and aspect	880m, north east to north west
Route length	One of the shorter scrambles on the Snowdon Horseshoe.
Conditions	Viable in most conditions. Wind and rain are less of a problem here than on Crib Goch.
Topo	See Route 69

With easy and satisfying scrambling up and down its broad-backed ridges, the traverse of the north east and north west ridges is usually undertaken as the last leg of the Snowdon Horseshoe. It is mentioned here in reverse as a route in its own right for completeness.

Approach
From Pen y Pass (SH 647 556), follow the Miners' Track to the shore of Llyn Llydaw.

Ascent
Turn left and follow a path near the shore, passing the valve house and crossing the stream outflow. Ascend the west flank of the north east ridge, rising steadily over

Llyn Llydaw and Llyn Teyrn from the Traverse of Lliwedd

scree and with some easy scrambling, to its crest. Follow a path on the left side of the crest, over Lliwedd Bach, to the summit of the East Peak. Continue along the rocky crest to the slightly higher summit of the West Peak. Descend the rock steps and terraces of the north west ridge – stay close to the crest for the best scrambling – to the cairned col of Bwlch Cilau at its foot.

It is best to cross the elongated col to Bwlch y Saethau by the circuitous edge on the right. Either ascend to Snowdon Summit via the East Ridge, the upper Watkin Path, or descend to Llyn Glaslyn via Y Gribin (Route 69).

Descent by this route
The traverse is slightly easier in reverse.

Descents and combinations
See Routes 55 and 69.

Route 71
West Peak via Bilberry Terrace 3S ✪✪✪

This wandering adventurous route ascends a devious but logical line up the huge face of the West Peak. The situations, atmosphere and scale are tremendous.

Location	West Buttress, Lliwedd (SH 623 534)
Grade	3S ✪✪✪
Approach time	1hr
Altitude and aspect	650m, north east
Route length	A long, meandering route with complex route-finding, it is a big undertaking for most parties. Allow plenty of time. Height gain approximately 250m.
Conditions	The buttress is rarely in good condition outside the period of May to October. Allow a few days to dry after wet weather. Best enjoyed early morning (when the face catches the sun) during dry summer weather. The rock is generally sound but expect to find some loose blocks and spikes.
Topo	See also Route 69

Scrambles in Snowdonia

> Long, varied and committing, Bilberry Terrace is the easiest route on the face. It should be attempted only in good conditions by skilful and confident scramblers familiar with the careful route-finding required to negotiate the serious situations found on its big cliffs. However, good belay anchors and runners are available to protect the most difficult sections (selection of nuts and slings needed).

Approach

Follow the Miners' Track from Pen y Pass to the stream outflow from Llyn Llydaw. Fork left and continue up the path until halfway up the first rise towards the north east ridge. Contour right along a clear narrow path until below the north east face. Ascend scree to below Central Gully, the shallow depression between the East and West buttresses.

From the top of a cone of red scree (just right of the mouth of Central Gully), ascend easily up right to a worn ledge below a 20m wall which bars access to the lower left end of the Bilberry Terrace – the heather ramp slanting upwards across the face from left to right. At this point Central Gully is about 30m to the left.

Ascent

Scramble up the wall – sustained but not too difficult – then step awkwardly right to gain the lower left end of the terrace. There is a belay a little higher. Scramble more easily up the terrace for 70m, crossing the narrows of a rock ramp, to the foot of a 5m corner (belay anchors above the ledge on the right).

Many will find this corner the hardest section of the route. Protect the crack and ascend the corner with conviction. Belay with nuts at its top or continue easily for 6m or so, trending left to a blunt spike.

Ignore the horrible wide crack above and instead traverse right (exposed but not too difficult) and climb a short, wide crack. Go up the terrace for 7m then, ignoring a grassy cul-de-sac, ascend rocks on the left to below a smooth wall. Now ascend a corner on the right to regain the terrace.

Continue up the terrace and over one short rise (ignoring a gully spanned by a rock splinter, which is well-worn as many parties go wrong here) to reach the notch behind a pinnacle on the apex of the buttress. This is Pinnacle Corner, the halfway point and the end of the easy route-finding.

Pass through the notch of the pinnacle, step across to grass ledges and follow them rightwards for 25m until below a spike 5m above the traverse line (a rib on the right bounds a depression). Exiting this area is not easy and involves a second crux. It is possible to ascend the depression above the spike directly to another good belay spike in 30m. Although it has gear placements, this escape is **very difficult on poor rock** and not recommended. A tricky indistinct rising leftwards traverse line from the depression is also possible. It is better, and more in keeping with the route, to continue the traverse

Route 71 – West Peak via Bilberry Terrace

Scrambles in Snowdonia

Stepping through Pinnacle Corner, midway up Bilberry Terrace

line rightwards 5m below the spike, step over the top of an odd shallow grassy gully and gain a ledge with a flat wobbly block on the bounding rib. Fix protection before making an intricate rightwards move using fingery holds on excellent rock to gain a wide left-slanting slabby and grassy ramp. Follow this easily to its top and a good belay. Stay right until it is possible to adopt a rising leftwards line above the aforementioned depression, passing good belay spikes en route, to gain – with relative ease – a delightful and obvious flat grassy shoulder on the ridge that rises up from Pinnacle Corner in 50m or so.

Trend 18m leftwards to another ridge and gain a second shoulder at a notch. There is an intricate descent on the shoulder followed by tricky leftward moves above a gully to reach easier ground. Cross the following depression with a rising leftwards line more easily via connecting ledges and in 30m or so reach a vague third shoulder on another ridge. Trend across yet another depression to a fourth shoulder on another ridge. Now, at last, some sort of upward escape is possible and various options present themselves. Continue up the obvious depression to the left, which can be followed to the summit, or better – but with slightly more suspect rock – the ridge further left can be followed over small spikes and pinnacles to the top.

Descents and combinations

See Route 55. Approached from Bwlch Ciliau, Route 68 is a possible – if demanding – addition to an already big day out!

Eifionydd

Passing the finger stone of Mynydd Drws y Coed on the Nantlle Ridge (Route 72)

Scrambles in Snowdonia

The small hills of Eifionydd exert a feeble pull on mountaineers. No cloud-piercing ridges here, no historically famous rock climbs. Climbers and hillwalkers come here – when they come at all – to relax on the sun-warmed rock of Craig Cwm Silyn or to stroll along the Nantlle Ridge.

There is even less to attract the scrambler. The most likely rock is either choked in vegetation or shattered into treacherous splinters. For this reason all described lines involve difficult scrambling, sometimes on very poor rock. More nervous energy has been expended checking routes in this area than twice their number on the Glyderau or Snowdon. The exception is the Nantlle Ridge, a simple ridge walk spiced with a few scrambly steps.

The main group of hills – those linked by the Nantlle Ridge – lie to the south of the B4418 between Penygroes and Rhyd Ddu. Mynydd Mawr lies in the angle made by this road and the A4085 from Rhyd Ddu to Caernarfon.

Craig Cwm Silyn (734m), the highest mountain on the Nantlle Ridge, has the most to offer in terms of rock climbs. These are concentrated on the magnificent twin rock prows of uncharacteristically sound rock which overlook Cwm Silyn on the west side of the mountain. One good and very long scramble on slightly dubious rock is found here. The crags on the east side of the mountain promise much but tend to return only disconcertingly wobbly and friable rock.

Eifionydd – Introduction

Mynydd Mawr (698m) is a shapely miniature mountain. It has two faces of interest to the scrambler: the bleached and crumbling south-facing cliffs of Craig y Bera; and the remote and dank north-facing cliffs of Craig Cwm Du. A route has been described on each, although neither escapes the doubtful rock for which these crags are renowned.

Access arrangements in Eifionydd are more restrictive and sensitive than elsewhere in the national park. For this reason it is wise to stick to the described approaches.

Scrambles in Snowdonia

Route 72
Nantlle Ridge

1- ✪✪✪

A delightful ridge walk on grass enlivened at intervals by sections of simple rock scrambling.

Location	Nantlle, Eifionydd
Grade	1- ✪✪✪
Circuit time	Roughly 7hrs for the whole double traverse.
Route length	18km
Conditions	Some sections are vulnerable to crosswinds, but otherwise the route is possible in most conditions. Popular during fine summer weekends.

The route is described as a double traverse to prolong interest and solve the logistical problem of arranging return transport. By this double traverse, the route provides an 18km ridge walk that includes isolated sections of easy scrambling, although an alternative return offers a partly circular route.

Approach
From Caernarfon or Beddgelert along the A4085 to a large car park on the main road, 500m south of Rhyd Ddu village (SH 571 526).

Ascent
Go through a swing gate opposite the car park entrance and follow the signed path to a junction with the Nantlle road (limited parking here).

Turn left immediately and follow the signed path onto the grassy flank of Y Garn. Turn right soon after crossing a ladder stile ('ridge' painted on a rock) and ascend steeply for 1.5km on a narrow path to the summit of **Y Garn**.

Follow the broad ridge southwards for 400m then ascend the narrow, rocky section – staying near the crest for maximum scrambling interest – to the summit of **Mynydd Drws y Coed**.

Continue along the narrow ridge as it descends then veers right (ignore a contouring path left here). Scruffy, easy scrambling leads to the flat summit of **Trum y Ddysgl**.

Route 72 – Nantlle Ridge

At an abrupt left turn on the Nantlle Ridge

Follow the grass ridge south west for 300m then fork right, descending, to cross a tremendous narrowing before rising gradually up its broad continuation to reach the obelisk at the summit of **Mynydd Tal y Mignedd** after 500m.

Walk south along the grass ridge for 400m then descend steeply on an eroded path to the double col of Bwlch Dros Bern. Ascend the rock nose at the far side of the col, scrambling up rocks just right of the crest for most interest (or directly above the stone wall at grade 2) – or avoid all this easily on the right. Continue up the good path beyond to the summit of **Craig Cwm Silyn**.

Follow a broad and featureless ridge south west for 1.5km to the final summit of **Garnedd Goch**.

Descent/Return by this route

Return to Rhyd Ddu by the same route. Scrambling sections are now taken in descent so there is a slight increase in difficulty.

Descents and combinations

- For a single traverse, leave a second vehicle at the road end at SH 496 511 (refer to Route 73 approach). From Garnedd Goch, descend a grass shoulder north-westwards of the dry stone wall, passing over a couple of stiles to a gate in the transverse stone wall. Go through the gate and turn left to follow the track to the road end.
- Alternatively, return along the Nantlle Ridge to the fork 280m south west of Trum y Ddysgl summit. Descend south along the crest of an initially steep grass ridge on a narrow path to the boggy col of Bwlch y Ddwy Elor. Cross a stile on the left and follow a good path and track, entering trees, to emerge later at a loose-surfaced forestry track. Follow this rightwards for a few metres then bear left on a track leading to a stream. Cross the stream by a bridge on the left and then turn right onto the main track. After a few metres turn left and follow a path northwards that becomes rough and stony across the base of the eastern slopes of Mynydd Drws y Coed and Y Garn. Enter a boggy area beyond a swing gate but then continue on a good path to rejoin the ascent route at the painted rock.

Craig Cwm Silyn

Route 73
Craig Fawr Rib (aka LMH) 3 ✪

A very long mountaineer's outing which begins scruffily but provides interesting positions and superb scenery higher up.

Location	Craig Cwm Silyn, Nantlle (SH 517 503)
Grade	3 ✪
Approach time	45min
Altitude and aspect	550m, north west
Route length	A very long route, with intricate sections. Suspect rock can slow parties down. If pitching sections allow considerable time. Height gain approximately 200m.
Conditions	Experienced hands are needed to tackle friable rock in some sections – remember, push don't pull! A helmet is recommended. Dries relatively quickly. Catches the afternoon and evening sun in summer.

Route 73 – Craig Fawr Rib (aka LMH)

Craig Cwm Silyn
73 Craig Fawr Rib

Scrambles in Snowdonia

> Twin rock prows dominate the rocky headwall above Cwm Silyn. That on the right is Craig yr Ogof, famous for the rock climbs on its slabby west face and vertical front nose. That on the left, Craig Fawr, is larger but more broken and therefore rarely climbed. This route ascends the slender rib on the right-hand side of Craig Fawr and can be used as a preliminary to an easterly traverse of the Nantlle Ridge by the energetic and fast. Mountaineering and rock climbing experience would be an asset **as loose rock predominates and requires caution**. A rope of at least 36m in length is desirable to reach the best belays on this rarely ascended route. An escape to easy ground can be made from any of the ledges between pitches, however.

Approach

From Nantlle on the B4418 between Rhyd Ddu and Penygroes. Go west from Nantlle and turn left after 2km onto the Llanllyfni road. Turn left again after 1.5km and follow this single-track road for 2km to the end of the surfaced section at SH 496 511 (park in the field just beyond the gate). Continue on foot until the track ends above the Llynnau Cwm Silyn. Contour above the lakes, crossing the hillside to the heather couloir between Craig yr Ogof and Craig Fawr. (Do not get drawn into following the well-walked path to the popular Craig yr Ogof; there is no path between Ogof and Fawr and the heathery traverse is difficult, frustrating and time-consuming.) To the left of the couloir and right of the line of the main crag is a heather rib, which leads into the first rocks of the rib proper.

Ascent

Heathery scrambling interspersed with moments of interest leads to a steep face. This is negotiated by a scrappy and difficult rising right-to-left line (it can be bypassed altogether by even scrappier scrambling on the right). Ascend the rib above centrally to reach an obvious broad heather platform.

From the heather platform, tackle the next rib on its right side then step left after 6m or so to gain its crest. Climb the crest – sustained but on good rock – to another level area. The crest of the next rib is best accessed via a small grassy recess on the left. Easy ground above is followed by a complex collection of ribs. Good mountain instinct is required to fashion the best line. The rib that bounds the deep recess of the left-hand gully is accessed via a hidden staircase on the left. As the rib's angle eases, two successive slabs beckon before a knife-edge with two block pinnacles leads to the summit plateau.

Route 73 – Craig Fawr Rib (aka LMH)

A lofty perch on the block pinnacles at the top of Craig Fawr Rib

Descents and combinations
- Refer to Route 72 for the simplest descent or combination.
- The well-used Great Stone Shoot gully (grade 1) on the west side of the Craig yr Ogof prow offers a return into Cwm Silyn. This can be identified from the edge of the summit plateau by the stone wall and fencing at its top. Where necessary, avoid awkward steps in the gully by descending the rib on its left (looking out), but avoid straying into the couloir even farther left.

Scrambles in Snowdonia

Mynydd Mawr

Route 74
Sentries' Ridge and Continuation 3- ✪✪✪

Excellent scrambling on suspect rock along a succession of narrow and pinnacled ridges.

Location	Craig y Bera, Mynydd Mawr (SH 545 540)
Grade	3- ✪✪✪
Approach time	1hr
Altitude and aspect	400m, south
Route length	A long but well-travelled route that tends to go by faster than might be expected. Nonetheless, a big undertaking for many parties. Height gain approximately 200m.
Conditions	Dries quickly on sunny or breezy days. Friable rock means a helmet is strongly advised.

Huge buttresses and pinnacled ridges cover almost the entire south flank of Mynydd Mawr, yet few climbers bother (or dare) to come here. Vast screes below the cliffs forewarn of the dangerously crumbly rock. Sentries' Ridge takes a well defined slender line to the right of the large central buttress. The scrambling is prolonged, sustained and varied. An ability to judge rock quality is more important than technical expertise. However, some of the gendarmes are difficult to climb when taken direct. Escape into an easy scree gully is possible at various points.

Approach
Take the A4085 to Rhyd Ddu. Park in the village or take the B4418 signed to Nantlle for 100m until there is parking space for a couple of cars at the start of a forestry track on the right. Follow the track for about 1km until a waymarked path splits off left. Take this, ascending to cross a stile at the forest boundary.

Turn right and ascend near the forest edge. Cross another stile at the highest corner of the plantation, then contour left on a small path across the southern flank of the

Route 74 – Sentries' Ridge and Continuation

Mynydd Mawr
74 Sentries' Ridge and Continuation

mountain all the way to scree below the cliffs. Pass below the first broken buttresses to a large recess from which rises a slender, pinnacled ridge between scree gullies.

Ascent

The true toe of the buttress is a steep wall. Bypass this with easy, heathery scrambling on its right side leading to the ridge crest and a first gendarme. Ascend this directly, including one awkward move, or turn it on the left, returning to the crest after about 6m. Continue up the slender ridge, passing directly over several pinnacles and a narrow bridge of clean rock which leads to a steep exit. Continue to a grass col at the end of the Sentries' Ridge as originally climbed by Archer Thomson in 1910.

Another ridge rises above. Scramble up the edge left of the central heather runnel, if necessary taking difficult sections on the wall overlooking the runnel to

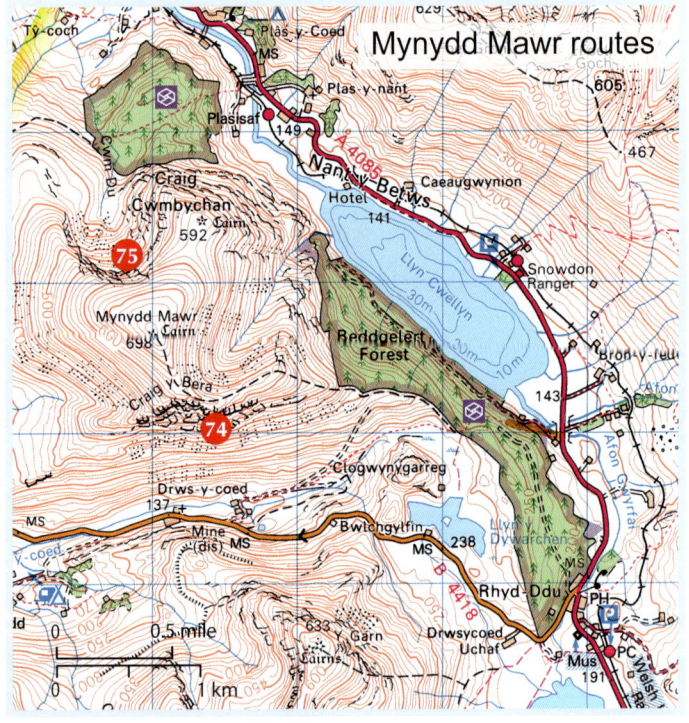

Route 74 – Sentries' Ridge and Continuation

Taking care on a slender section of Sentries' Ridge

minimise the consequences of a slip. Above a heather col, scramble up another shorter ridge for about 20m to a tunnelled notch.

The ridge above the notch is steeper and more difficult than its predecessors, although the rock is better than appearances suggest. Ascend it directly.

Above is a mirror image of the ridge above the grass col; scramble up its right edge to easier ground. Continue up the remainder of the ridge, probably turning the most shattered gendarmes, to heather slopes above the cliff. The path to the summit is nearby; walk north west up the broad grassy ridge for about 500m.

Descents and combinations

Do not descend this route. To return to Rhyd Ddu, descend the spur eastwards above the cliffs, rejoining the approach path at the forestry plantation. Route 75 could be hunted out to elongate the day.

Beneath Bear Tower on Bear Buttress. Crazy Pinnacle visible upper right

Route 75
Bear Buttress   3S ✪

A committing and satisfying mountaineering route in a superb remote setting.

Location	Craig Cwm Du, Mynydd Mawr (SH 539 551)
Grade	3S ✪
Approach time	1hr 15min
Altitude and aspect	520m, north
Route length	A bigger undertaking than might be expected. Allow plenty of time. Height gain approximately 140m.
Conditions	Care needed with suspect rock. The lichenous rock and some down-sloping holds are slippery in poor weather. Conversely, friction is excellent in dry conditions. North-facing, so allow several dry days after prolonged rain.

This route follows a logical line up a series of ribs culminating in Bear Tower next to the tottering Crazy Pinnacle. After a difficult start on the generally good rock of the lower buttress, this intimidating and sustained scramble finishes precariously on technically easier but less stable terrain. Suspect rock means only the most foolhardy would forego a rope, and extra care should be taken placing protection – although one doubts if draping slings over those rickety spikes would ultimately do any good.

For map, see Route 74.

Approach
From the A4085 Caernarfon to Beddgelert road. Park at a lay-by at SH 547 563 and cross the track over the bridge 20m towards Caernarfon. After a few minutes turn right on a signed footpath and follow it uphill, entering the forest at a gate. Continue up through the forest until the path dips. Go over a stile and cross a meadow between two plantations. Beyond a ladder stile, turn sharp left and follow the wall to a stream. Follow the stream bank into Cwm Du, heading left of the large heather mound and gaining good views of the crescent-shaped cliffs of the headwall. Bear Buttress is on the far left side of the cwm. Take your pick between steep boulder chutes or heather-tugging to gain the base of the cliff. Higher on the approach the unmistakable 10m Crazy Pinnacle near the top of the crag will come into view. Bear Buttress is immediately to the left of this, with the start of the route in the gully to the left.

Mynydd Mawr
75 Bear Buttress

Ascent

Gain the first rib with difficulty by traversing right from about 10m or so up the scree of the gully. Continue over a spiky ridge and a 5m finger until below a maze of ribs and walls. After a short, vegetated interlude, twin ribs separated by a V-groove stand slightly to your left. Scramble directly up the right-hand rib on its left side (avoid recourse to the left-hand rib; it is unstable). Ascend the next difficult step from the right.

Above is the blunt-fronted mass of Bear Tower. Scramble precariously over ledges until below a group of overhangs on Bear Tower (Crazy Pinnacle is at this level over the gully on the right). Now trend leftwards and up until it is possible to go out left onto the nose to gain the top of the tower with a few breath-holding moves. Easy scrambling leads to the summit slopes directly ahead.

Descents and combinations

- Follow the clifftop path westwards, soon curving north, to a mine entrance. From here an old path starts promisingly but soon entails awkward heather-bashing, descending north east then east to join the approach at the stream that drains Cwm Du.
- A slightly longer but considerably easier descent is to continue on the main path from the mine west north west until a clear path heading north east is intersected. Follow this to a wall and continue eastwards to join the approach at the stile.
- Alternatively, a descent to access the start of Sentries' Ridge (Route 74) could be added to the day's itinerary.

Outlying Areas

Stepping off the Table (Route 79)

The Moelwyns

Route 76
*Moel Siabod Ridge Circuit
(including Daear Ddu Ridge)*

1- ✪✪✪

A rewarding introductory outing with simple scrambling on scenic ridges.

Location	Moel Siabod
Grade	1- ✪✪✪
Circuit time	4hr 30min
Route length	9km
Conditions	Quick drying, sound solid rock – about as safe as a scramble ever can be.

Seen from the mountains of northern Snowdonia, the 872m Moel Siabod looks pretty uninspiring. On closer inspection, however, the mountain reveals some first-rate easy scrambling on its summit ridge and on Daear Ddu, the south eastern approach. Here, the more challenging scrambling is always avoidable and there is plenty of scope for finding your own route amid the rocky steps of the broad easy-angled ridge. This is an ideal scramble for novices and energetic youngsters, but the length of the circuit and the height gain involved should not be underestimated. A good warm-up for those aspiring to scramble on the longer Snowdonian horseshoes.

Approach
From Capel Curig, head south east along the A5 for about a mile towards Betws-y-Coed. Park in the Bryn Glo car park near **Pont Cyfyng** (SH 734 572); additional parking in a lay-by just before the car park.

Ascent/Descent
Cross the impressive gorge of the Afon Llugwy by the road bridge at **Pont Cyfyng**, then take the second track on the right, starting up steeply through woods with a

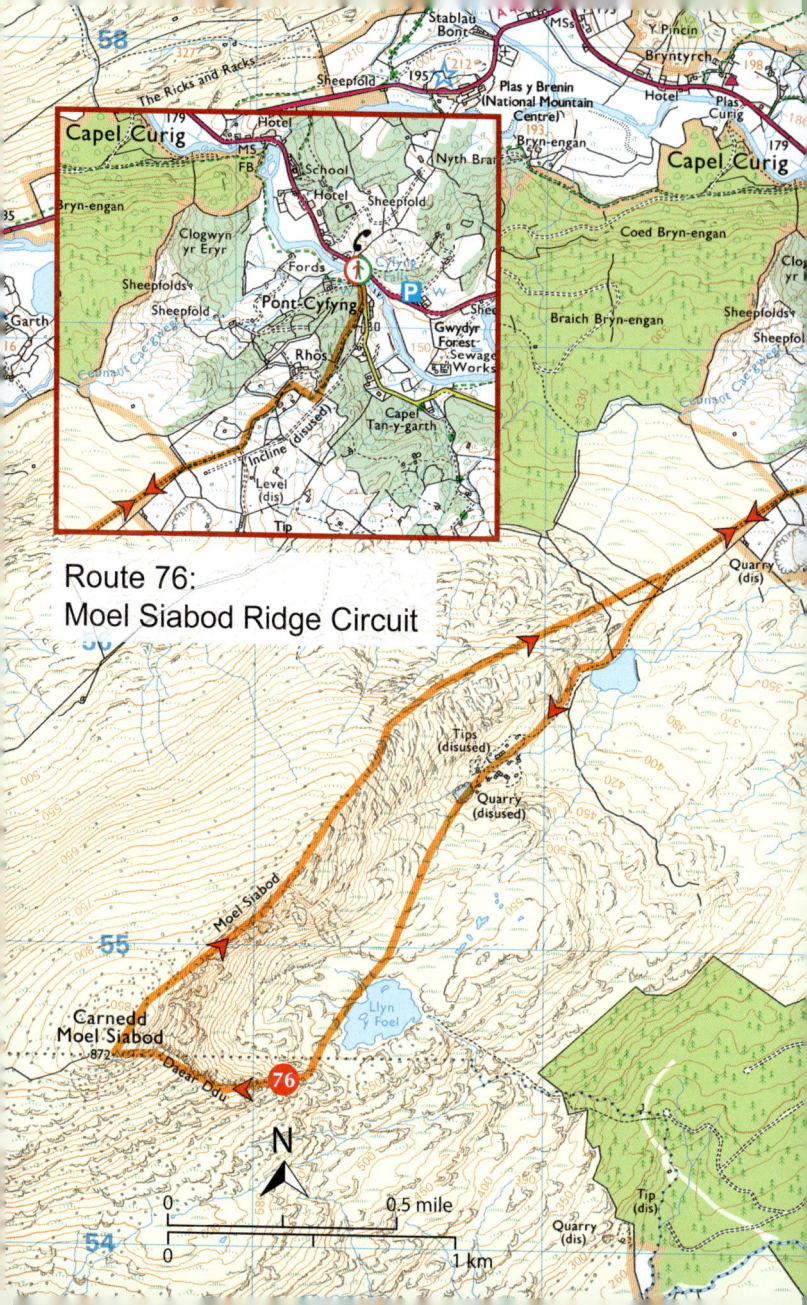

Scramblers nearing the top of the Daear Ddu Ridge

short signed detour avoiding a farmyard. The track then crosses open moorland. After 2km, bear left at a fork, traversing under the flanks of the north east ridge, to reach a small **lake** and eventually a crater containing an eery black **quarry pool**. Continue left of the pool upwards over a shoulder into the cwm and to **Llyn y Foel**. Daear Ddu, the south east ridge, can be seen rising at the opposite side of the lake. Gain the ridge by skirting the often-boggy right side of the lake. (The path continuing beyond the ridge swings round to approach the summit from the south and avoids any scrambling.)

The ridge is well-used, although in parts a path avoids some of the most entertaining scrambling. Keeping to the well-worn rocky steps on the ridge crest or towards its right side provides a surprising amount of hands-on interest. An initial polished V-groove set at an amenable angle on the broad crest has been well-travelled, although its top-out is hard at the grade and easier worthwhile alternatives exist round to its right. Continue to the top of the ridge.

At the summit cairn, head along the lengthy north east ridge for 1km. This is initially broad but becomes rockier and provides several easy scrambling sections if the final knobbly summit with its impressive sloping slabs is reached directly.

Follow the north east ridge down to meet the outbound route after 1.5km at a stile on the flattest section of the track from Pont Cyfyng.

The Rhinogs

The Rhinogs are the unassuming, rough-and-ready wilds of Snowdonia. The terrain is less tamed and the scrambling opportunities far fewer. The two routes described offer rewarding excursions through exceptional surroundings.

Route 77
South Face of Rhinog Fawr 2- ✪

Intermittent scrambling on terraced gritstone in a less-frequented area of Snowdonia.

Location	Rhinog Fawr (SH 663 283)
Grade	2- ✪
Approach time	1hr
Altitude and aspect	370m, south
Route length	A meandering, moderately long route with opportunities for exploratory scrambling – although if the easiest lines are opted for it can go fairly quickly. Height gain approximately 350m.
Conditions	The route catches the sun throughout the day. Rock quality is generally sound gritstone, although the route is not well-travelled and care should be taken with occasional balanced blocks.

A wandering line of limited exposure that gives a scenic introduction to the Rhinogs. It is not especially challenging and nearly all difficulties have easier alternatives or can be bypassed altogether. Conversely, there is scope for hunting out short problems. As such it is well suited to mixed-ability parties. The rugged descent from the summit, which goes via Llyn Du, completes a picturesque round.

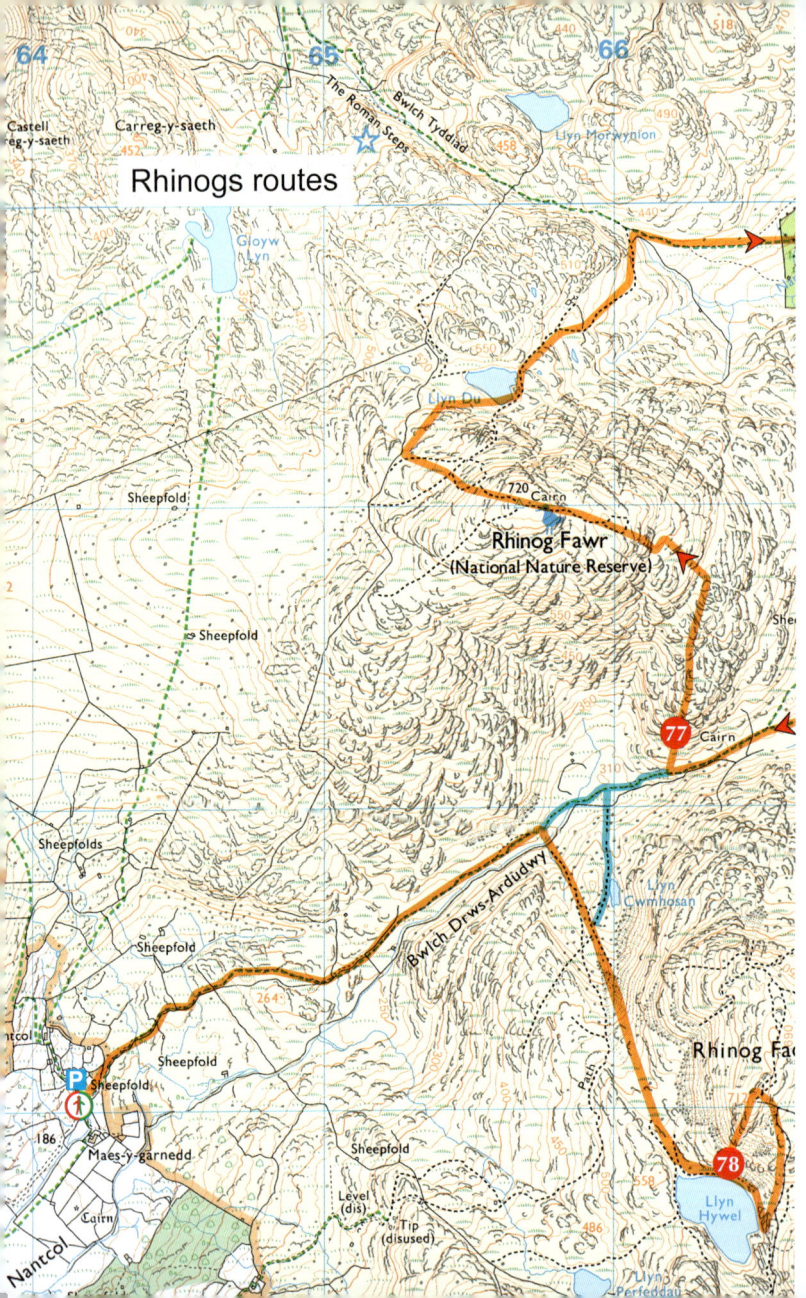

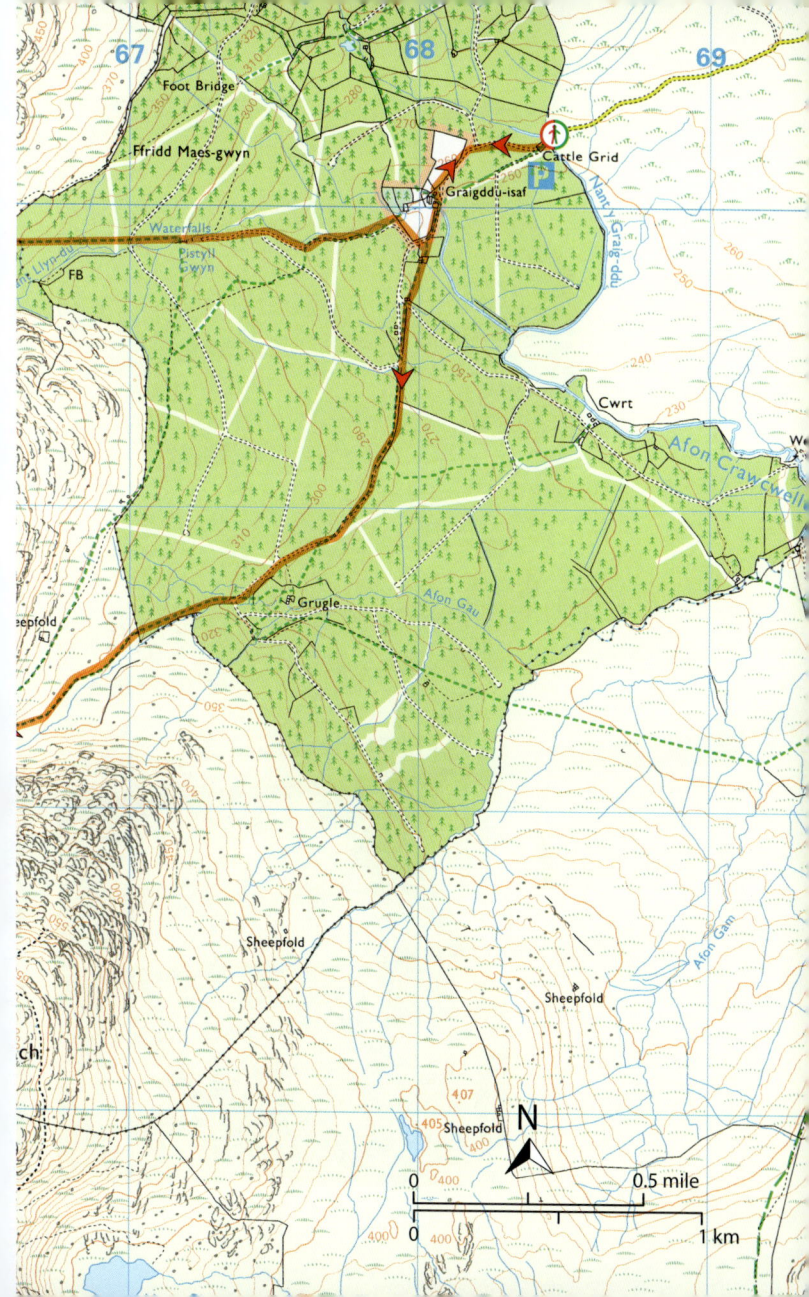

Route 77 – South Face of Rhinog Fawr

Approach
Two approaches are possible:
- From the east: follow the A470 from Blaenau Ffestiniog south past Lyn Trawsfynydd. After 4km at SH 713 306 turn right (west) on an easily missed gated minor road (the gate is after 50m). Continue on this for 3km to its conclusion, where parking for eight or so vehicles can be found at a gate (SH 684 302). The direct bridleway from the parking area heading south west is a quagmire. Fortunately, a permissible surfaced track leaves the parking area on the right. Follow this for 200m, then bear left at a fork signposted Bwlch Drws-Ardudwy to pass the **Graigddu-Isaf** farm. Stay on the main forest track for 1.5km, initially southwards before curving west towards the mountains. At a sharp bend take a well-surfaced path heading west towards the col between Rhinog Fach and Rhinog Fawr. A large **cairn** marks the top of Bwlch Drws-Ardudwy. Continue beyond this for 300m, descending slightly to reach the narrowest part of the pass and the remnants of a hard-to-spot collapsed wall.
- From the west: this hike is especially scenic and would be recommended, but even in the driest spells it is an exceptionally boggy approach. Follow the A496 to Llanbedr. At the Victoria Inn take the minor road east on the north side of the river, signposted Cwm Nantcol. Follow the narrow road and signs to Cwm Nantcol through increasingly picturesque scenery to reach the farm of **Maes-y-garnedd** (SH 642 270; parking £2 per day in 2016). The South Ridge of Rhinog Fach (Route 78) can be seen due east of the parking area, while the broad tiered rock of Rhinog Fawr can be seen across the pass to the north east. Take the signposted footpath north east from the grassy parking area and continue up the ancient narrow way through **Bwlch Drws-Ardudwy**. After descending to an unmistakable broad flat boggy area, hike up towards the high point of the pass, looking out for a hard-to-spot broken wall after 400m.

Ascent
Boulder-hop up the hill towards the very left-hand end of the first of a series of tiered rock walls. Gain a ledge and follow it easily rightwards, passing between the face and a block beneath an obvious jutting overhang, then work upwards on amenable ledges to reach level ground. The next tier is characterised by a band of ivy and a small tree at mid-height. A timid left-to-right break below and to the right of the tree enables this tier to be overcome easily. However, a better grade 2 challenge weaves up a series of corners and V-grooves on the steeper blocky buttress to the right.

The next tier of rock has a short and uninviting gully in it. Climb the rib on the right of the gully (an exit rightwards on a heather ledge halfway up gives a gentle line), overcoming a 2.5m step with a harder-than-it-looks slanting ledge at mid-height and a tricky mantelshelf leftwards towards the gully before reaching the top.

Creeping behind the block beneath the jutting overhang on the first tier

Route 77 – South Face of Rhinog Fawr

The hillside now levels out. Hike rightwards past a couple of cairns over broad sweeps of rock paving and follow the crest of the ridge round towards the second part of the route after 500m.

The most substantial collection of rock on the upper face has a gully in its middle. Head leftwards, crossing the base of the gully to reach the right foot of a smooth, steep little buttress. The buttress is too difficult to tackle direct, so find an amenable traverse line in its bottom quarter to gain its left side. It is now possible to work pleasantly up the left side of the buttress on good holds. Keep roughly 10m to the gully's left and, passing a sharp-pointed flake set against the rock en route, reach a broad heather platform. The better rock across the gully now beckons: venture into the gully and join a path. Where it narrows, locate a bilberry ledge and follow this rightwards for 3m. Access slabby rock above by trending leftwards with an awkward start. The scrambling soon peters out and the top of **Rhinog Fawr** lies 500m to the west along a good path.

Descent

- To return to the eastern approach: From the summit, head north west on a clear path. Continue on this path for 250m or so until another path branches off on the right. Follow this towards a dry stone wall. Where this forks, head right and continue down the path with the dry stone wall always to your left until the large **Llyn Du** is spotted. The path passes this on raised ground by its east side. Beyond the lake, trend leftwards (north east). At the next fork stay right and pass through a dry stone wall. The path is at times hard to follow and some boggy ground may be encountered before the main path east from Bwlch Tyddiad is met. Continue east until a well-surfaced path through felled forest is joined that leads back to the **Graigddu-Isaf** farm.
- To return to the western approach: From the summit, head south west on a clear path. After 500m or so a wall is crossed by means of a stile. Stay on the path, heading generally south west over stiles, to reach the farm at **Nantcol**, where a track leads back to the parking area.

Scrambles in Snowdonia

Route 78
South Ridge Variant, Rhinog Fach (aka Hywel Ridge) 3- ✪✪

A scenic venture to a remote cwm escaped by a distinctive gritstone ridge.

Location	Rhinog Fach (SH 664 268)
Grade	3- ✪✪
Approach time	1hr 20min
Altitude and aspect	590m, south west
Route length	A moderately long route that, if solo, can fly by a little too quickly. Parties pitching the route will take plenty of time. Approximately 120m height gain.
Conditions	A stepped gritstone ridge with generally sound rock quality – although some wobbly blocks need caution. Relatively quick drying, however, exceedingly difficult in or immediately after rain (in summer allow half a day to dry). Catches the sun throughout the day.

The South Ridge of Rhinog Fach saw its first recorded ascent in 1935. At that time it was known as the Hywel Ridge and given the now obsolete grade of 'Mild Difficult'. Over the years two short difficult sections were added and the route was both renamed and regraded to become a contrived Severe rock climb. The ridge is far better suited to the scrambler, its exposure being limited and its difficulties short-lived and always escapable. The line described in this book is in the spirit of the original ascent; a fine outing claimed in 1935 to be 'the best mountaineering route between Snowdon and Cadair Idris on the N-S line'. Set above the attractive Llyn Hywel, where wild brown trout may be seen breaking the surface to snap dragonflies from the air, the South Ridge and summit of Rhinog Fach give expansive views of Cardigan Bay, the Llyn Peninsula and a tapestry of interlocking hills and mountains across a wide swathe of Snowdonia.

Approach
- As for the first Route 77 approach to the Bwlch Drws-Ardudwy. Continue descending for 600m west of the large cairn to an unmistakable broad flat boggy area. Two stiles 300m apart each allow the dry stone wall on its south west side to be crossed. Cross the wall by the first stile on the left (SH 659 280). Head

Scrambles in Snowdonia

up the path beyond to pass the small **Llyn Cwmhosan**. After a short descent, continue up the cwm, keeping to the most-walked path to reach **Llyn Hywel**. Cross the stream outflow and, with a spot of boulder-hopping en route, reach the right-hand toe of the ridge.

- As for the second Route 77 approach to the broad flat area. Crossing the stream to reach a stile on the right can be a challenge after heavy rain (but if you have come from Cwm Nantcol then your feet will probably already be sodden!). The path beyond the stile follows the stream up on its left side and is soon joined by the approach from the east – see above.

Ascent

The steep broken face of the lowest rib is precarious if tackled front on. So move round to its right-hand side and climb steeply leftwards on surprisingly good holds to

On the South Ridge with the Hywel Slabs and Llyn Hywel glinting in the sun

Route 78 – South Ridge Variant, Rhinog Fach

reach its crest near the top. (A scrappy alternative heads up the scree on the right and misses the rib altogether by ascending a smooth wall on spaced ledges.)

Head up the ridge for 20m or so to reach a lightning symbol off-width crack. This is steep, often greasy and gives a tussle best suited to the rock climber. Instead, find an easier alternative much to the right. The next steep rib is tackled directly. Starting at a slight niche on the front right, climb steeply on excellent holds and step left where necessary to follow the most amenable line to its top.

Continue more easily up the ridge for 50m or so until meeting a steep buttress rising up from a gully on the right, separated by a grassy runnel from a shorter buttress on the left that has an overhang above a V-groove. (The Severe rock climb ascends the awkward V-groove to an excellent hold beneath the overhang, crosses the grassy runnel to reach a perched block on the right buttress and climbs the blank wall airily above.) A number of scrambling options are possible here:

- Ignore the V-groove altogether and climb the amenably angled slab immediately to its left, exiting steeply rightwards (taking care with suspect rock) to reach the top of the shorter buttress above the overhang.
- Climb the V-groove but exit left under the overhang.
- The perched block can be gained by the scrambler at grade 3, but the blank wall above it is too hard, so moving onto the wall left of the arête and picking an easier line on worryingly suspect and unappealing rock is possible.

Head up the ridge more easily until reaching a final substantial rock barrier. This can be overcome with difficulty, starting on its right end and moving leftwards. A more amenable blocky line can be found on its left side. The summit of **Rhinog Fach** is reached after a few more metres.

Descent

- It is best to follow the wall east off the summit until a path beside another wall leads south for 500m to reach a col and clear path leading back down to the east side of **Llyn Hywel**.
- In good visibility it is possible to follow a steep path running parallel to the route on its north west side. When this appears to lead rightwards towards a long stretch of scree, follow a faint grassy path carefully back left, crossing the ascent route just above its first rib to meet the boulders and scree near the start.

Cadair Idris

Route 79
Cyfrwy Arête
(including Table Direct option)

3 ✪✪✪ or 3S ✪✪✪

A classic mountaineering route that is strong on atmosphere.

Location	Cyfrwy, Cadair Idris (SH 705 135)
Grade	3 ✪✪✪ or 3S ✪✪✪
Approach time	1hr 15min
Altitude and aspect	640m, north east
Route length	Allow plenty of time if incorporating Table Direct into the itinerary. The ridge itself can go by more quickly than anticipated. Nonetheless, this is a route of substantial length. Height gain approximately 200m.
Conditions	Quick drying on the arête. In contrast to many of the surrounding routes the rock is sound, although occasional loose material may be encountered. The rock on Table Direct is good and takes no significant drainage, but it catches less sunlight and can be marginally slower to dry. All options can be climbed in the wet, but are appreciably harder in or after rain.

Stretching the arms of this guide to the deep south of the national park enables us to gather in the most famous route of any grade in southern Snowdonia and a worthy excursion to the summit of a mountain steeped in Welsh myth and legend. First climbed by Owen Glynne 'the Only Genuine' Jones in 1888, the nature of the Cyfrwy Arête is very much a hard scramble with passages of easy rock climbing rather than a sustained rock climb. By following the traditional line and bypassing its steepest section, the route becomes grade 3. If climbing the hardest part of the Arête proper, along with the Table Direct approach, the route is a 3S/Diff (see alternative ascent below).

Route 79 – Cwfrwy Arête

263

Cadair Idris
79 Cyfrwy Arête

Table Direct option

Route 79 – Cwfrwy Arête

Approach

From Dolgellau, follow a minor road south west uphill (signposted Cadair Idris as it leaves the town) for roughly 4km to the National Trust car park (toilets) at **Ty-Nant** (SH 698 153). From the exit of the car park turn right and follow the road for 100m. Turn left up the **Pony Path**, passing through woods and out to the open hillside. Continue up, eventually passing through a dry stone wall. After 200m reach a second dry stone wall with a gate. Go through this but leave the Pony Path after 20m and pick up a grassy path heading towards the Cyfrwy Arête. Avoid the temptation of direct routes over wretched loose scree and instead follow the path to **Llyn y Gadair**. (If intending to include Table Direct on your itinerary the approach splits here – see below.) To access the Cyfrwy Arête above Table Direct, follow the path beside the lake until 80m left of the line of the arête. Follow a snaking scree path uphill until nearly level with the unmistakable large notch in the arête and slightly above a nearby cairn. Traverse easily across the scree for 50m, then follow a path curving down under the nose to a platform on the arête. A faint 'CA' has been scratched into a rock beneath a rib.

Ascent

Head directly up the rib above the 'CA' and follow polished holds sweeping a course over pinnacles and blocks to reach the Table – a broad leaning platform separated from the rest of the ridge by a distinct notch. Facing the mountain, two descents to the notch are possible, and both feel a little unnerving as the wall is undercut slightly. The right-hand descent (looking down) leads to the highest part of the notch and is the best, its rock being sound and necessary holds appearing as you step down.

From the notch, a small shelf to the left of the imposing wall is reached with surprising ease by means of a diagonal crack (the shelf boasted a prominent pinnacle until recently). The traditional route of the Cyfrwy Arête now tackles the wall directly above the shelf at 3S (see 3S alternative below). This steep wall can be craftily dodged at grade 2, thereby maintaining an overall grade 3 option for the whole arête: from the shelf sneak leftwards for 10m and climb the obvious line above by means of a series of ledges to rejoin the crest of the ridge above its hardest section, appreciating that this is a less-travelled line and therefore taking care with its rock. Continue up the crest until confronted by a triangular wall. This is overcome by a right-to-left sloping ramp. This is a stiff little section (it can be circumvented by accessing the left edge from a grassy platform). Straightforward scrambling now leads to the top, where 700m to the east **Penygadair** (the summit of Cadair Idris) beckons; it is reached by an obvious path.

Alternative ascent 3S/Diff (including Table Direct approach)

We have included a description of Table Direct (3S/Diff) for roped parties keen to double the amount of interest without a big increase in standard. Despite the reputation of Table Direct as a harder preliminary extension, it receives a 3S/Diff grade for its steepness rather than the difficulty of its moves. These are firmly of a traditional Moderate standard and will be familiar to scramblers who have tackled some of the harder routes in this book. Surprisingly, the hardest part of Table Direct is easier than the – avoidable – 3S section on the Arête proper. Nonetheless, a rope is strongly advised.

Approach

From **Llyn y Gadair**, head up the hillside towards the arête before trending round to its right-hand (north) side (take care on loose scree and boulders here). Work upwards to pass between a pinnacle rib on the left and a curving pinnacle ridge sweeping down from the main face on the right to access a ledge beneath a large leaning rectangular block.

Ascent

Standing beneath the imposing steep wall of Table Direct it feels unlikely that an amenable route could possibly sneak up such terrain – have faith. It is best tackled in two pitches, although intermediate stances are possible and protection is excellent throughout. Climb a shallow square-cut recess immediately right of the leaning rectangular block on well-travelled holds. Trend easily rightwards for a few metres until grass pushes you left. A groove above is tackled direct or by surprisingly good holds on the face to its left. Eschew the first ledge above the groove and move up left to a larger ledge beneath a steep block-filled corner and belay (27m). Climb the block-filled corner – not as difficult as it looks – to an optional stance (15m). Then continue up, taking care with spikes, to a ledge below a smooth wall and the end of Table Direct (10m). Follow the path down the ledge for a few metres to reach the broad platform and start of the Cyfrwy Arête route.

Follow the primary Cyfrwy Arête route description, passing over the Table and out of the notch to reach the small shelf below the steep wall. Ignoring the dodge, the wall above the shelf is tackled more or less directly and passes through vertiginous terrain that many will find a tad harder than anything on Table Direct – although protection is good (16m). Continue as for the primary route description.

Descent

From the summit of Cadair Idris, descend west for nearly 2km on the **Pony Path** to the col separating Cadair Idris from Tyrrau Mawr. At the col, stay on the Pony Path as it passes through a gate and descends, initially northwards, back to the start of the route. (The Fox's Path, which leaves the summit of Cadair Idris on its east side and descends scree back to Llyn y Gadair, is severely eroded and not much fun.)

Conwy

Route 80
Penmaenbach Arête

1+ ✪✪

A unique and substantial scramble up a coastal peak on a dramatic line which has caught the eye of many a passing motorist.

Location	Penmaenbach, off the A55 north of Penmaenmawr (SH 743 781)
Grade	1+ ✪✪
Approach time	10min
Altitude and aspect	20m, west
Route length	With a short approach, this sustained and direct line allows height to be gained rapidly. A good and very satisfying choice for a shortish outing. Height gain approximately 230m.
Conditions	Often remains dry when it is raining inland. The rock is of generally good quality. There is a little gorse en route. Part of the approach is on a footpath on private land; there were no access issues in 2016 but if this situation changes, the route should be approached from the right of way south of the caravan park starting from the minor road at SH 742 769.

Purists might baulk at the inclusion of a coastal outing that nestles in the foothills of the national park above the busy A55, but this outlying scramble will surely win over its would-be detractors. Its clean line, sea views and tendency to stay dry when Ogwen is covered in rainclouds, mean that it is well worth an hour or two of anyone's time. The scrambling starts at sea-level and is interesting and sustained at the grade throughout. Penmaenbach summit at 245m makes a surprisingly serene spot to gaze out beyond the quiet heathery fell-top across Conwy Bay up the Welsh coast and across to Anglesey. The whole area is deservedly part of Snowdonia National Park and it would seem churlish to grumble about the proximity of the A-road.

Route 80 – Penmaenbach Arête

Approach

From the village of Penmaenmawr, follow the main street east through Dwygyfylchi parallel to the coastal A55. Keep going east, as if you intend to rejoin the A55. Just before the road filters traffic back onto the A55, a large lay-by just after a big caravan site at Pendyffryn Hall provides ample parking. From the lay-by head up the road towards the caravan park. On the opposite side of the road to where a sign points westwards at the entrance to a field for tents, take a small track that initially threads between two sections of the caravan park. This becomes narrower after 50m. Turn left at a toilet block, skirting the back of the caravan site to end up on a grassy path heading north east over a stile. After 300m you will meet the foot of the crags. Ignore steeper walls and continue a little further to where the obvious curving ridge starts, just right of scree slopes and just above the level of the path.

Ascent

Scramble carefully up the exposed curving crest of the ridge, passing most difficulties on the right. At a steep blocky overhanging tower that appears to bar the way, pass this awkwardly via a ramp on its left side. Continue up the most continuous rock as the angle gradually eases. At a wide scree-filled col, take the rib and runnel on

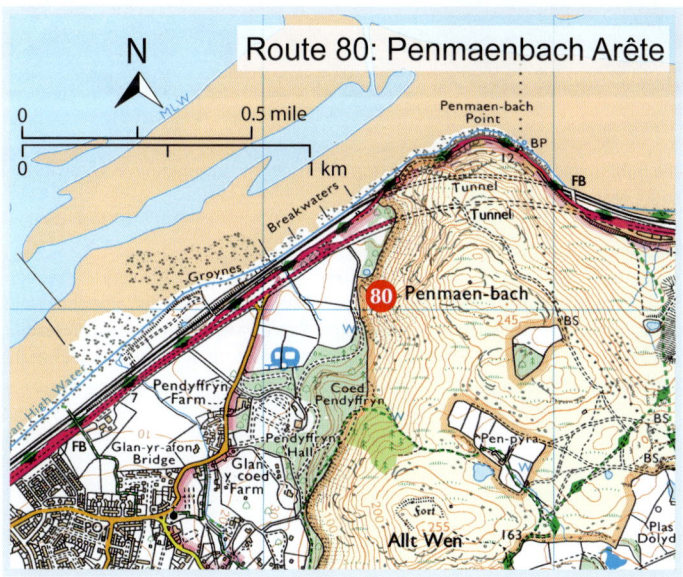

On the beginning of Penmaenbach Arête

the right up more broken rock to the top of the fell. The true summit is a little further south east.

Descent
Continue in the same direction from the summit on a faint path. At a very large sheepfold this joins a more distinct traversing path. Take this past another large sheepfold, at the far corner of which there is a wide gully. Pick up a faint path in the gully leading down the side of a wood. Eventually this enters the woods and emerges back at the caravan site.

Appendix A
Summary of routes in grade order

Route	Mountain	Area	Grade	Star rating	Route number	Page
Southern Ridge Circuit	Carneddau	Carneddau	1-	✪✪✪	1	31
Seniors' Gully	Glyder Fawr	Glyderau	1-	✪	43	148
Moel Siabod Ridge Circuit	Moelwyns	Outlying	1-	✪✪✪	76	248
Nantlle Ridge	Eifionydd	Eifionydd	1-	✪✪✪	72	234
Cwm Glas Ridge	Crib y Ddysgl	Snowdon group	1-	✪	63	206
Traverse of Lliwedd	Lliwedd	Snowdon group	1	✪✪	70	225
North Ridge of Crib Goch	Crib Goch	Snowdon group	1	✪	57	191
East Ridge of Crib Goch	Crib Goch	Snowdon group	1	✪	56	189
Seniors' Ridge	Glyder Fawr	Glyderau	1	✪	42	146
South Ridge Direct	Tryfan West Face	Glyderau	1	✪	29	112
Gribin Ridge	Glyder Fawr	Glyderau	1	✪	38	135
False Gribin	Glyder Fawr	Glyderau	1	✪	39	138
Crib Lem (Llech Ddu Spur)	Carnedd Dafydd	Carneddau	1	✪✪✪	5	43
Little and North Gullies	Tryfan East Face	Glyderau	1	✪✪	15	79
Crib y Ddysgl	Crib y Ddysgl	Snowdon group	1	✪✪	60	198
Y Gribin and the East Ridge	Snowdon	Snowdon group	1	✪✪	69	222
North Ridge Tryfan	Tryfan West Face	Glyderau	1	✪✪✪	19	87
Bristly Ridge	Glyder Fach	Glyderau	1	✪✪✪	30	115
Cwm Bochlwyd Horseshoe	Glyderau	Glyderau	1	✪✪✪	8	56
The Snowdon Horseshoe	Snowdon group	Snowdon group	1	✪✪✪	55	185
Traverse of Crib Goch	Crib Goch	Snowdon group	1	✪✪✪	59	196
Nor' Nor' Groove	Tryfan East Face	Glyderau	1+	✪	13	75
East Gully	Glyder Fach	Glyderau	1+	✪	35	127
South Arête	Foel Goch	Glyderau	1+	✪	51	170
Cwm Glas Mawr Approach	Crib y Ddysgl	Snowdon group	1+ or 3S	✪	61	200

Scrambles in Snowdonia

Route	Mountain	Area	Grade	Star rating	Route number	Page
Eastern Terrace of Clogwyn du'r Arddu	Crib y Ddysgl	Snowdon group	1+	✪✪	66	213
Penmaenbach Arête	Conwy	Outlying	1+	✪✪	80	267
Milestone Gully Approach	Tryfan West Face	Glyderau	2-	✪✪	21	95
Main Gully	Glyder Fach	Glyderau	2-	✪✪	32	122
South Face of Rhinog Fawr	Rhinogs	Outlying	2-	✪	77	251
Llechog Ridge	Crib y Ddysgl	Snowdon group	2-	✪	65	211
Y Gully	Tryfan West Face	Glyderau	2	✪	28	111
Eastern Ridge of Black Ladders	Carnedd Dafydd	Carneddau	2	✪	6	47
North Buttress Variant	Tryfan East Face	Glyderau	2	✪✪	14	77
Notch Arête	Tryfan West Face	Glyderau	2	✪✪✪	27	108
Direct Approach to Seniors' Ridge	Glyder Fawr	Glyderau	2	✪	44	149
North West Face Route	Glyder Fawr	Glyderau	2	✪✪	46	154
East Ridge Y Garn	Y Garn	Glyderau	2	✪✪	50	168
Llechog Buttress	Crib y Ddysgl	Snowdon group	2	✪✪	64	208
Tregalan Couloir	Snowdon	Snowdon group	2	✪	68	219
The Ridge (Atlantic Ridge)	Carnedd y Filiast	Glyderau	2+	✪✪	54	177
Esgair Felen Direct	Glyder Fawr	Glyderau	2+	✪	48	161
Broad Gully Ridge	Pen yr Ole Wen	Carneddau	2+	✪	3	37
Craig yr Ysfa Amphitheatre	Carnedd Llewellyn	Carneddau	2+	✪	7	50
Nor' Nor' Gully	Tryfan East Face	Glyderau	2+	✪	12	73
Idwal Staircase and Continuation	Glyder Fawr	Glyderau	2+	✪✪✪	45	152
Braich Ty Du Face	Pen yr Ole Wen	Carneddau	2+	✪✪	2	33
Bryant's Gully	Glyder Fawr	Glyderau	2+	✪✪✪	47	157
Bastow Buttress Variant	Tryfan East Face	Glyderau	2+	✪✪✪	10	68
South Gully	Tryfan East Face	Glyderau	3-	✪	17	83
South Ridge Variant, Rhinog Fach	Rhinogs	Outlying	3-	✪✪	78	258
Sentries Ridge and Continuation	Mynydd Mawr	Eifionydd	3-	✪✪✪	74	240
Craig Lloer Spur	Pen yr Ole Wen	Carneddau	3-	✪✪	4	41
Needle's Eye Arête	Foel Goch	Glyderau	3	✪	52	173

Appendix A – Summary of routes in grade order

Route	Mountain	Area	Grade	Star rating	Route number	Page
Western Terrace of Clogwyn du'r Arddu	Crib y Ddysgl	Snowdon group	3	✪	67	217
Milestone Continuation	Tryfan West Face	Glyderau	3	✪✪	22	95
Milestone Buttress Approach	Tryfan West Face	Glyderau	3	✪✪	20	93
Tryfan Bach Approach	Tryfan East Face	Glyderau	3	✪✪✪	9	61
Nor' Nor' Buttress Variant	Tryfan East Face	Glyderau	3 or 3S	✪✪	11	70
South Buttress	Tryfan East Face	Glyderau	3	✪✪	18	85
West Face Route	Tryfan West Face	Glyderau	3	✪	24	101
V Buttress	Tryfan West Face	Glyderau	3	✪✪	25	105
V Arête	Tryfan West Face	Glyderau	3	✪	26	106
Main Gully Ridge	Glyder Fach	Glyderau	3 or 2	✪✪✪	33	124
Cneifion Arête	Glyder Fawr	Glyderau	3	✪✪✪	40	142
Dolmen Ridge	Glyder Fach	Glyderau	3	✪✪✪	37	132
Craig Fawr Rib	Craig Cwm Silyn	Eifionydd	3	✪	73	236
Maybe Tower Rib	Glyder Fawr	Glyderau	3	✪	41	144
Clogwyn y Person Arête	Crib y Ddysgl	Snowdon group	3 or 3S	✪✪✪	62	203
Pinnacle Rib Variant	Tryfan East Face	Glyderau	3	✪✪	16	81
The Chasm Face	Glyder Fach	Glyderau	3	✪✪✪	31	118
East Gully Ridge	Glyder Fach	Glyderau	3	✪✪✪	34	125
Cyfrwy Arête	Cadair Idris	Outlying	3 or 3S	✪✪✪	79	262
West Peak via Bilberry Terrace	Lliwedd	Snowdon group	3S	✪✪✪	71	227
Wrinkled Tower	Tryfan West Face	Glyderau	3S	✪✪✪	23	99
Shark Buttress	Glyder Fach	Glyderau	3S	✪✪✪	36	129
Jammed Boulder Gully	Crib Goch	Snowdon group	3S	✪✪	58	193
Bear Buttress	Mynydd Mawr	Eifionydd	3S	✪	75	245
Yr Esgair	Foel Goch	Glyderau	3S	✪	53	175
Devil's Kitchen and the Sheep Walk	Y Garn	Glyderau	3S or 1-	✪✪✪	49	165

Appendix B
Longer combination ideas

Scrambles in Snowdonia lends itself to those searching for big days and high-quality link-ups that maintain as much height as possible. Along with the classic Southern Ridge Circuit and the Cwm Bochlwyd and Snowdon Horseshoes, other possible link-ups include:

Carneddau Round: Using the Southern Ridge Circuit (Route 1) as a link route, ascend either Route 2, 3 or 4 to reach the summit of Pen yr Ole Wen. Descend Route 5 then ascend Route 6. Dependent on time, either return to Ogwen or incorporate Route 7.

Glyderau Round (grade 2-): Ascend either Milestone Gully (Route 21) or Nor' Nor' Groove (Route 13), then use Routes 19 and 29 to reach Bwlch Tryfan. Access Glyder Fach losing minimal height using the second approach option for Route 31. Ascend Main or East Gully (Routes 32 or 35). Either descend the Gribin Ridges (Routes 38 and 39) or head onwards to the summit of Glyder Fawr and descend the Seniors' Routes 42 and 43.

Snowdon Round: Ascend either Route 64 or 65 on Llechog then ascend either Route 66 or 67 on Clogwyn Du'r Arddu to reach the summit of Snowdon. Descend either Route 63 or – better but somewhat herculean – descend/reverse Routes 60 and 59, then descend Route 57.

Appendix C
Useful contacts

Emergencies
Dial 999 or 112 and ask for police, mountain rescue.

Weather
For mountain weather forecasts, www.metoffice.gov.uk and www.mwis.org.uk are the most useful. There are also local weather forecasts and limited information posted in the window of the toilet complex at Ogwen and in the foyer of the café/toilet complex at Pen-y-Pass.

Guiding and courses
The following can provide information:

British Mountaineering Council:
tel 0161 445 6111,
www.thebmc.co.uk

The National Mountain Centre
at Plas y Brenin: tel 01690 720214,
www.pyb.co.uk

Tourist information
Snowdonia National Park:
tel 01766 770274,
www.eryri-npa.gov.uk

Appendix C – Useful contacts

Welsh Tourist Board:
www.visitwales.com

Snowdonia information:
www.visitsnowdonia.info

Betws y Coed Information Centre:
Royal Oak Stables, LL24 0AH,
tel 01690 710426

Beddgelert Information Centre:
Canolfan Hebog, LL55 4YD,
tel 01766 890615

Dolgellau Tourist Information Centre:
Stryd Fawr, LL40 1PU,
tel 01341 422888

Llanberis tourist information:
Hwb Eryri Electric Mountain, LL55 4UR,
tel 07867976183

Transport
Sherpa Bus timetables:
www.visitsnowdonia.info

National Rail Enquiries:
www.nationalrail.co.uk

Indoor climbing
Beacon Indoor Climbing Centre,
Caenarfon: tel 01286 677322,
www.beaconclimbing.com

The National Mountain Centre at Plas y Brenin: tel 01690 720214,
www.pyb.co.uk

Accommodation
The following budget options are well placed for the scrambles in this book. Only camping, hostels and bunkhouses are included and the list is by no means exhaustive. Plentiful accommodation can be found in Llanberis, Beddgelert and Betwys y Coed.

Camping

Ogwen
Gwern Gof Uchaf: LL24 0EU,
tel 01690 720294,
www.tryfanwales.co.uk

Gwern Gof Isaf: LL24 0EU,
tel 01690 720276,
www.gwerngofisaf.co.uk

(Both situated close to Tryfan, with easy access to the Glyderau and Carneddau.)

Capel Curig area
Garth Farm:
Capel Curig, LL24 0ES,
tel 01690 720212

Dolgam, just east of Capel Curig:
LL24 0DS, tel 01690 720228,
www.dolgam-snowdonia.co.uk

Llanberis Pass
Ty Isaf: Nant Peris, LL55 4UN,
tel 01286 870494

Cae Gwyn: LL55 4UN, tel 01286 870718

Rhyd Ddu/Beddgelert
Snowdon Base Camp (for Nantlle):
LL54 6TL, tel 01766 890321,
www.snowdoninn.co.uk

Tal-y-mignedd (for Mynydd Mawr):
LL54 6BT, tel 01286 880374

Bryn Gloch (for Mynydd Mawr):
LL54 7YY, tel 01286 650216
www.northwalescamping.co.uk

Hafod y Llan
(for Snowdon's Watkin Path):
www.hafodyllancampsite.co.uk

Dolgellau
Torrent Walk: LL40 2AB,
tel 01341 422269

Scrambles in Snowdonia

Hafod Dywyll: LL40 1TR,
tel 01341 423444,
www.hafoddywyllcampsite.co.uk

Youth Hostels

YHA Idwal: LL5 3LZ,
tel 0345 371 9744
(perfect for accessing the Glyderau)

YHA Pen y Pass: LL55 4NY,
tel 0345 371 9534
(popular for scrambles on Snowdon)

The following hostels are also useful

YHA Snowdon Ranger
near Rhyd Ddu: LL54 7YS,
tel 0345 371 9659

YHA Bryn Gwnant
off the A498 east of Beddgelert:
LL55 4NP, tel 0345 371 9108

YHA Llanberis:
LL55 4SR, tel 0345 371 9645

YHA Betwys y Coed:
LL24 0DW, tel 01690 710796
(slightly further afield)

YHA Kings near Dolgellau:
LL40 ITB, tel 0345 371 9327
(further afield, ideal for Cadair Idris).

Further details of all these at
www.yha.org.uk

Bunkhouses and independent hostels

Ogwen
Gwern Gof Uchaf: LL24 0EU,
tel 01690 720294,
www.tryfanwales.co.uk

Gwern Gof Isaf: LL24 0EU,
tel 01690 720276,
www.gwerngofisaf.co.uk

Capel Curig area
Plas Curig Hostel
(tel 01690 720225,
www.snowdoniahostel.co.uk)
is well placed for Moel Siabod.

Llanberis area
Ben's Bunkhouse in Nant Peris
(www.bensbunkhouse.co.uk),

Pete's Eats, Llanberis
(www.petes-eats.co.uk)

or Jesse James' Bunkhouse
off the A4244 north of Llanberis.

Numerous other options exist, many of which cater primarily for groups.

Rhyd Ddu
Cwellyn Arms Bunkhouse:
LL54 6TL, tel 01766 89032,
www.snowdoninn.co.uk

Beddgelert
Hafod y Llan
(www.hafodyllancampsite.co.uk)
near the start of Snowdon's Watkin Path has a bunkhouse.

LISTING OF CICERONE GUIDES

BRITISH ISLES CHALLENGES, COLLECTIONS AND ACTIVITIES

Great Walks on the England Coast Path
Map and Compass
The Big Rounds
The Book of the Bivvy
The Book of the Bothy
The Mountains of England and Wales:
Vol 1 Wales
Vol 2 England
The National Trails
Walking the End to End Trail

SHORT WALKS SERIES

Short Walks Hadrian's Wall
Short Walks Lake District — Keswick, Borrowdale and Buttermere
Short Walks Lake District — Windermere Ambleside and Grasmere
Short Walks Lake District — Coniston and Langdale
Short Walks in Arnside and Silverdale
Short Walks in Nidderdale
Short Walks in Northumberland: Wooler, Rothbury, Alnwick and the coast
Short Walks on the Malvern Hills
Short Walks in Cornwall: Falmouth and the Lizard
Short Walks in Cornwall: Land's End and Penzance
Short Walks in the South Downs: Brighton, Eastbourne and Arundel
Short Walks in the Surrey Hills
Short Walks on Dartmoor — South: Ivybridge and Princetown
Short Walks on Exmoor
Short Walks Winchester
Short Walks in Pembrokeshire: Tenby and the south
Short Walks in Dumfries and Galloway
Short Walks on the Isle of Mull
Short Walks on the Orkney Islands
Short Walks on the Shetland Islands

SCOTLAND

Ben Nevis and Glen Coe
Cycling in the Hebrides
Cycling the North Coast 500
Great Mountain Days in Scotland
Mountain Biking in Southern and Central Scotland
Mountain Biking in West and North West Scotland
Not the West Highland Way Scotland
Scotland's Best Small Mountains
Scotland's Mountain Ridges
Scottish Wild Country Backpacking
Skye's Cuillin Ridge Traverse
The Borders Abbeys Way
The Great Glen Way
The Great Glen Way Map Booklet
The Hebridean Way
The Hebrides
The Isle of Mull
The Isle of Skye
The Skye Trail
The Southern Upland Way
The West Highland Way
Walking Ben Lawers, Rannoch and Atholl
Walking in the Cairngorms
Walking in the Pentland Hills
Walking in the Scottish Borders
Walking in the Southern Uplands
Walking in Torridon, Fisherfield, Fannichs and An Teallach
Walking Loch Lomond and the Trossachs
Walking on Arran
Walking on Harris and Lewis
Walking on Jura, Islay and Colonsay
Walking on Rum and the Small Isles
Walking on the Orkney and Shetland Isles
Walking on Uist and Barra
Walking the Cape Wrath Trail
Walking the Corbetts Vol 1 South of the Great Glen
Walking the Corbetts Vol 2 North of the Great Glen
Walking the Fife Pilgrim Way
Walking the Galloway Hills
Walking the John o' Groats Trail
Walking the Munros
Vol 1 — Southern, Central and Western Highlands
Vol 2 — Northern Highlands and the Cairngorms
Walking the West Highland Way
West Highland Way Map Booklet
Winter Climbs in the Cairngorms
Winter Climbs: Ben Nevis and Glen Coe

NORTHERN ENGLAND ROUTES

Cycling the Reivers Route
Cycling the Way of the Roses
Hadrian's Cycleway
Hadrian's Wall Path
Hadrian's Wall Path Map Booklet
The Coast to Coast Cycle Route
The Coast to Coast Map Booklet
The Coast to Coast Walk
The Pennine Way
Pennine Way Map Booklet
Walking the Dales Way
The Dales Way Map Booklet

LAKE DISTRICT

Bikepacking in the Lake District
Cycling in the Lake District
Great Mountain Days in the Lake District
Joss Naylor's Lakes, Meres and Waters of the Lake District
Lake District Winter Climbs
Lake District: High Level and Fell Walks
Lake District: Low Level and Lake Walks
Mountain Biking in the Lake District
Outdoor Adventures with Children — Lake District
Scrambles in the Lake District —
North
South
Trail and Fell Running in the Lake District
Walking The Cumbria Way
Walking the Lake District Fells —
Borrowdale
Buttermere
Coniston
Keswick
Langdale
Mardale and the Far East
Patterdale
Wasdale
Walking the Tour of the Lake District

NORTH-WEST ENGLAND AND THE ISLE OF MAN

Cycling the Pennine Bridleway
Isle of Man Coastal Path
The Lancashire Cycleway
The Lune Valley and Howgills
Walking in Cumbria's Eden Valley
Walking in Lancashire
Walking in the Forest of Bowland and Pendle
Walking on the Isle of Man
Walking on the West Pennine Moors
Walking the Ribble Way
Walks in Silverdale and Arnside

NORTH-EAST ENGLAND, YORKSHIRE DALES AND PENNINES

Cycling in the Yorkshire Dales
Great Mountain Days in the Pennines
Mountain Biking in the Yorkshire Dales
The Cleveland Way and the Yorkshire Wolds Way
The Cleveland Way Map Booklet
The North York Moors
Trail and Fell Running in the Yorkshire Dales
Walking in County Durham

Walking in Northumberland
Walking in the North Pennines
Walking in the Yorkshire Dales:
  North and East
  South and West
Walking St Cuthbert's Way
Walking St Oswald's Way and Northumberland Coast Path

DERBYSHIRE, PEAK DISTRICT AND MIDLANDS

Cycling in the Peak District
Dark Peak Walks
Scrambles in the Dark Peak
Walking in Derbyshire
Walking in the Peak District —
  White Peak East
  White Peak West

WALES AND WELSH BORDERS

Cycle Touring in Wales
Cycling Lon Las Cymru
Great Mountain Days in Snowdonia
Hillwalking in Shropshire
Mountain Walking in Snowdonia
Offa's Dyke Path
Offa's Dyke Path Map Booklet
The Pembrokeshire Coast Path
Pembrokeshire Coast Path Map Booklet
Scrambles in Snowdonia
Snowdonia: 30 Low-level and Easy Walks — North, South
The Cambrian Way
The Snowdonia Way
The Wye Valley Walk
Walking Glyndwr's Way
Walking in Carmarthenshire
Walking in Pembrokeshire
Walking in the Brecon Beacons
Walking in the Wye Valley
Walking on Gower
Walking the Severn Way
Walking the Shropshire Way
Walking the Wales Coast Path

SOUTHERN ENGLAND

20 Classic Sportive Rides in South East England
20 Classic Sportive Rides in South West England
Cycling in the Cotswolds
Mountain Biking on the North Downs
Mountain Biking on the South Downs
The North Downs Way
North Downs Way Map Booklet
Walking the South West Coast Path
South West Coast Path Map Booklet
  — Vol 1: Minehead to St Ives
  — Vol 2: St Ives to Plymouth
  — Vol 3: Plymouth to Poole
Suffolk Coast and Heath Walks
The Cotswold Way
The Cotswold Way Map Booklet
The Kennet and Avon Canal
The Lea Valley Walk
The Peddars Way and Norfolk Coast Path
The Pilgrims' Way
The Ridgeway National Trail
The Ridgeway Map Booklet
The South Downs Way
The South Downs Way Map Booklet
The Thames Path
The Thames Path Map Booklet
The Two Moors Way
Two Moors Way Map Booklet
Walking Hampshire's Test Way
Walking in Cornwall
Walking in Essex
Walking in Kent
Walking in London
Walking in Norfolk
Walking in the Chilterns
Walking in the Cotswolds
Walking in the Isles of Scilly
Walking in the New Forest
Walking in the North Wessex Downs
Walking on Dartmoor
Walking on Guernsey
Walking on Jersey
Walking on the Isle of Wight
Walking the Dartmoor Way
Walking the Jurassic Coast
Walking the Sarsen Way
Walks in the South Downs National Park
Cycling Land's End to John o' Groats

ALPS CROSS-BORDER ROUTES

100 Hut Walks in the Alps
Alpine Ski Mountaineering Vol 1 — Western Alps
The Karnischer Hohenweg
The Tour of the Bernina
Trekking the Tour du Mont Blanc
Tour du Mont Blanc Map Booklet
Trail Running — Chamonix and the Mont Blanc region
Trekking Chamonix to Zermatt
Trekking in the Alps
Trekking in the Silvretta and Ratikon Alps
Trekking Munich to Venice
Walking in the Alps

FRANCE, BELGIUM, AND LUXEMBOURG

Camino de Santiago — Via Podiensis
Chamonix Mountain Adventures
Cycling London to Paris
Cycling the Canal de la Garonne
Cycling the Canal du Midi
Mont Blanc Walks
Mountain Adventures in the Maurienne
Short Treks on Corsica
The Grand Traverse of the Massif Central
The Moselle Cycle Route
Trekking in the Vanoise
Trekking the Cathar Way
Trekking the GR10
Trekking the GR20 Corsica
Trekking the Robert Louis Stevenson Trail
The GR5 Trail
The GR5 Trail —
  Vosges and Jura
  Benelux and Lorraine
Via Ferratas of the French Alps
Walking in Provence — East
Walking in Provence — West
Walking in the Auvergne
Walking in the Brianconnais
Walking in the Dordogne
Walking in the Haute Savoie: North
Walking in the Haute Savoie: South
Walking on Corsica
Walking the Brittany Coast Path
Walking in the Ardennes

PYRENEES AND FRANCE/SPAIN CROSS-BORDER ROUTES

Shorter Treks in the Pyrenees
The Pyrenean Haute Route
The Pyrenees
Trekking the Cami dels Bons Homes
Trekking the GR11 Trail
Walks and Climbs in the Pyrenees

SPAIN AND PORTUGAL

Camino de Santiago: Camino Frances
Costa Blanca Mountain Adventures
Cycling the Camino de Santiago
Mountain Walking in Mallorca
Mountain Walking in Southern Catalunya
Spain's Sendero Historico: The GR1
The Andalucian Coast to Coast Walk
The Camino del Norte and Camino Primitivo
The Camino Ingles and Ruta do Mar
The Mountains Around Nerja
The Mountains of Ronda and Grazalema
The Sierras of Extremadura
Trekking in Mallorca
Trekking in the Canary Islands
Trekking the GR7 in Andalucia
Walking and Trekking in the Sierra Nevada
Walking in Andalucia
Walking in Catalunya —
  Barcelona
  Girona Pyrenees
Walking in the Picos de Europa
Walking La Via de la Plata and Camino Sanabres
Walking on Gran Canaria
Walking on La Gomera and El Hierro
Walking on La Palma
Walking on Lanzarote and Fuerteventura
Walking on Tenerife
Walking on the Costa Blanca
Walking the Camino dos Faros
Portugal's Rota Vicentina